Internet Explorer 4 For Windows® For Dummies®

COMPUTER
BOOK SERIES
FROM IDG

Internet Explorer Toolbar Buttons

Toolbar Button	What It Does
Back	Goes back to the previously displayed page
Forward	Returns to the page where you were before you went back
Stop	Stops downloading the current page
Refresh	Downloads a fresh copy of the current page
Home	Goes to your designated start page
Search	Calls up the Search bar
Favorites	Calls up the Favorites bar
History	Calls up the History bar
Channels	Calls up the Channels bar
Fullscreen	Switches to full screen view
Mail	Summons Outlook Express for Internet e-mail or news
Print	Prints the current page
Edit	Summons FrontPage Express to edit the Web page

Internet Explorer Keyboard Shortcuts

Keyboard Shortcut	What It Does
Backspace	Back (previous page)
Shift+Backspace	Forward (next page)
Shift+F10	Display the pop-up menu for a link
Ctrl+Shift+Tab	Move to the next frame
F5	Refresh the current page
Esc	Stop downloading
Ctrl+O	Go to a new page
Ctrl+N	Open a new window
Ctrl+S	Save the current page
Ctrl+P	Print the current page

Outlook Express Buttons

Outlook Express Button	What It Does
Compose Message	Composes a new e-mail message
Reply to Author	Sends a message back to the author of an incoming message
Reply to All	Sends a message to everyone to whom the original message was addressed
Forward Message	Forwards a message to another user
News groups	Lets you choose a newsgroup
Send and Receive	Delivers any pending e-mail and checks for new e-mail

...For Dummies: #1 Computer Book Series for Beginners

Internet Explorer 4 For Windows® For Dummies®

COMPUTER
BOOK SERIES
FROM IDG

Cheat Sheet

Essential Connection Information

If you don't know what to put in the following blanks, call your Internet service provider for help.

My user ID: _____

My password: *(No! Don't Write It Here!)*

Phone number I dial to access the Internet:

_____

My e-mail address:

_____

Customer service phone number:

_____

DNS Server IP Address: ____ . ____ . ____ . ____

SMTP Server Address:

_____

POP3 Server Address:

_____

News Server Name:

_____

Microsoft Chat Buttons

Microsoft Chat Button	What It Does
	Switches to Comics View
	Switches to Text View
	Sends your message to the chat
	Sends your message to the chat as a thought
	Says something privately to another chat user
	Sends your message to the chat as an action

Web Addresses to Remember

URL	What It Is
www.microsoft.com/ie/ie40	Internet Explorer 4.0 home page
www.microsoft.com/ie/ie40/download	Internet Explorer download site (where you can get Internet Explorer 4 and other add-ons)
home.microsoft.com	The Microsoft customizable home page
www.microsoft.com/sitebuilder	The Microsoft SiteBuilder Network home page, with lots of good information about creating Web pages for Internet Explorer 4
www.yahoo.com	The Yahoo! search service
www.lycos.com	The Lycos search service
www.altavista.digital.com	The AltaVista search service

IDG
BOOKS
WORLDWIDE

...For Dummies: #1 Computer Book Series for Beginners

INTERNET EXPLORER 4
FOR WINDOWS®
FOR
DUMMIES®

by Doug Lowe

IDG Books Worldwide, Inc.
An International Data Group Company

Foster City, CA ♦ Chicago, IL ♦ Indianapolis, IN ♦ Southlake, TX

Internet Explorer 4 For Windows® For Dummies®

Published by
IDG Books Worldwide, Inc.
An International Data Group Company
919 E. Hillsdale Blvd.
Suite 400
Foster City, CA 94404
www.idgbooks.com (IDG Books Worldwide Web site)
www.dummies.com (Dummies Press Web site)

Library of Congress Catalog Card No.: 97-80309

ISBN: 0-7645-0121-6

Printed in the United States of America

10 9 8 7 6 5 4

1DD/RW/QR/ZX/IN

Distributed in the United States by IDG Books Worldwide, Inc.

Distributed by Macmillan Canada for Canada; by Transworld Publishers Limited in the United Kingdom; by IDG Norge Books for Norway; by IDG Sweden Books for Sweden; by Woodslane Pty. Ltd. for Australia; by Woodslane Enterprises Ltd. for New Zealand; by Longman Singapore Publishers Ltd. for Singapore, Malaysia, Thailand, and Indonesia; by Simron Pty. Ltd. for South Africa; by Toppan Company Ltd. for Japan; by Distribuidora Cuspide for Argentina; by Livraria Cultura for Brazil; by Ediciencia S.A. for Ecuador; by Addison-Wesley Publishing Company for Korea; by Ediciones ZETA S.C.R. Ltda. for Peru; by WS Computer Publishing Corporation, Inc., for the Philippines; by Unalis Corporation for Taiwan; by Contemporanea de Ediciones for Venezuela; by Computer Book & Magazine Store for Puerto Rico; by Express Computer Distributors for the Caribbean and West Indies. Authorized Sales Agent: Anthony Rudkin Associates for the Middle East and North Africa.

For general information on IDG Books Worldwide's books in the U.S., please call our Consumer Customer Service department at 800-762-2974. For reseller information, including discounts and premium sales, please call our Reseller Customer Service department at 800-434-3422.

For information on where to purchase IDG Books Worldwide's books outside the U.S., please contact our International Sales department at 415-655-3200 or fax 415-655-3295.

For information on foreign language translations, please contact our Foreign & Subsidiary Rights department at 415-655-3021 or fax 415-655-3281.

For sales inquiries and special prices for bulk quantities, please contact our Sales department at 415-655-3200 or write to the address above.

For information on using IDG Books Worldwide's books in the classroom or for ordering examination copies, please contact our Educational Sales department at 800-434-2086 or fax 817-251-8174.

For press review copies, author interviews, or other publicity information, please contact our Public Relations department at 415-655-3000 or fax 415-655-3299.

For authorization to photocopy items for corporate, personal, or educational use, please contact Copyright Clearance Center, 222 Rosewood Drive, Danvers, MA 01923, or fax 508-750-4470.

is a trademark under exclusive license to IDG Books Worldwide, Inc., from International Data Group, Inc.

About the Author

Doug Lowe lives in sunny Fresno, California (where the motto is "At least it's a *dry* heat"), with his wife Debbie, daughters Rebecca, Sarah, and Bethany, and female Golden Retrievers Nutmeg and Ginger. He works full-time creating outstanding literary works such as *Internet Explorer 4 For Windows For Dummies* and wonders why he hasn't yet won a Pulitzer Prize or had one of his books made into a movie starring Harrison Ford so he can retire. Doug really thinks that Harrison Ford would be excellent as the Dummies Guy and thinks that John Kilcullen's people should call Harrison's people real soon before someone else steals the idea.

In between writing computer books, which leaves about three free hours per month, Doug enjoys golfing and makes it a point to play at least once each decade. Hiking is also a favorite hobby, so much so that Doug really would like to write *Backpacking For Dummies* but hasn't had the time to write a proposal yet because these computer books just keep coming up. Maybe someday.

ABOUT IDG BOOKS WORLDWIDE

Welcome to the world of IDG Books Worldwide.

IDG Books Worldwide, Inc., is a subsidiary of International Data Group, the world's largest publisher of computer-related information and the leading global provider of information services on information technology. IDG was founded more than 25 years ago and now employs more than 8,500 people worldwide. IDG publishes more than 275 computer publications in over 75 countries (see listing below). More than 60 million people read one or more IDG publications each month.

Launched in 1990, IDG Books Worldwide is today the #1 publisher of best-selling computer books in the United States. We are proud to have received eight awards from the Computer Press Association in recognition of editorial excellence and three from *Computer Currents'* First Annual Readers' Choice Awards. Our best-selling *...For Dummies*® series has more than 30 million copies in print with translations in 30 languages. IDG Books Worldwide, through a joint venture with IDG's Hi-Tech Beijing, became the first U.S. publisher to publish a computer book in the People's Republic of China. In record time, IDG Books Worldwide has become the first choice for millions of readers around the world who want to learn how to better manage their businesses.

Our mission is simple: Every one of our books is designed to bring extra value and skill-building instructions to the reader. Our books are written by experts who understand and care about our readers. The knowledge base of our editorial staff comes from years of experience in publishing, education, and journalism — experience we use to produce books for the '90s. In short, we care about books, so we attract the best people. We devote special attention to details such as audience, interior design, use of icons, and illustrations. And because we use an efficient process of authoring, editing, and desktop publishing our books electronically, we can spend more time ensuring superior content and spend less time on the technicalities of making books.

You can count on our commitment to deliver high-quality books at competitive prices on topics you want to read about. At IDG Books Worldwide, we continue in the IDG tradition of delivering quality for more than 25 years. You'll find no better book on a subject than one from IDG Books Worldwide.

John Kilcullen
John Kilcullen
CEO
IDG Books Worldwide, Inc.

Steven Berkowitz
Steven Berkowitz
President and Publisher
IDG Books Worldwide, Inc.

Dedication

This book is dedicated to Bethany. May all your explorations be fruitful.

Author's Acknowledgments

I'd like to thank project editor Kelly Oliver, who showed great patience as deadlines came and went, and manuscripts didn't, until Microsoft finally made beta versions of the software available. Thanks also to Jim McCarter for his excellent tech review, and to copy editor Linda Stark for correcting all my spelling errors and other silly mistakes.

Publisher's Acknowledgments

We're proud of this book; please register your comments through our IDG Books Worldwide Online Registration Form located at http://my2cents.dummies.com.

Some of the people who helped bring this book to market include the following:

Acquisitions, Development, and Editorial

Project Editor: Kelly Oliver

Acquisitions Editor: Michael Kelly

Copy Editor: Linda S. Stark

Technical Editor: Jim McCarter

Editorial Manager: Leah P. Cameron

Editorial Assistant: Donna Love

Production

Project Coordinator: E. Shawn Aylsworth

Layout and Graphics: Steve Arany, Cameron Booker, Lou Boudreau, Linda M. Boyer, Maridee V. Ennis, Angela F. Hunckler, Todd Klemme, Anna Rohrer, Brent Savage, M. Anne Sipahimalani, Michael A. Sullivan

Proofreaders: Arielle Carole Mennelle, Christine Berman, Michelle Croninger, Joel K. Draper, Nancy Price, Rebecca Senninger, Janet M. Withers

Indexer: Sherry Massey

Special Help: Tamara S. Castleman, Senior Copy Editor; Elizabeth Netedu Kuball, Copy Editor; Clark Scheffy, Project Editor

General and Administrative

IDG Books Worldwide, Inc.: John Kilcullen, CEO; Steven Berkowitz, President and Publisher

IDG Books Technology Publishing: Brenda McLaughlin, Senior Vice President and Group Publisher

Dummies Technology Press and Dummies Editorial: Diane Graves Steele, Vice President and Associate Publisher; Mary Bednarek, Acquisitions and Product Development Director; Kristin A. Cocks, Editorial Director

Dummies Trade Press: Kathleen A. Welton, Vice President and Publisher; Kevin Thornton, Acquisitions Manager; Maureen F. Kelly, Editorial Coordinator

IDG Books Production for Dummies Press: Beth Jenkins, Production Director; Cindy L. Phipps, Manager of Project Coordination, Production Proofreading, and Indexing; Kathie S. Schutte, Supervisor of Page Layout; Shelley Lea, Supervisor of Graphics and Design; Debbie J. Gates, Production Systems Specialist; Robert Springer, Supervisor of Proofreading; Debbie Stailey, Special Projects Coordinator; Tony Augsburger, Supervisor of Reprints and Bluelines; Leslie Popplewell, Media Archive Coordinator

Dummies Packaging and Book Design: Patti Crane, Packaging Specialist; Lance Kayser, Packaging Assistant; Kavish + Kavish, Cover Design

♦

The publisher would like to give special thanks to Patrick J. McGovern, without whom this book would not have been possible.

♦

Contents at a Glance

Cartoons at a Glance

By Rich Tennant

page 197

page 159

"Well heck, all the boy did was launch a search on the Web and up comes Tracy's retainer, your car keys, and my bowling trophy here on a site in Seattle!"

page 9

"It's a letter from the company that installed our in-ground sprinkler system. They're offering Internet access now."

page 97

page 297

"He's our new Web Bowzer."

page 37

page 231

Fax: 978-546-7747 • E-mail: the5wave@tiac.net

Table of Contents

Introduction

Microsoft has done it again. Just when you thought you had your computer and the Internet all figured out, here comes a new version of your trusted friend, Internet Explorer.

Welcome, Internet Explorer 4.0. Think about it as, "Internet Explorer, Fore!" because you don't want this new version of Internet Explorer to hit you in the head when you're not looking. That would be bad.

But I have good news! You discovered just the right book. Help is here, within these humble pages.

This book can direct your attention toward Internet Explorer's landing spot so that you can get out of the way. Or, if you can't move with the speed of cyberspace you can at least hold the book over your head like a helmet.

There's a lot to figure out about Internet Explorer 4.0: new features such as channels, subscriptions, Active Desktop, Outlook Express, and the list goes on and on. If you're a Web developer or an aspiring HTML author, there's FrontPage Express and Dynamic HTML to contend with.

This book tackles all these subjects and more, in plain English and with no pretense. No lofty prose here. The language is friendly. You don't need a graduate degree in computer science to get through it. I have no Pulitzer ambitions for this book, but it would be cool if it were made into a movie starring Harrison Ford.

I even occasionally take a carefully aimed potshot at the hallowed and sacred traditions of Internetdom, just to bring a bit of fun to an otherwise dry and tasteless subject. If that doesn't work, I throw in an occasional lawyer joke.

Why Another Internet Book?

Unfortunately, when it comes right down to it, Internet Explorer — like the Internet itself — isn't as easy to use as *they* would have you believe. Alas, Internet Explorer is nothing more than a computer program, and like any computer program, it has its own commands to master, menus to traverse, icons to decipher, nuances to discover, and quirks to work around. Bother.

Oh, and then take the Internet itself. Frankly, the Internet is a sprawling mess. It's filled with klutzy interfaces, programs that don't work the way they should, and systems that were designed decades ago. Finding the information you need on the Internet can be like the proverbial search for a needle in a haystack. The Internet is everything they say it is except easy to use.

That's why you need this book to take you by the hand and walk you step-by-step through all the details of using Internet Explorer 4.0. This book doesn't bog you down with a bunch of puffed-up techno-jargon that makes you feel like your head is about to explode. Instead, this book spells out what you need to know in language that promises not to rap your urge to know more.

Sure, plenty of books about the Internet already crowd the computer section of your local bookstore. IDG Books Worldwide, Inc. even has several excellent books available: *The Internet For Dummies,* 2nd Edition is an especially good general introduction to the Internet. But if you are using — or are planning to use — Internet Explorer, you need to know more than generic Internet stuff. You need to know specifically how to use the features of Internet Explorer 4.0. Many of these features are unique to Internet Explorer 4.0 and are not found in any other Web browser.

How to Use This Book

The beauty of this book is that you don't have to read it through from start to finish. You wouldn't dare pick up the latest Clancy or Grisham novel and skip straight to page 173. But with this book, you can. That's because this book works like a reference. You can read as much or as little of it as you need. You can turn to any part of the book and start reading, and then put the book down after finding the information you needed and get on with your life.

On occasion, this book directs you to use specific keyboard shortcuts to get things done. I indicate such key combinations like this:

Ctrl+Z

which means to hold down the Ctrl key while pressing the Z key, and then release both together. Don't type the plus sign.

Sometimes, I tell you to use a menu command. For example, you may see something like this:

File⇨Open

which means to use the keyboard or mouse to open the File menu and then choose the Open command. (The underlined letters are the keyboard hot keys for the command. To use them, first press the Alt key. In the preceding example, you press and release the Alt key, press and release the F key, and then press and release the O key.) Whenever I describe a message or information you see on-screen, it looks like this:

```
Are we having fun yet?
```

Anything you are instructed to type appears in bold, like so: Type **puns** in the field. You type exactly what you see, with or without spaces.

Internet links are shown <u>underlined</u>, the way they appear on-screen in Internet Explorer. Internet addresses (technically known as *URLs*) appear like this: www.whatever.com.

Another little nicety about this book is that when I tell you to click one of those little toolbar buttons on Internet Explorer's screen, a picture of the button appears in the margin. Seeing what the button looks like helps you find it on-screen.

This book rarely directs you elsewhere for information — just about everything you need to know about using Internet Explorer is in here. However, two other books may come in handy from time to time. The first is *Windows 95 For Dummies* by Andy Rathbone (published by IDG Books Worldwide, Inc.), which is helpful if you're not sure how to perform a Windows 95 task such as copying a file or creating a new folder. The second book is *The Internet For Dummies* by John R. Levine, Carol Baroudi, and Margaret Levine Young (also published by IDG Books Worldwide, Inc.), which is helpful if you decide to venture into the dark recesses of Internet.

Foolish Assumptions

I'm making only three assumptions about you:

- ✔ You use a computer.
- ✔ You use Windows 95 or its replacement, Windows Ninety-Something.
- ✔ You access (or are thinking about accessing) the Internet with Internet Explorer 4.0.

Nothing else. I don't assume that you're a computer guru who knows how to change a controller card or configure memory for optimal usage. Such technical chores are best handled by people who like computers. Hopefully, you are on speaking terms with such a person. Do your best to keep it that way.

How This Book Is Organized

Inside this book are ample chapters arranged into seven parts. Each chapter is broken down into sections that cover various aspects of the chapter's main subject. The chapters have a logical sequence, so reading them in order makes sense (if you're crazy enough to read this entire book). But you don't have to read them that way. You can flip open the book to any page and start reading.

The following sections give you the lowdown on what's in each of the seven parts.

Part I: Preparing for an Internet Expedition

The two chapters in this part deal with really introductory stuff: what the Internet is and how to get connected to it. Part I is the place to start if you haven't visited the Internet before and you're not sure what the World Wide Web is, what www.microsoft.com means, or how to connect your computer to the Internet.

Part II: Embarking on a World Wide Web Adventure

This part is the heart and soul of the book. Its chapters show you how to use the basic features of Internet Explorer to untangle the World Wide Web. You find out how to "surf the Web" like a pro using the Internet Explorer 4 Web browsing features, how to look up information on the Web, how to build a library of your favorite Web sites so you don't always have to hunt them down, and how to get help when you're stuck. You also figure out how to use one of the Internet Explorer 4 hot new features called channel subscriptions, which enables you to access special Web channels that can download new information to your computer automatically while you sleep.

Part III: Outlook Express and Other Ways to Talk

The chapters in this part show you how to use three Microsoft programs that work alongside Internet Explorer to access those parts of the Internet that fall outside the World Wide Web. You can discover how to use Outlook Express to send and receive e-mail and to participate in Internet newsgroups, Microsoft Chat to access online chat areas, and NetMeeting to use voice communications on the Internet and work collaboratively with other Internet users.

Part IV: Customizing Your Explorations

The four chapters in this part show you how to configure Internet Explorer by tweaking its options so that it suits your working style. This stuff is best read by people who like to show their computers who's the boss.

Part V: The Active Desktop

One of the more intriguing new features of Internet Explorer 4 is the Active Desktop, which allows Internet Explorer to take over your Windows 95 desktop so that your computer looks and acts as if it is a part of the World Wide Web. The two chapters in this part show you how to set up the Active Desktop and how to customize it to your needs.

Part VI: Building Your Own Web Pages

If you're someone who enjoys creating your own Web pages, check out the four chapters in this part. Here, you find out how to create your own Web pages using Microsoft FrontPage Express, which comes free with Internet Explorer 4. Then, you find out how to post your HTML documents to a Web site using the new Web Publishing Wizard. And for the technically inclined, you learn how to incorporate the new Dynamic HTML features into your Web pages and how to create your own channel using the Microsoft CDF file format.

Part VII: The Part of Tens

This wouldn't be a *...For Dummies* book if it didn't include a collection of chapters with lists of interesting snippets: Ten Hot Features of Internet Explorer 4.0, My Top Ten Web Site Picks, and so on.

Glossary

People use so much techno-babble when they discuss the Internet that I decided to include an extensive glossary of online terms, free of charge. With this glossary in hand, you can beat the silicon-heads at their own game.

Icons Used in This Book

As you read all this wonderful prose, you occasionally encounter the following icons. They appear in the margins to draw your attention to important information.

Uh-oh, some technical drivel is about to come your way. Cover your eyes if you find technical information offensive.

This icon points out traps you may fall into if you're not careful. Heed these warnings and all shall go well with you, with your children, and with your children's children.

Pay special attention to this icon — it points to some particularly useful tidbit, perhaps a shortcut or a way of using a command that you may not have considered.

This icon points out important information to definitely remember as you use the Internet Explorer features being discussed. The information may not be totally new to you; it may just remind you of something you've temporarily forgotten.

 This icon points out a new feature of Internet Explorer 4.0, for those Internet Explorer 3.0 veterans in the audience.

Where to Go from Here

The Internet is an exciting new computer frontier, and Internet Explorer is hands-down the best way to experience the Internet. So where do you go from here? Online, of course. With this book at your side, you can visit the world from your desktop. Happy exploring!

Part I
Preparing for an Internet Expedition

The 5th Wave — By Rich Tennant

"Well heck, all the boy did was launch a search on the Web and up comes Tracy's retainer, your car keys, and my bowling trophy here on a site in Seattle!"

In this part . . .

*T*he Internet is one of the best things to happen to computers since the invention of the On button. Everyone and his uncle is going online these days. Even television commercials are in on the act — it's amazing how many ads flash Internet addresses at the end. The Internet promises to revolutionize the way we do business, the way we buy cars, the way kids learn at school, even the way we shop for groceries.

The two chapters in this part give you a gentle introduction to the Internet. In Chapter 1, you get a crash course on what the Internet is and why everyone is so excited about it. Then, in Chapter 2, you find out how to get yourself connected so that you don't miss out on all the excitement.

Chapter 1

Welcome to the Internet

. . . .

. . . .

*O*nce upon a time, there were seven stranded castaways lost on a desert isle somewhere in the Pacific. They were completely cut off from civilization: no television, no newspapers, and worst of all — gasp — no Internet access! What would they do?

Fortunately, they had a genius among them: a professor, who figured out a way to access the Internet using an old radio, a few coconut shells, and electricity generated by a makeshift stationary bicycle. The professor set up a Web page announcing the location of the island, but the hapless first mate, Gilligan, somehow managed to crash the server only moments before a Coast Guard sailor was about to access their home page.

So what's the point of this story? Simply that just about everyone — even the crew of the S.S. Minnow — is cruising the Internet these days. If you want to join the tour, but you're afraid you know even less about the Internet than Gilligan, this chapter is for you. It provides a brief introduction to what the Internet is and why you would want to use it. So grab your pith helmet, and let's start exploring!

What Is This Internet Thing?

The Internet is an enormous computer network that links tens of millions of computers all across the planet. The Internet allows you, sitting at your own private computer in a small town in Iowa, to access computers in Moscow or Geneva or Tokyo or Washington, D.C. The Internet is the most exciting thing to happen to computers since the invention of the mouse.

Most people are actually referring to the Internet when they talk about the *Information Superhighway*. The Information Superhighway is supposed to allow every man, woman, and child in the United States — indeed, on the entire planet — to access every conceivable bit of information that has ever been discovered, instantly and without error.

Is the Internet Really As Big As They Say It Is?

The simple fact is, no one really knows just how big the Internet actually is. That's because no one really owns the Internet. But several organizations make it their business to periodically try to find out how big the Internet is. The science is far from exact, but these organizations are able to come up with pretty reasonable estimates.

The best known of these Internet bean counters is Network Wizards, which does a survey every year. In January of 1997, Network Wizards found that the Internet connected 828,000 separate computer networks and that more than 16 million separate computers existed on the Internet. When compared with the 1996 numbers, the 1997 survey shows that the Internet has almost doubled in size in the past year. Or to put it another way, a new computer was added to the Internet every five seconds.

Truth is, estimates such as Network Wizards' are probably low. Consider that three of the large online services — America Online, CompuServe, and The Microsoft Network — together support more than 10 million users. No one knows exactly how many of these subscribers actually use the Internet. Still, the indisputable point is that the Internet is big — and getting bigger every day.

If you find these figures interesting, you can check up on the latest Internet statistics from Network Wizards by accessing its Web site, www.nw.com.

Unfortunately, the Information Superhighway is, at best, a promise of what the future holds. Currently, the Internet still requires a fairly major investment in computer equipment (a decent computer for accessing the Internet still costs around $1,500). And although an enormous amount of information is available on the Internet, the entire contents of the Internet amounts to only a tiny fraction of human knowledge, and what information is there is haphazardly organized and difficult to sift through.

Still, a tiny fraction of all human knowledge is worth having, even if it is poorly organized. And that's why the Internet has become so popular. People love to "surf the Web" (I explain what the *Web* is later in this chapter), hoping to glean some useful bit of information that will make their investment of online time and money worthwhile.

Plus, the Internet is just downright fun.

The Internet: A Network of Networks

The Internet is actually a network of networks. The world is filled with computer networks. Large and small businesses have networks that connect the computers in their offices. Universities have networks that students and faculty can access. Government organizations have networks. And many people belong to online services such as CompuServe, America Online, or The Microsoft Network; these online services are themselves large computer networks.

The Internet's job is to connect all these networks together to form one gigantic mega-network. In fact, the very name *Internet* comes from the fact that the Internet allows connections among distinct computer networks.

The Internet consists of several hundreds of thousands of separate computer networks. These networks in turn connect a whopping 16 million computers to one another.

Who Invented the Internet?

Some people are fascinated by history. They love to watch Ken Burns specials about the Civil War or baseball and subscribe to cable TV just to get the History Channel. If you're one of those history buffs, you may be interested in the following chronicle of the Internet's humble origins.

In the summer of 1969, the four mop-topped singers from Liverpool were breaking up. The war in Vietnam was escalating. Astronauts Neil Armstrong and Buzz Aldrin walked on the moon. And the Department of Defense built a computer network called ARPANET to link its defense installations with several major universities throughout the United States.

In the early 1970s, ARPANET was getting difficult to manage, so it was split into two networks: one for military use, called MILNET, and the other for nonmilitary use. The nonmilitary network retained the name ARPANET. To link MILNET with ARPANET, a new network link, called *Internet Protocol,* or IP, was invented.

The whole purpose of IP was to allow these two networks to communicate with one another. Fortunately, the designers of IP realized that it wouldn't be long before other networks wanted to join in the fun, so they designed IP to allow for more than two networks. In fact, their ingenious design allowed for tens of thousands of networks to communicate via IP.

The decision was a fortuitous one, as the Internet quickly began to grow. By the mid-1980s, the original ARPANET reached its limits. Just in time, the National Science Foundation (NSF) decided to get into the game. NSF had built a network called NSFNET to link its huge supercomputers. (*Supercomputers* are those behemoth computers — the kind of computers that, even today, fill entire rooms and are used to calculate the orbits of distant galaxies, discover new prime numbers, and play chess masters like Kasparov to a draw.)

NSFNET replaced ARPANET as the new background for the Internet. Around that time, magazines such as *Time* and *Newsweek* began writing articles about this new phenomenon called the Internet, and the Net (as it became nicknamed) began to grow like wildfire. Soon NSFNET couldn't keep up with the growth, so several private commercial networks took over management of the Internet backbone. The Internet has doubled in size every year for quite a few years now, and who knows how long this dizzying rate of growth will continue.

If the story of the Internet has a moral, it is that the Internet has probably been so successful precisely because it's not strictly a commercial or government venture. No one is really in charge of the Internet. Instead, the Internet sprang up pretty much on its own. No rules dictate who can and who cannot join the Internet, and no one can kick you or anyone else off the Internet. Kinda warms your cockles, doesn't it?

The Internet Has Many Faces

The Internet is not a single, monolithic entity that has a consistent look and feel for all of its services. Quite the contrary. Over the years, many different services have sprung up on the Internet, each with its own style and appearance. Microsoft Internet Explorer has features that enable you to access most, but not all, of these services.

The World Wide Web

The most popular Internet venue is the World Wide Web, usually called *the Web* for short. The Web is to the Internet what Windows is to DOS: a graphical interface to what otherwise would be a bland and boring place.

The Web enables you to view the information that is available on the Internet using fancy graphics and formatted text, and even incorporates trendy multimedia such as sounds and video.

Information on the World Wide Web is organized into documents called *pages*. A single Web page can be as short as one word, or it can contain hundreds of lines of text. Most pages contain no more information than you can comfortably squeeze onto an $8^1/2$-x-11-inch printed page.

Each page on the Web can contain text, graphics, sounds, videos, and — most important — links to other Web pages with related information. For example, a page that contains information about frogs may contain links to other pages with information about princes, muppets, or hallucinogenic substances.

Every Web site has a *home page,* which is the starting point for exploring information available at the Web site. The home page may have links to additional pages at the same site, as well as to pages on different Web sites. Thus, clicking a link may take you to an entirely different Web site that's located halfway around the world from the one you were accessing, without jet lag, airsickness, or even a noticeable hesitation!

That's the neat thing about surfing the Web. It allows you to travel the world without leaving your home — and without long-distance charges! Your Internet service provider charges you a flat monthly or hourly rate, whether you're retrieving data from a Web site four miles or four *thousand* miles from your computer.

To access the Web, you need a special program called a Web browser. A *Web browser* knows how to display the special formats and codes used to send information over the World Wide Web. The Web browser reads these special codes over the Internet and translates them into fancy displays and beautiful pictures for your screen. The browser also enables you to follow the links from one Web page to another, simply by clicking the link.

Just as you can choose among many different word processing or spreadsheet programs, you have your choice of many different Web browsers to use. Internet Explorer 4 is the latest and greatest Web browser program from Microsoft. Figure 1-1 shows Internet Explorer 4 in action, displaying a page from the World Wide Web.

Internet Explorer isn't the only Web browser on the block, of course. Another popular Web browser is Netscape's Navigator. Netscape and Microsoft are in a neck-and-neck race to see who can create the best browser software — kind of like the way Microsoft and WordPerfect were in a race to see who could create the best word processing software a few years ago. Obviously, this book is about exploring the Internet using Internet Explorer. If you use Netscape, you should probably be reading *Netscape and the Worldwide Web For Dummies,* 2nd Edition (published by IDG Books Worldwide, Inc.), by Paul Hoffman instead.

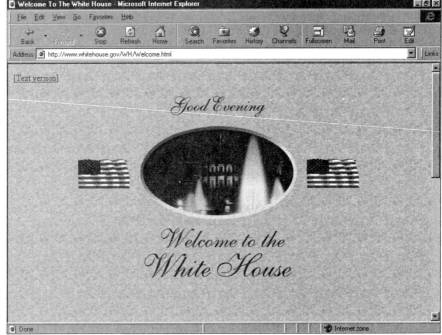

Figure 1-1:
Internet
Explorer 4
displays
pages from
the World
Wide Web,
including
this one,
the White
House's
own home
page.

Netscape distributes the latest version of Navigator, 4.0, in a suite of Internet programs called Netscape Communicator. In addition to Navigator, Communicator includes an electronic mail program, a newsgroup program, a special program to help you create your Web pages, and more.

Web browsers such as Internet Explorer aren't limited to accessing just the World Wide Web. In fact, you can access most of the other parts of the Internet directly from Internet Explorer or from programs that come with Internet Explorer.

Electronic mail

Electronic mail (sometimes called *e-mail*) lets you exchange private messages with any other user on the Internet, no matter where in the country or world that user lives. Unlike the postal service, Internet e-mail is delivered almost instantly. And unlike Federal Express, you don't have to pay $13 for fast delivery. In fact, Internet e-mail is probably the least expensive yet most efficient form of communication available.

E-mail is not just for sending short notes to your friends, either. You can use e-mail to send entire files of information to coworkers. For example, I used Internet e-mail to send the document files for this book to my editor at IDG Books Worldwide, Inc., and she in turn used e-mail to send me back corrections and technical questions.

Many programs are available for reading Internet e-mail, including Microsoft Exchange, which comes with Windows 95, and Microsoft Outlook, which comes with Microsoft Office 97. However, Internet Explorer comes with its own e-mail program in the form of a scaled-back version of Outlook, called Outlook Express. Figure 1-2 shows Outlook Express in action. I show you how to use Outlook Express to read e-mail in Chapter 8.

Newsgroups

Newsgroups are online discussion groups — places where users with common interests gather to share ideas. Thousands of newsgroups exist, covering just about every topic imaginable. You can find newsgroups that discuss obscure computer topics, fan clubs for various celebrities, online support groups, and who knows what else.

Most Internet newsgroups are distributed over *Usenet,* a network of special server computers that contain the special software needed to handle newsgroups. As a result, you sometimes see the terms *Usenet* and *newsgroups* used together. However, you can access some newsgroups that aren't a part of Usenet.

As luck would have it, Outlook Express, the handy e-mail program that comes with Internet Explorer 4, is also adept at handling Internet newsgroups. Figure 1-3 shows Outlook Express accessing a newsgroup — in this case, the newsgroup happens to be devoted to the subject of amateur softball. I give you the ins and outs of using Outlook Express to participate in newsgroup discussions in Chapter 9.

Don't be confused by the term *news* in newsgroups. Newsgroups are *not* a news service designed to give you accurate, up-to-date, and unbiased information about current events. Newsgroups are places where people with common interests can share opinions. In this sense, newsgroups are more like talk radio than a news program.

File Transfer Protocol (FTP)

File Transfer Protocol, or FTP as it is usually called, is the Internet equivalent of a network file server. FTP is the Internet's primary method of moving files around. Thousands of FTP sites make their files available for downloading. All you have to do is sign in to the FTP site, find the file you want to download, and click.

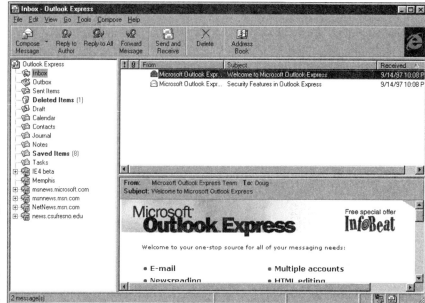

Figure 1-2:
Using
e-mail with
Outlook
Express.

Internet Explorer has built-in support for FTP, so you can easily log in to an FTP site and download files to your computer. In fact, you don't have to do anything special to access FTP from Internet Explorer; you may not even be aware that you're using FTP.

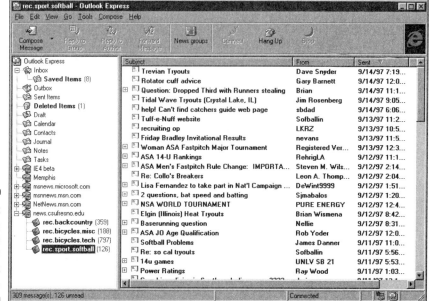

Figure 1-3:
Accessing
newsgroups
with
Outlook
Express.

Telnet

Telnet is a way of connecting to another computer on the Internet and actually running programs on that computer, as if your computer were a terminal attached to the other computer. Telnet is one of the many Internet services that is rapidly losing popularity as the World Wide Web becomes more popular. However, some Internet sites are still available only via Telnet. Most of these seem to be public libraries, so if you want to search the card catalog of your local public library, you may need to learn how to use Telnet.

Although Telnet may be a bit archaic for Internet Explorer's taste, if you're using Windows 95, you already have a built-in program that lets you Telnet to other computer sites.

Internet Relay Chat (IRC)

Internet Relay Chat, or IRC, is an online feature that enables you to talk with other Internet users live. IRC is kind of like a huge online party line; it's the Internet feature that keeps many users connected into the wee hours of the morning, chatting with other cyberjunkies around the planet.

Be warned: The Internet is not censored

No censorship exists on the Internet. If you look hard enough, you can find just about anything on the Internet — not all of it wholesome. In addition to information about fly-fishing, knitting, and the solar system, you can find photographs of men and women in various states of dress and undress, and often engaged in unmentionable acts that would make Hugh Hefner blush.

Unfortunately, you can't do much about the content on the Internet. Congress has introduced legislation that would ban indecent content from the Internet, but the Supreme Court has ruled such legislation unconstitutional. After all, indecency is a pretty ambiguous concept, and the First Amendment pretty much prohibits Congress from banning any but the most obscene materials from publication on any medium.

However, just because Congress can't prevent people from publishing offensive material on the Internet doesn't mean that you have to view it. One of the new developments on the Internet is a voluntary system of ratings that lets you know whether an Internet site contains offensive material. Internet Explorer enables you to control whether you (or anyone in your household) can view such material. The solution's not perfect, but it does go a long way toward controlling the amount of offensive material kids are exposed to. In Chapter 13, I describe Internet Explorer controls for blocking offensive material.

Internet Explorer 4 comes with a program called Microsoft Chat that enables you to participate in IRC chats. Microsoft Chat, which I cover in Chapter 10, is one of the more unusual programs you can expect to encounter. As you chat on the Internet, it actually draws a comic strip on-screen, using comic-book style characters to represent the different people you are conversing with.

Gopher

Gopher was an early attempt to make the Internet easy to use. Before gopher, people had to use cryptic commands to access the Internet. Gopher presented Internet information using a series of text-based menus.

Gopher has been largely replaced by the World Wide Web, which is easier to use because of its graphic nature. The good news is that Internet Explorer can handle what few gopher sites still exist. In fact, Internet Explorer presents gopher as if it were a part of the World Wide Web. So you probably won't even notice when you display a gopher page.

Chapter 2

Getting Connected with Internet Explorer

● ●

In This Chapter

▶ Finding out whether you're already connected to the Internet

▶ Getting connected, if you aren't so lucky

▶ Comparing various Internet pricing plans to get the best deal

▶ Setting up your Internet connection with the Internet Connection Wizard

● ●

The hardest part about using the Internet is figuring out how to get connected to it the first time. After you figure that out, the rest is easy. (Well, *relatively* easy. Nothing about computers is easy!)

This chapter explores the various options for connecting your computer to the Internet using Internet Explorer 4. With luck, you discover that you're already connected to the Internet and Internet Explorer is set up on your computer, so you can skip this chapter and get on with the fun. If you're not so fortunate, read on to find out to get the job done.

You May Already Be on the Internet . . .

It's true. You may have been on the Internet for years now and not realized it. And you may have already won $10 million from Publisher's Clearinghouse, and maybe tomorrow you'll get struck by lightning, and your IQ will double.

Actually, the possibility that you already have access to the Internet isn't that outlandish. Here are some reasonable scenarios:

✔ If you subscribe to one of the major online services such as America
Online, CompuServe, or The Microsoft Network, you already have
access to the Internet. Each of these online services provides a link to
the Internet. In the past, online services provided only limited access to
the Internet and were among the more expensive methods of connecting to the Net. But nowadays, the major online services offer full
Internet access at competitive prices.

✔ If you use a computer at work, and that computer is a part of a local
area network (LAN), and the LAN is connected to the Internet, you may
be able to access the Internet via the LAN. Talk to your resident network guru to find out.

✔ The computers at many schools are connected to the Internet. If you're
a student, you may be able to bribe your teachers into letting you
access the Internet. You may even get extra credit for using the
Internet — especially if you use it to do your homework.

✔ Some public libraries have computers that are connected to the Net.
With access at a public library, you probably won't be able to set up
your own account to send and receive private e-mail. But you may be
able to access newsgroups and the World Wide Web.

What about the Unlucky Rest of Us?

If you don't have access to the Internet through one of the sources listed in
the preceding section, you have no alternative but to set up your own
Internet access at home. Unfortunately, you can't do so without having to
contend with at least some of the boring technical details.

Following are a few general tips I want to offer before I get into the details of
setting up your Internet access:

✔ Upgrade to one of the latest and greatest versions of Windows:
Windows 95 or Windows NT 4.0. One of the favorable things about
these new versions of Windows is that they have built-in support for
the Internet. Setting up Internet access for Windows 3.1 is much more
difficult; besides, you need one of the newer versions of Windows to
experience all the features of Internet Explorer 4.0. This book assumes
that you are running Windows 95 or Windows NT 4.0.

✔ Make sure that your computer is located near a telephone outlet.

✔ If you have a friend who already has access to the Internet, treat him to
lunch and pick his brain (well, not literally). Find out what kind of
modem he has, who his Internet service provider (ISP) is, how much he
is paying for it, what he likes best about it, what he hates about it, what
he would do differently, who he thinks played the best Batman, and
whether he thinks O.J. really did it.

✔ If you have a friend who happens to be a computer expert, see if you can bribe her into helping you set up your Internet access. Don't offer cash; barter is better. Offer to mow her lawn or wash her car.

First, You Need a Modem

The first thing you need to connect your computer to the Internet is a *modem*. If your computer is brand new, you're lucky: It probably already has a modem in it. In that case, all you have to do is plug the modem into the telephone jack using a phone cord, and you're ready to go.

If your computer doesn't have a modem, you have to purchase and install one yourself. The basic rule of modem-buying is this:

Buy the fastest modem you can afford.

Modems come in a variety of speeds, but the two common speeds being hawked at computer stores these days are 33,600 bps and 56,000 bps. Bps stands for *bits per second* and is simply a measure of how fast the modem can pump data through the phone lines. (The term *baud* is sometimes used as a substitute for bps. Both have pretty much the same meaning.)

✔ The slower but less expensive modems are the 33,600 bps variety. You often see these modems referred to as 33.6 or V.34 (pronounced *vee-dot-thirty-four*). If you shop around, you can find 33.6 modems for as little as $50.

✔ The faster modems are the 56,000 bps modems, also known as 56K. A decent 56K modem should cost in the neighborhood of $150 or $200. Before you make such an investment, be sure to check with your Internet service provider or online service to find out if it supports 56K transmission and whether one brand of 56K modem is preferred over others.

✔ If your computer has an older modem in it, watch out. Older modems may not be fast enough to efficiently access the World Wide Web. If you're working with an older 14,400 bps modem or — heaven forbid — a 2,400 bps modem, you need to replace it with a faster model.

Most modems also enable you to send and receive faxes. Because this feature is handy and doesn't increase the cost of the modem, make sure that the modem you buy includes fax support.

What about ISDN?

ISDN, which stands for *Integrated Services Digital Network*, is a digital rather than analog phone line. ISDN allows data to be sent much faster than a conventional phone line — up to 128 Kbps rather than 56 Kbps (kilobytes per second). As an added plus, a single ISDN line can be logically split into two separate channels, so you can carry on a voice conversation while your computer is connected to the Internet.

Sounds great. The only catch is that it's expensive. An ISDN connection doesn't require a modem. Instead, a special ISDN adapter is used, and that will set you back at least $250. In addition, you have to pay the phone company anywhere from $50 to $200 to install the ISDN line, and you pay a monthly fee ranging from $25 to $50 (depending on your area). On top of that, you may be billed by the minute for usage. For example, in my area, an ISDN line costs $24.95 per month, plus usage fees of about a penny a minute.

Over the next few years, the cost of ISDN will probably come down. Until then, ISDN will be used mostly by die-hard computer geeks.

If you're not a die-hard computer geek, but still want to learn more about ISDN, check out *ISDN For Dummies*, 2nd Edition, by David Angell (published by IDG Books Worldwide, Inc.).

A fairly recent alternative to ISDN for high-speed Internet access is Internet cable modems, which enable you to connect to the Internet via your local cable television company. Cable modems are lightning fast — from 500 Kbps to 10,000 Kbps. When I wrote this, cable modem service was available in only a few dozen cities in the United States. If cable modems catch on, however, service should be available in most cities within a year or so.

Your modem must be connected to a phone line so your computer can access the outside world. Unfortunately, whenever you use the Internet, the modem ties up your phone line. Anyone calling your number gets a busy signal, and you can't use the phone to call out for pizza. If being deprived of telephone privileges while you're online proves to be a problem, you can always have the phone company install a separate phone line for your modem.

If the thought of installing a modem nauseates you, pack up your computer and take it to your friendly local computer shop. The folks there can sell you a modem and install it for you for a small charge.

Next, You Need a Service Provider

An *Internet service provider,* or ISP, is a company that charges you, usually on a monthly basis, for access to the Internet. The ISP has a bunch of modems connected to phone lines that you can dial into. These modems are connected to a computer system, which is in turn connected to the Internet via a high-speed data link. The ISP's computer acts as a liaison between your computer and the Internet.

Typically, an ISP provides you with the following services in exchange for your hard-earned money:

- **Access to the World Wide Web via one of two types of connections — a PPP connection or a SLIP connection:** You don't have to worry about the technical differences between these two types of connections; you just have to know which type you have so you can configure your software properly.

- **Electronic mail:** You will be assigned an e-mail address that anyone anywhere on the Internet can use to send you mail. You can use Microsoft's Outlook Express, which comes with Internet Explorer 4, to access your e-mail. See Chapter 8 for more information.

- **Access to Internet newsgroups:** In the newsgroups, you can follow ongoing discussions about your favorite topics. Read all about newsgroups in Chapter 9.

- **Software to access the Internet:** In many cases, this software includes Microsoft Internet Explorer. Or it may include a different Web browser, such as Netscape Navigator. (If Internet Explorer isn't provided by your ISP, you can obtain it free from Microsoft after you set up your Internet connection. Find out how later in this chapter, under "Finally, You Need Internet Explorer.")

- **Technical support, the quality of which varies greatly:** If you have trouble with your Internet connection, try calling your ISP's technical support line. If you're lucky, an actual human being who knows something about computers will pick up the phone and help you solve your problem. Next best: You're put on hold, but someone will eventually answer and help you. Not so good: The technical support line is always busy. Worse: You get a recording that says, "All our support engineers are busy. Please leave a message and we'll get back to you." Yeah, right.

Basically two types of companies provide access to the Internet: commercial online services such as America Online, CompuServe, and The Microsoft Network, and independent Internet service providers. The following sections describe the pros and cons of both types of providers and the Internet access they provide.

Online services

All the major online services allow you to connect to the Internet. On the plus side, you gain access to unique content that's available only to members of the online service. On the minus side, you pay for this extra service. The following paragraphs describe the pricing plans of the three major online services.

- ✔ **America Online (AOL):** The most popular online service, America Online boasts something like 8 million users. AOL has several pricing plans. The Standard Monthly plan gives you unlimited access to AOL and the Internet for $19.95 per month; if you prepay 12 months, the rate drops to $17.95 per month. The Light Usage plan gives you three hours per month for $4.95, with each additional hour costing $2.95. And the Limited Usage plan gives you five hours for $9.95 per month, again with each additional hour costing $2.95.

- ✔ **CompuServe:** Running second in online service popularity is CompuServe, which claims more than 5 million users. CompuServe has two pricing plans. The Standard Plan gives you five free hours per month for $9.95, with each additional hour costing $2.95 (it's the same as America Online's Limited Usage plan). The Super Value plan gives you 20 hours per month for $24.95, with each additional hour costing $1.95.

- ✔ **The Microsoft Network (MSN):** MSN is Microsoft's attempt to challenge America Online and CompuServe. The Microsoft Network offers two price plans: Premier, which gives you five hours of connect time each month for $6.95, with each additional hour costing $2.50; and Premier Flat Rate, which gives you unlimited hours for $19.95 per month.

If you opt to use an online service as your Internet service provider, you need to carefully select the correct pricing plan for the number of hours you intend to use the service. To make the point, Table 2-1 shows the monthly cost for each of the preceding plans for monthly usage of 10, 20, 40, and 60 hours. As you can see, the actual monthly cost varies tremendously depending on which plan you select.

Table 2-1	Pricing Plans Compared			
Price Plan	*10 hours*	*20 hours*	*40 hours*	*60 hours*
America Online Standard	$19.95	$19.95	$19.95	$19.95
America Online Light Usage	$25.60	$55.10	$114.10	$173.10

Price Plan	10 hours	20 hours	40 hours	60 hours
America Online Limited Usage	$24.70	$54.20	$113.20	$172.20
CompuServe Standard	$24.70	$54.20	$113.20	$172.20
CompuServe Super Value	$24.95	$24.95	$63.95	$102.95
The Microsoft Network Premier	$19.45	$44.95	$94.95	$144.95
The Microsoft Network Premier Flat Rate	$19.95	$19.95	$19.95	$19.95

I hear too many horror stories about families that have signed up for America Online or CompuServe, expecting the monthly bill to be only $9.95, only to discover a $200 bill the first month. The problem is that the kids discover the Internet some evening and end up spending three or four hours online every night for two weeks before the parents catch on.

My advice is that if you sign up for an online service, always start off with the frequent user plan. Such a plan may cost you $10 or $15 more if you end up not using it as much as you expect, but that's a lot better than paying $50 to $100 more if you end up using it more than you expect. And make sure all family members, including the kids, understand how the pricing works.

Are the online services worth it?

Because you can access the Internet in less expensive ways, this question naturally comes up: "Are the extra features you get with an online service worth the extra cost?" This may sound like a cop-out, but there's no right or wrong answer to that question. It all depends on whether you use and benefit from the additional features provided by online services.

One major advantage of online services is their organization. The Internet is a sprawling mess, and sometimes it's hard to find what you want. In contrast, online services are well organized. Information in online services is neatly arranged according to topic. Not so on the Internet.

Another benefit you can probably expect from your online service is customer service support. CompuServe and America Online both have large support staffs that can help make sure that you get on and stay on the Internet without a lot of technical headaches. The quality of technical support that comes with an ISP varies greatly from one ISP to the next.

Still, if you subscribe to an online service and then discover that you use it only to access the Internet, you may be better off canceling your online service subscription and signing up with a simple Internet service provider instead.

Internet service providers

The alternative to using a commercial online service is to sign up with an Internet service provider, or ISP. ISPs provide the same Internet access that online services do, but they don't provide their own additional content. ISPs are invariably less expensive than commercial online services because they don't have the added expense that results from providing their own proprietary services.

Technically, any company that provides you with Internet access is an ISP, including commercial online services. However, I prefer to use the term ISP to refer to a company that specializes in providing only Internet access, without providing a separate online service of its own.

The changing role of online services

The sudden growth of the Internet has had a profound impact on established online services such as CompuServe and America Online, and even on newer online services, such as The Microsoft Network. In the past, online services required that you use software provided by the online service to access the information available at the service. For example, to access America Online, you must use special software provided by America Online. CompuServe and The Microsoft Network work the same way.

All that is changing, however. Online services are discovering that users prefer to choose access software — so the providers are slowly but surely moving their services to a format that allows users access with standard Internet Web browsers such as Netscape Navigator and Internet Explorer.

Now, these developments don't mean that online services are becoming part of the World Wide Web, or that you can look forward to free CompuServe or America

Online access. The online services will continue to offer distinctive subscriber-only features, such as discussion forums, file libraries, stock quote services, and reference databases.

The gradual change means a move toward using the same software to access an online service and the World Wide Web, and picking which browser program you prefer to use to access your online service.

These changes are evolving slowly. You can't change the software used by four or five million subscribers all at once. But the change is certain, and within a few years, all the major online services will allow you to use Internet Explorer or any other Web browser to access their content.

In fact, The Microsoft Network is already at that point. The latest version of MSN is Web-based, so that you can move seamlessly between Internet Web sites and The Microsoft Network without changing browsers.

You can choose from nationally known service providers such as NETCOM or AT&T WorldNet Service, or you can select a local ISP. To find the ISPs in your area, check the *Yellow Pages* under Computers — Online Services and Internet.

Most ISPs offer unlimited access for $15 to $20 per month. Some offer a limited hour plan for slightly less (for example, 40 hours for $10). Either way, the cost of using an ISP is likely to be less than using a commercial online service, unless you end up using the Internet for only a few hours each month.

Both America Online and The Microsoft Network allow you to access their services for a low monthly fee ($9.95 for AOL, $6.95 for MSN) provided that you use your own Internet service provider. In other words, you can access America Online or The Microsoft Network by dialing in to your own ISP rather than by dialing one of AOL's or MSN's access numbers.

Finally, You Need Internet Explorer

Naturally, before you can begin to use Internet Explorer, you must install it on your computer. The section explains how.

As you may know, Internet Explorer is free. You can download it from any of several sites on the Internet, and you can use it without charge. There are no restrictions on how you can use it: At home or at the office, Internet Explorer is completely free.

How can the good people at Microsoft afford to distribute Internet Explorer for free? Because they're hoping that the browser will catch on like wildfire. Internet Explorer 3 was a huge success. Microsoft hopes to build on that success by offering Internet Explorer 4 at the same irresistible rate.

For sure, Microsoft plans to make plenty of money from Internet Explorer — not by selling Internet Explorer itself, but by establishing Internet Explorer 4 as the standard Internet browser, used by more people than any other browser. Microsoft then plans to make its money by selling the development tools that Web authors and software developers need to create interesting content — viewable only with Internet Explorer.

Here are some of the ways you can obtain Internet Explorer 4:

✔ If you already have Internet access using another program (such as Netscape Navigator or an earlier version of Internet Explorer), you can download Internet Explorer 4 from the Microsoft Internet Explorer download page at www.microsoft.com/ie/ie40. Note that the download for Internet Explorer can take several hours. Better go to the local video store and rent a movie before proceeding. Or start the download just before you go to bed. The download should be finished by morning.

✔ If you recently purchased a new computer, Internet Explorer 4 is probably already installed.

✔ You can subscribe to an Internet service provider that uses Internet Explorer as its default browser. But make sure that the service uses the latest version of Internet Explorer; some ISPs offer only older versions of Internet Explorer.

Internet Explorer has been through several major revisions. The current version, Internet Explorer 4.0, is among the more powerful Web browsers available. If you have an earlier version (3.0, 2.0, or 1.0), be sure to upgrade to Version 4.0 as soon as possible. You can find Internet Explorer 4.0 available for download at `www.microsoft.com/ie/ie40`.

After you download the Internet Explorer file, exit from your Web browser; open the folder you downloaded into, and double-click the file's icon. The Internet Explorer setup program then installs Internet Explorer for you. (Depending on the browser you use, Internet Explorer may automatically install itself after the download finishes. If so, just sit back and enjoy the ride.)

If you don't want to contend with an hours-long download, you can get Internet Explorer 4 on CD-ROM directly from Microsoft. Just give them a call at 1-800-426-9400. Have your credit card ready; the Internet Explorer 4 CD-ROM costs about $5.

To actually install the downloaded Internet Explorer 4 on your computer, just follow the instructions that appear when you call up the `www.microsoft.com/ie/ie40` download page. If you get Internet Explorer 4 on a CD-ROM, insert the CD-ROM in your CD-ROM drive and follow the instructions that appear on-screen.

The Internet Explorer 4 Setup program asks you several questions before it installs Internet Explorer on your computer. For starters, the Setup program asks if you want to install all of Internet Explorer or just part of it. You have three choices:

✔ **Browser Only Installation:** Installs just the Internet Explorer 4 Web browser. This option requires the least amount of disk space and downloads from Microsoft's Web site fastest, but you don't get any of the Internet Explorer 4 extra goodies such as Outlook Express or Microsoft Chat.

✔ **Standard Installation:** Installs the Internet Explorer 4 Web browser plus Outlook Express. This takes longer to download and requires more disk space than the Browser Only Installation, but not as much as the Full Installation option.

✔ **Full Installation:** Installs all of Internet Explorer 4: the Web browser, Outlook Express, Microsoft Chat, NetMeeting, FrontPage Express, NetShow, and the Web Publishing Wizard.

If you have plenty of disk space on your computer and don't mind a long download (as in several hours long), I suggest you opt for the Full Installation so you'll be able to use all the Internet Explorer 4 features. If you choose a Standard Installation or Browser Only Installation, you can always return to the download page later and pick up the components you didn't install the first time.

Setup also asks if you want to install an optional feature called the Active Desktop. This feature changes the way the Windows 95 desktop and My Computer windows work. You can read all about it in Chapters 16 and 17. If you choose not to install the Active Desktop now, you can always install it later if you want to.

Now You Can Set Up Your Internet Connection

In the old, pre-Windows 95 days, setting up a connection to the Internet was a complicated affair best handled by computer experts with pocket protectors and tape on their glasses. Now, with Windows 95 and Internet Explorer 4, configuring your computer to connect to the Internet is a simple, straightforward process. All you have to do is run a special program called the *Internet Connection Wizard*. The Wizard handles all the configuration details for you.

To run the Internet Connection Wizard, follow these steps:

1. **Gather the information you need to configure your Internet connection.**

    You need the following information, which your Internet service provider should be able to supply:

    - The name of your Internet service provider

    - The telephone number you dial to connect to the Internet

    - The name and password you must use to access the system

    - Your IP address, unless an IP address is assigned automatically each time you log on

    - The DNS server address, which looks like a bunch of numbers with periods where they don't belong, as in 123.4.56.789

    - Your e-mail address and the address of your e-mail server

2. Fetch your Windows 95 installation disks or CD-ROM.

You may not need these, but the Internet Connection Wizard sometimes asks for them. Better keep them handy just in case.

3. Start the Internet Connection Wizard.

Click the Start button on the taskbar and choose Programs➪ Internet Explorer➪Connection Wizard. When you start the Internet Connection Wizard, the dialog box shown in Figure 2-1 greets you.

Figure 2-1:
The Internet Connection Wizard.

4. Click Next >.

The Internet Connection Wizard displays the dialog box shown in Figure 2-2, which gives you three choices for configuring your computer for the Internet.

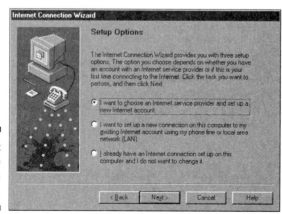

Figure 2-2:
You have three choices.

- The first option enables you to set up a new Internet connection. Choose this option if you don't already have any type of Internet connection or an account with an Internet service provider. The Internet Connection Wizard uses your modem to dial into a Microsoft computer that maintains a list of Internet service providers. A list of ISPs in your area appears, and you are granted the privilege of signing up with one of these providers and having your connection configured automatically.

- The second option assumes that you have an account with an Internet service provider, but you haven't yet configured your computer to access the account. The Internet Connection Wizard asks you to enter information about your account so that it can configure your Internet connection.

- Pick the third option if your computer has been configured for the Internet and you want to retain your current settings.

5. **Choose the second option (assuming that you already have an Internet account) and then click Ne<u>x</u>t >.**

   The Internet Connection Wizard displays the dialog box shown in Figure 2-3, asking whether you plan to connect to the Internet via a modem and phone line or through a local area network.

6. **Check the appropriate connection option and then click Ne<u>x</u>t >.**

   Assuming you are connecting via a phone line, the Wizard displays a dialog box similar to the one shown in Figure 2-4.

7. **Click Ne<u>x</u>t >.**

   The dialog box shown in Figure 2-5 appears.

8. **Type the phone number for your service provider and then click Ne<u>x</u>t >.**

   The dialog box shown in Figure 2-6 appears next.

Figure 2-3:
The Internet
Connection
Wizard asks
how you
will connect
to the
Internet.

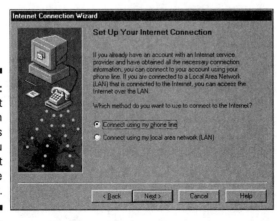

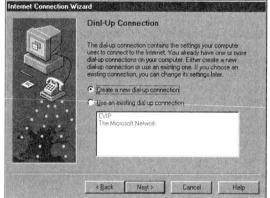

9. Type your name and password, and then click Ne_x_t>.

Your password is not displayed when you type it, so you don't need to worry about anyone watching over your shoulder. When you click Next>, the Internet Connection Wizard displays the dialog box shown in Figure 2-7.

Figure 2-7:
I'd say
"No" if I
were you.

10. If you need to change any of the advanced settings for your Internet connection, click the _Y_es option, and then click Ne_x_t> and enter the information for the advanced settings you need.

In most cases, you can skip these advanced settings. You should use the advanced settings only if your ISP uses a SLIP connection rather than a PPP connection, or if your ISP tells you to set your browser to use a specific IP or DNS server address. The good news is that you don't have to know anything about what SLIP connection, IP address, or DNS server address means. Just type the information provided by your Internet service provider and get on with it.

11. Click Ne_x_t>.

The dialog box shown in Figure 2-8 appears.

12. Type a name for your connection, and then click Ne_x_t>.

You see a series of dialog boxes that enable you to configure the Outlook Express program, which comes with Internet Explorer 4, so that it can handle your e-mail and Internet newsgroups.

13. Type the information requested on each of the Outlook Express configuration screens, clicking Ne_x_t> to move from one screen to the next.

You need to type in your e-mail address and the name of your e-mail and Internet News servers. This information should be supplied to you by your Internet service provider.

Eventually, the dialog box shown in Figure 2-9 appears.

Figure 2-8:
Type a name for your connection.

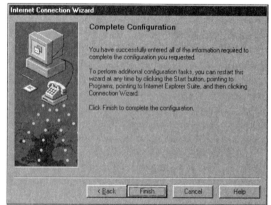

Figure 2-9:
It's about time.

14. Click Finish.

Your computer grinds and whirls for a moment, and then the Internet Connection Wizard disappears — finally!

Now, you can access the Internet by double-clicking the Internet Explorer icon that appears on your desktop. (If you opted to install the Active Desktop option when you installed Internet Explorer, you don't have to double-click the icon; a single click does the trick.) When the Connection Manager dialog box appears, click Connect and start exploring!

Part II
Embarking on a World Wide Web Adventure

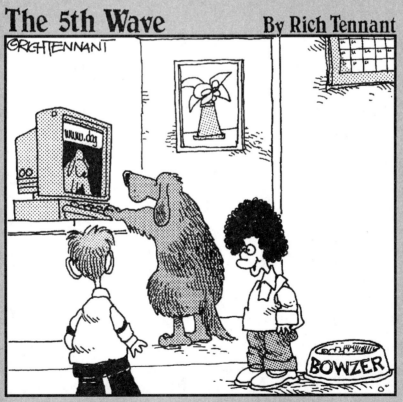

The 5th Wave   By Rich Tennant

"He's our new Web Bowzer."

In this part . . .

This is the part of the book where you discover the basics of using Internet Explorer: how to start it, how to use Internet Explorer to browse the World Wide Web, how to look for and find the information you're interested in, how to keep track of your favorite places, and how to get help when you don't know what you're doing.

This is just the beginning of your Internet explorations. After you have these basics under your belt, you'll be ready to take on the most advanced topics covered in the rest of this book. But, as a great king once advised, it is best to begin at the beginning, and go on until you come to the end, and then stop. So grab your pith helmet and prepare for Web Wonderland!

Chapter 3
Pushing Off

· ·

In This Chapter

▶ Starting Internet Explorer

▶ Understanding World Wide Web addresses

▶ Displaying pages on the World Wide Web

▶ Saving and printing Web pages

▶ Downloading files from the Internet

▶ Finding information on a page

▶ Exiting Internet Explorer and disconnecting from the Internet

· ·

*W*hen you have your Internet connection in place and Internet Explorer installed, you're ready to begin your Internet explorations. This chapter shows you how to use Internet Explorer's basic features to surf the Web. You won't gather intimate knowledge about all the nuances of using Internet Explorer — I save some of the more exotic features for later chapters. In this chapter, I focus on the foundation: how to start Internet Explorer, how to explore the Web, and so on.

Starting Internet Explorer

The first step to surfing the Web using Internet Explorer is starting the program. There are at least three ways to start Internet Explorer:

Internet
Explorer

✔ Double-click the Internet Explorer icon that appears on your desktop.

(If you don't have this icon on your desktop, you probably need to install Internet Explorer — read Chapter 2. If you chose to install the Active Desktop feature when you installed Internet Explorer, you need to click the Internet Explorer only once — double-clicking the icon isn't required. You can find out more information about the Active Desktop feature in Chapter 16.)

✔ Click the Start button on the taskbar, and then choose Programs⇨ Internet Explorer⇨Internet Explorer.

 ✔ Click the small Launch Internet Explorer Browser icon that appears in the taskbar.

Whichever method you opt for, Internet Explorer grinds and churns for a moment and then displays the Dialing Progress dialog box, as shown in Figure 3-1.

Figure 3-1:
The Dialing
Progess
dialog box.

After the Dialing Progress dialog box appears, your computer automatically dials the phone number of your ISP. If the modem volume is turned up, you hear a dial tone, the familiar tones as the number is dialed, two or three rings, and then a few moments of rather obnoxious squealing as the modems establish their connection.

After a connection is established, the Internet Explorer window appears and goes directly to your start page, as shown Figure 3-2.

 You can resize the Internet Explorer window just as you would any other window. I usually like to work with Internet Explorer maximized so that it fills the entire screen and displays as much of each Web page as possible. To maximize a window, click the Maximize button in the upper-right corner of the Internet Explorer window.

After Internet Explorer dials into your ISP, you may be faced with a window in which you must type log-in information (see Figure 3-3). For example, my ISP requires me to type in my user ID and password, even though the Connection Manager knows my user ID and password. If your ISP tells you to type similar information, you have to follow its instructions.

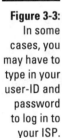

Figure 3-2:
Welcome to
Internet
Explorer 4!

Figure 3-3:
In some
cases, you
may have to
type in your
user-ID and
password
to log in to
your ISP.

Typing the log-in information every time you access the Internet is a big-time hassle. Fortunately, Windows 95 lets you create a special file, called a *dial-up script,* which supplies the information automatically whenever you dial up your ISP. Creating a dial-up script isn't rocket science, but it's a little more advanced than this chapter can handle. When you grow weary of typing this log-in information every time you call up your ISP, skip ahead to Chapter 15, which explains in detail how to create a dial-up script.

Making Sense of the Internet Explorer Screen

Before showing you how to actually explore the Internet, let me pause for a moment to examine all the bells and whistles that Microsoft has loaded on the Internet Explorer window. Figure 3-4 shows the Internet Explorer window, maximized for your viewing pleasure, with some of the more important parts labeled for easy identification.

The following items on the Internet Explorer screen are worthy of note:

✓ **Title bar:** At the very top of the window, the title bar always displays the name of the Internet page you are currently viewing. For example, in Figure 3-4, the title is "Internet Start - Microsoft Internet Explorer."

Figure 3-4: The different parts of the Internet Explorer 4 screen.

- **Menu bar:** Just below the title bar lives the menu bar, as in any Windows program. Internet Explorer's deepest secrets are hidden within the menus located on the menu bar. Several of these menus are familiar: File, Edit, View, and Help. Two of the menus — Go and Favorites — provide features that are unique to Internet Explorer.

- **Standard toolbar:** Beneath the menu bar is the Standard toolbar, which contains buttons you can click to perform common tasks. The purpose of each of these buttons is summarized in Table 3-1, but don't feel as though you need to understand these buttons at first. As you gain experience with Internet Explorer, the function of each of these buttons becomes apparent.

- **Address toolbar:** Beneath the Standard toolbar is the Address toolbar, which displays the Internet address (called a URL) of the page currently being displayed in the Address box. You can click the down-arrow button on the right end of the Address box to see addresses of pages you recently visited. (If you don't understand Internet addresses, don't worry. I explain them later in this chapter, under the heading "Understanding Web addresses.")

- **Links toolbar:** To the right of the Address toolbar, you find the word Links. Clicking this word reveals Internet Explorer's Links toolbar, which houses a collection of five of your favorite Internet locations that you can access with just a click of the mouse.

To save space, the Address toolbar and the Links toolbar are shown in the same horizontal bar in the Internet Explorer window. Initially, only the Address toolbar is fully visible, with the Links toolbar shrunk down so that only the word *Links* is visible. To access the Links toolbar, double-click the word *Links*. The Links toolbar expands and the Address toolbar shrinks so that both are visible. Double-click *Links* again to expand the Links toolbar to the full width of the horizontal bar, shrinking the Address toolbar so that only the word *Address* is visible. Double-click *Links* a third time to shrink the Links toolbar again so the entire Address toolbar is visible. (You can also resize the Links toolbar by dragging the word *Links* across the horizontal bar. Or, you can drag the word *Links* down so that the Links toolbar appears on a separate line beneath the Address toolbar.)

- **Status bar:** The status bar, located at the bottom of the window, periodically displays useful information, such as what Internet Explorer is trying to do or how much progress it has made downloading a large file.

- **Scroll bars:** Located at the right and bottom of the window, the scroll bars appear and disappear as needed. Whenever Internet Explorer can't display all the information on an Internet page on a single screen, a scroll bar appears so that you can scroll to the hidden information.

One other feature of the Internet Explorer screen that's important to know about but that isn't visible in Figure 3-4 is the new Explorer bar. The Explorer bar occupies the left side of the main Internet Explorer window area and comes and goes as needed. It appears when you click the Search, Favorites, History, or Channels buttons in the Standard toolbar. You see the Explorer bar in action in several places throughout this book.

Table 3-1	Internet Explorer Standard Toolbar Buttons
Button	*What It Does*
Back	Moves back to the most recently displayed page
Forward	Moves forward to the page you most recently moved back from
Stop	Cancels a time-consuming download
Refresh	Forces Internet Explorer to obtain a fresh copy of the current page
Home	Takes you to your start page
Search	Allows you to quickly search the Internet for topics of interest
Favorites	Displays a list of your favorite Internet locations
History	Displays a list of sites you have recently visited
Channels	Displays the Internet channels you have subscribed to (For more information about channels and subscriptions, refer to Chapter 6.)
Fullscreen	Switches to full screen view so that more of the Web page is visible.
Mail	Calls up the Outlook Express program so you can send and receive e-mail

Button	What It Does
Print	Prints the current page
Edit	Lets you edit the current Web page

Oh, the Places You'll Go!

As its name implies, the chief function of Internet Explorer is to enable you to explore the Internet. To do so, you need to know how to get around — that is, how to navigate from one Internet location to another. The following sections explain Internet Explorer's navigation features.

Understanding Web addresses

Just as every house in a neighborhood has a street address, every page of the World Wide Web has an Internet address. Because the Web has so many pages, simply assigning a name to each page on the Web would quickly become unmanageable. As a result, Web addresses are constructed using a method called the *Uniform Resource Locator* (URL).

URLs are becoming commonplace in our society. Just think about how many times you've seen addresses such as `www.whatever.com` appear at the end of a television advertisement. These days, every company that advertises seems to have a Web page.

To use Internet Explorer effectively, you need to know how to compose URL Web addresses. Entering URLs isn't hard, but it takes some practice.

A URL consists of three parts, written as follows:

```
protocol://host-address/resource-name
```

- ✔ For World Wide Web pages, the *protocol* portion of the URL is always `http` (http stands for *HyperText Transfer Protocol,* but you don't need to know that to use URLs).
- ✔ The *host-address* is the Internet address of the computer on which the Web page resides (for example, `www.dummies.com`).

✔ The final part, the *resource-name,* is a name assigned by the host computer to a specific Web page or other file. In many cases, this name contains additional slashes that represent directories on the host system. Most of the time, you can omit the resource-name completely if you simply want to display the home page for a company's Web site.

Here are some examples of complete URLs:

```
http://www.yahoo.com
```

```
http://www.cbs.com/lateshow/lateshow.html
```

```
http://asylum.cid.com/hhgttg/hhgttg.html
```

Notice that all Internet addresses also must be prefixed by `http://`. However, Internet Explorer cleverly adds the `http://` automatically, so you don't have to type it yourself. Throughout this book, I leave off the `http://` from any World Wide Web address.

Because Internet Explorer always allows you to omit the protocol part (`http://`), and because you can often omit the resource name, the only URL component you really need to worry about is the Internet address. Internet addresses themselves consist of three components, separated from one another by periods, usually called *dots*.

✔ The first part of the Internet address is almost always `www`, to indicate that the address is for a page on the World Wide Web.

✔ The second part of the Internet address is usually a company or organization name, sometimes abbreviated if the full name is too long. Sometimes, this second part actually consists of two or more parts in itself, separated by periods. For example, in the address `www.polis.iupui.edu`, the second part is `polis.iupui`.

✔ The third and final part of an Internet address is a category that indicates the type of organization the name belongs to. The most common categories are

- **gov:** Government agencies

- **com:** Private companies

- **edu:** Educational institutions

- **org:** Organizations

- **net:** Networks

Putting these three address parts together, you get addresses such as `www.microsoft.com`, `www.nasa.gov`, and `www.ucla.edu`.

Following the links

The most popular method of navigating through the Internet is by following links. A *link* is a bit of text on one Web page that leads you to another Web page. A link may lead to another page at the same Web site, or it may lead to a page at a different Web site altogether.

You can easily identify the text links on a Web page because they're underlined and displayed in colors different from the rest of the text. (The default colors are blue for links you have yet to view and purple for links you already visited; however, you can change the color of your links if you want.) For example, Figure 3-4 had four text links:

what Microsoft is doing to protect information online

rich medium for hoaxes and misinformation

commonsense steps to protect yourself

attempts to connect in a variety of conditions

In addition to text links, many Web pages contain graphical links — graphics that you can click to jump to another Web page. Unlike text links, graphical links are not identified with a special color or underlining. But you can spot them by watching the mouse pointer as you glide it over the graphic. If the mouse pointer changes from an arrow to a pointing finger, you know that you found a link.

In some graphical links, the page you are taken to depends on where in the graphic you click. For technical reasons you don't want to know, this type of graphical link is called an *image map*.

In most cases, Web-page designers try to make their graphical links obvious by including text next to them. For example, Figure 3-5 shows the Web page for the National Park Service, which sports the following graphical links:

✔ Links to the Past

✔ Park Smart

✔ Info Zone

✔ Nature Net

✔ Lying Lightly on the Land

✔ Visit Your Parks

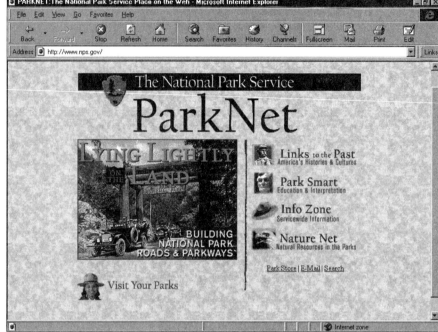

Figure 3-5:
The
National
Park
Service
page,
loaded with
graphic
links.

You can tell where a link leads by moving the mouse pointer over it. This displays a message in the status bar indicating the address of the page that will be displayed if you click the link. For example, if you point the mouse at the Links to the Past link on the National Park Service page, the status bar displays the following message:

```
http://www.cr.nps.gov
```

Yes, you can go back

Exploring links on the Web can be like exploring paths in the woods. You see a link that looks promising, so you take it. The page the link leads to has other links that seem interesting, so you pick one and take it. And so on, until pretty soon you're lost. You should have marked your path with bread crumbs.

Fortunately, Internet Explorer allows you to retrace your steps easily. Two buttons on the Standard toolbar exist for just this purpose:

✔ The Back button moves backward along the path you've taken. Clicking this button retraces the links you followed, only backward. You can click the Back button several times in a row if necessary to retrace your steps through several links.

✔ The Forward button moves you forward along your path. As long as you keep plowing ahead, this button is grayed out — meaning you can't use it. However, after you begin to retrace your steps with the Back button, the Forward button becomes active. Clicking the Forward button takes you to the page where you were when you clicked the Back button.

The Internet Explorer 4 bag of nifty new features includes a pair of down-arrows, situated next to the Back and Forward buttons. You can click these arrows to reveal a list of Web pages you recently visited, in the order in which you visited them. This feature enables you to return directly to any page you've visited, without having to retrace your steps one page at a time.

It's all history now

Internet Explorer automatically keeps track of the pages you visited not only during your current Internet session, but also in past sessions. To quickly return to one of these pages, click the History button on the Standard toolbar. The History bar appears on the left side of the Internet Explorer window, as shown in Figure 3-6.

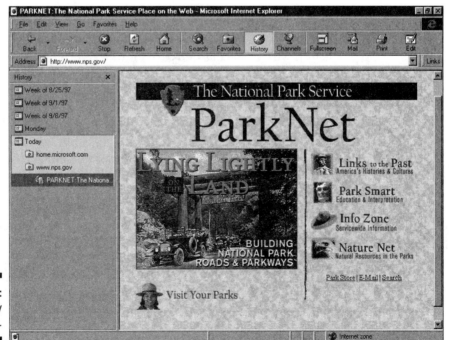

Figure 3-6: The History bar.

As you can see, the History bar lists the Web pages you've visited today and in past weeks. To return to a page, first click Today or one of the previous week's history folders. A list of Web sites appears, showing all previous stops on your Web page tour. You can then click the site you want to revisit.

Don't forget that every place you visit is recorded in the history folder. Thus, the history folder provides a record of where you've been and what you've seen . . . and that can be incriminating!

If your kid denies that he's been sneaking peaks at www.playboy.com, pop up the history folder and find out. Pretty tricky, eh? (Of course, if the kids read this book, they'll know about this trick. Better tear out this page before anyone else sees it.)

Exploring the Web can be fun, but sometimes the exploration turns out to be a wild goose chase. Fortunately, Internet Explorer can bail you out if you find yourself hopelessly lost. Just click the Home button, and you're instantly transported to your start page. Then you can start over with a clean slate.

If you want to change your start page, may I recommend Chapter 14?

Going to a specific page

What if a friend gives you the address of a Web page you want to check out? No problem. To visit a specific Web page for which you know the address, all you have to do is follow these simple steps:

1. **Click the mouse in the Address box, which you can find in the Address toolbar.**

   Refer back to Figure 3-4.

2. **Type the address of the Web page you want to retrieve.**

3. **Press Enter.**

Internet Explorer 4 sports a new feature called AutoComplete that is designed to make it even easier to type Web addresses. The AutoComplete feature keeps track of Web addresses you recently typed. Then, AutoComplete watches as you type Web addresses and tries to anticipate which address you are typing. As soon as it thinks it knows, it automatically fills in the rest of the address.

For example, if you recently visited www.microsoft.com then you type www.mi, AutoComplete automatically fills in www.microsoft.com as the complete address. If you visited www.yahoo.com then you type www.ya,

AutoComplete fills in www.yahoo.com. If the address AutoComplete suggests is indeed the address you wanted to type, just press Enter. Otherwise, keep typing — the address suggested by AutoComplete is erased the instant you type another letter.

Another new feature in Internet Explorer 4 is that you don't have to type the www. that comes before most Web addresses and the .com that comes after most addresses. Instead, you can just type the middle portion of the Web address and then press Ctrl+Enter instead of just the Enter key. When you press Ctrl+Enter, Internet Explorer automatically adds http://www. and .com to your Web addresses.

For example, suppose you want to go to the Microsoft Web site. You could do that by typing **www.microsoft.com** in the Address box and pressing the Enter key. Or, to save time, you could just type **microsoft** and press Ctrl+Enter. Internet Explorer changes microsoft to http:/www.microsoft.com and then retrieves the page.

Note that this trick won't work for government or educational Web pages because their addresses end in .gov or .edu rather than .com.

Many Web addresses are complicated — complicated enough that typing them without making a mistake is difficult. Fortunately, if you already have the Web address in another document, such as a word processing document or e-mail message, you can always copy and paste it into Internet Explorer's Address box. Assuming that Internet Explorer is already running and that you have opened the word processing document or other document that contains the address you want to copy in another window, you can paste the address into Internet Explorer by following these steps:

1. **From Internet Explorer, press Alt+Tab and then open the document or e-mail message that contains the address you want to copy.**

2. **Highlight the entire address and then press Ctrl+C to copy the address to the Windows Clipboard.**

   If you're a mouse fan, you can select Edit⇨Copy.

3. **Press Alt+Tab again to return to Internet Explorer.**

   You may have to press Alt+Tab several times to bring up Internet Explorer, depending on what other programs are currently running.

4. **Click in the Address box in the Address toolbar.**

5. **Press Ctrl+V to paste the address.**

   Or, use the Edit⇨Paste command.

6. **Press Enter.**

Refreshing a Page

The first time you access a Web page, Internet Explorer copies the entire page over the network from the Web site to your computer. Depending on the size and complexity of the page and the speed of your connection, this process can take a few seconds or a few minutes.

To avoid repeating this download, Internet Explorer saves the information for the page in a special area of your hard disk known as the *cache* (pronounced like *cash*). The next time you retrieve the same page from the Web, your computer gets the page directly from your hard disk rather than download it again from the Web site. Thus, you get to see the page much faster.

What happens if the page has changed since the last time you downloaded it? Most Web pages don't change very often, but some do. In fact, some pages change daily or even more often. For such pages, you can force Internet Explorer to refresh its view of the page.

 To refresh a page, all you have to do is click the Refresh button and then twiddle your thumbs while Internet Explorer downloads the page. Refreshing a page takes longer than grabbing it from your hard disk, but at least you know that the information is current.

 The Subscriptions feature is a popular new offering with Internet Explorer 4 It lets you tell Internet Explorer that you want certain pages to be refreshed for you automatically, without requiring you to actually visit the page. With Subscriptions, you can designate that a page be refreshed at a certain time every day (for example, midnight). Then, you can view the page at a more reasonable hour without having to sit and wait while the page downloads to your computer. You find everything you need to know about the Subscriptions feature in Chapter 6.

Stop! Enough Already!

Every once in a while, you wander into a Web page you could do without. The link that led you to the page may have looked interesting, but after you get there, the page isn't what you expected. According to Murphy's Law, that page will also be the page that has a 200K graphic that takes forever to download.

 Fortunately, you're not forced to sit there and wait while a large graphic you don't want downloads. All you have to do is click the Stop button, and Internet Explorer cancels downloading the current page. The portion of the page that has already made it to your computer continues to be displayed, but anything that hasn't yet arrived won't. You can then click the Back button to go back to the previous page.

Sometimes, you go to a page that appears to remain blank while a large graphic is downloading. In many cases, simply scrolling the page a bit reveals text that has already been downloaded to your computer, but which (for some reason) Internet Explorer has yet to display. Any time you find yourself staring at a blank page that appears to be in the midst of downloading a large graphic, try clicking in one of the scroll bars just to see whether any text is hiding.

Working in Full Screen View

The Internet Explorer menus and toolbars are nice, but sometimes they get in the way — especially when you're viewing a Web page that is chock full of information. To see more of the Web and less of Internet Explorer's menus and toolbars, switch to full screen view by clicking the Fullscreen button (shown in the margin).

Figure 3-7 shows how the National Park Service Web page appears when displayed in full screen view. As you can see, the menu bar, address bar, and status bar have completely disappeared, and the Standard toolbar has been reduced to a smaller toolbar at the very top of the screen. To return Internet Explorer to its normal view, just click the Fullscreen button again.

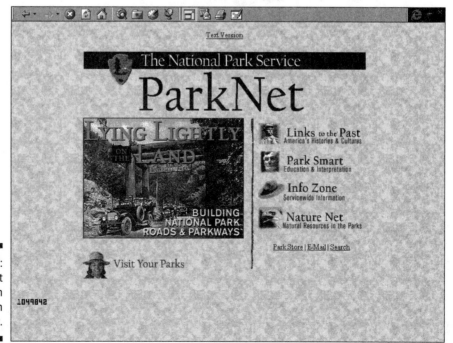

Figure 3-7: Internet Explorer in full screen view.

Printing a Web Page

If you find a page with really interesting information that you want to have a hard copy of, all you have to do is print the page. Make sure that your printer's turned on and ready to go, and then follow these steps:

1. **Choose File⇨Print.**

   The Print dialog box appears, as shown in Figure 3-8.

2. **Stare at the Print dialog box for a moment.**

   If you have more than one printer at your disposal, make sure that the correct printer is selected in the Name drop-down list. If you want to print more than one copy of the page, change the Number of Copies setting.

3. **Click OK.**

4. **Wait a moment while your printer grinds and whirls.**

A faster way to print a Web page — assuming that you want only one copy and you know that the correct printer has already been selected as your default printer — is to simply click the Print button.

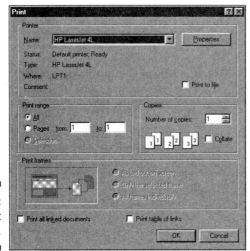

Figure 3-8:
The Print
dialog box.

Changing the Font Size

If you consistently find that the text displayed on the Internet is too small, you may want to visit your ophthalmologist. On the other hand, if every once in awhile you come across a page you have to squint at to see, the problem may not be with your eyes; it could be that the text is simply displayed too small.

Fortunately, Internet Explorer provides a simple solution for too-small text. To change the font size choose the View➪Fonts command. This command leads to another menu that lists five font sizes: Largest, Larger, Medium, Smaller, and Smallest. Click the size you want.

You can also use the Font button to change the font size. When you click the Font button, all the text on a page jumps to a larger size. Each time you click the Font button, the text size increases — until you get to the largest possible size. Then, clicking the Font button once more returns you to the smallest size.

Unfortunately, the Font button is not normally displayed in the Internet Explorer Standard toolbar. To display the Font button, choose the View➪Internet Options command to display the Internet Options dialog box, and then click the Advanced tab. Scroll down the list of options until you find the Show Font Button option. Then, click the check box that appears next to Show Font Button and click OK. The Font button now appears on your toolbar.

Saving a Page

You can save the contents of any Web page to a file on your computer by following these steps:

1. **Choose File➪Save As.**

   A dialog box like the one shown in Figure 3-9 appears.

2. **Select a suitable location for the file.**

   By default, Internet Explorer saves the file in your Windows folder. If this is not an appropriate location, you can browse your way to a better locale.

3. **Type a name for the file you want to save in the File Name field.**

Figure 3-9:
The Save
As dialog
box.

4. Choose the file type in the Save as Type field.

You have two choices: HTML (which saves the page complete with formatting) and Text File (which saves the text without the formatting information).

5. Click the Save button.

If you don't want to save the entire page as a text file, you can select the text you want to save and then press Ctrl+C to copy it. Next, switch to a word processing program, such as Microsoft Word, open an existing document or create a new document, and then press Ctrl+V to paste the copied text into the document.

Saving a Picture

You can save any picture you see in a Web site as a graphic file on your hard disk. To save a picture, all you have to do is follow these steps:

1. Right-click the picture you want to save.

A pop-up menu appears.

2. Choose the Save Picture As command.

A standard Save As dialog box appears.

3. Navigate to the folder in which you want to save the file.

4. Type a new filename for the file if you don't like the one that is supplied.

5. Click the Save button.

Note that you can also choose to use the picture as your desktop wallpaper. Simply right-click the image and then select Set As Wallpaper.

Beware of copyright protections when you save a graphic. Many images, especially artwork, photographs, and company logos, are copyrighted. If you save a graphic that may be protected by copyright law, be sure to get the owner's permission before you use the graphic.

Downloading a File

One of the main reasons many people use the Internet is to download files — that is, to copy files from other computer systems and place them on their own computers. The Internet offers many types of files for downloading: documents, pictures, sounds, movies, animation, and programs.

Internet Explorer makes downloading files easy. In fact, the only hard part is finding the file you want to download. The best way to find a file to download is to use one of the search services described in Chapter 4. For example, if you want to download the popular computer game Doom, use any of the search services to search for the word Doom. You're sure to find several sites from which you can download the file.

To actually download a file, just follow these steps:

1. **Find a Web site that contains a file that you want to download.**

   You may have to use one of the search services described in Chapter 4. Usually, a search leads you to a page that includes a link that you can click to download the file. This link usually, but not always, gives you some indication of how large the file is. For example, Figure 3-10 shows a page at `www.microsoft.com` from which you can download a program called the Word 6.0/95 Binary Converter (this program enables you to easily convert documents from Word 95 to Word 6.0 format). You can see that clicking the Download Now link downloads this 623KB file.

2. **Click the link to download the file.**

   Internet Explorer grinds and churns for a moment. Eventually, the dialog box shown in Figure 3-11 appears.

3. **Make sure the Save This Program to Disk option is selected, and then click OK.**

   If you want to run the program immediately after you download it, click the Run This Program from the Internet option instead.

   Assuming you chose the Save This Program to Disk option, a Save As dialog box appears. (If you chose Run This Program from the Internet instead, you can skip ahead to Step 5.)

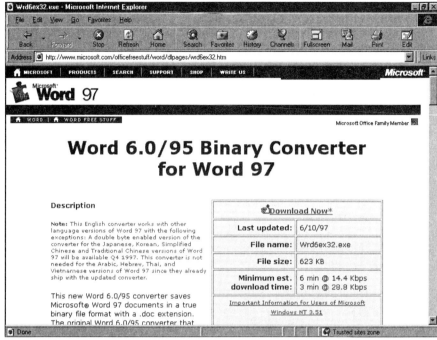

Figure 3-10:
Clicking the
Download
Now link
on this
page will
download a
623KB file.

4. In the Save As dialog box, select the folder where you want the file to be saved. Then click Save.

A dialog box displays a progress bar that enables you to monitor the download progress, as shown in Figure 3-12.

Figure 3-11:
The File
Download
dialog box.

5. Wait until the download is finished.

If you chose the Save This Program to Disk option in Step 3, you're done. If you chose the Run This Program from the Internet option instead, the program you downloaded runs immediately.

Figure 3-12:
Downloading
a file.

Here are some pertinent points to ponder when performing a download:

✔ You should always make sure that you have enough disk space on your hard drive before downloading a large file. Nothing is more frustrating than discovering that you have only 3MB of free disk space an hour into a 4MB download.

✔ To check your free disk space, double-click the My Computer icon on your desktop and then click the icon for your C drive. The My Computer window displays the amount of free space on the C drive in the status bar at the bottom of the window.

✔ You don't have to twiddle your thumbs while the file is downloading. In fact, as I write this, I'm downloading a 4MB file from the Internet. To continue with other work, simply click anywhere outside the File Download dialog box. The dialog box kindly steps out of the way, allowing you to work with other programs while the download continues. You can even use Internet Explorer to browse other Web sites while the download takes its sweet time.

Finding Text

Sometimes, you stumble across a large page of text that you know contains some useful tidbit of information, but you can't seem to locate what you want among all those words. When this happens, you can use the Find command to locate text on the page. Simply follow these steps:

1. **Choose Edit⇨Find (or press Ctrl+F).**

   The Find dialog box appears, as shown in Figure 3-13.

2. **In the Find What text box, type the text that you want to find.**

3. **Click Find Next.**

   Internet Explorer finds the first occurrence of the text on the current page. The Find dialog box remains active so that you can quickly find additional occurrences of the text.

Figure 3-13:
The Find
dialog box.

4. **Keep clicking Find Next until you find the text you want.**

5. **Click Cancel to close the Find dialog box.**

Keep in mind that the Find command searches for text only on the current page; it does not search the Internet for other text references to what you're trying to find. To do that type of search, you must use one of the search services described in Chapter 4.

Exiting Internet Explorer

After you finish browsing the Web, you can exit Internet Explorer using any of the following techniques:

  ✔ Choose File⇨Close.

  ✔ Click the Close button, which is located at the top right corner of the Internet Explorer window. (It's the one with an X in it.)

  ✔ Press Alt+F4.

 After closing Internet Explorer, you should disconnect from your Internet service provider. To do so, double-click the modem connection icon that is displayed in the right corner of the Windows 95 taskbar (shown in the margin) to bring up the Connected dialog box that you see in Figure 3-14. Then click the Disconnect button.

 Be aware that connect time charges continue to accumulate if you close Internet Explorer but forget to disconnect from your ISP. The extra time won't hurt if you pay a flat monthly rate with unlimited access, but if you're paying $2.50 or $2.95 per hour, you don't want to remain accidentally connected overnight!

Figure 3-14:
The
Connected
dialog box.

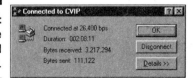

Chapter 4

Searching the Web

● ●

In This Chapter

▶ Searching for information on the Web with Internet Explorer's Search bar

▶ Searching in the Address box

▶ Using search services such as AltaVista, Yahoo!, and Lycos

● ●

*M*any people think of the Internet as a vast library of online information, but the Internet hardly resembles a library. Libraries are run by compulsive neat freaks known as *librarians,* whose mission in life is to make sure that, at least within their libraries, there is a place for everything and everything is in its place. In the old days, librarians devoted much of their energy to maintaining the ever-useful card catalog, which served as a crude but effective index to every book in the library. Nowadays, most libraries have replaced their card catalogs with more sophisticated online card catalogs. So, not only is every book in the library indexed in the catalog, but you can also find any book by searching for it according to author, title, or subject.

Contrary to popular belief, the Internet is nothing like a library; no one person or organization is officially in charge of the Internet. Anyone can put anything on the Internet, and no one is responsible for making sure that new entries are cataloged in any way, shape, or form.

Fortunately, all is not lost. Several excellent search services are available to help you locate information on the Internet. Although none of these services is truly comprehensive, several of them come pretty close. No matter what you're looking for, these services are likely to turn up a few Internet sites that pertain to that topic.

And Internet Explorer 4 makes it easier than ever to use these search services. A special Search bar enables you to access the most popular services quickly. This chapter shows you how it works.

Finding Stuff Fast

The easiest way to locate information on the Internet is to use the *Search bar*. The Search bar is a pane that appears on the left side of the Internet Explorer window when you click the Search button on the Standard toolbar. It's designed to enable you to snoop around for information via a search service while simultaneously viewing a Web page.

To use the Search bar, follow these directions:

1. **Click the Search button on the Standard toolbar.**

   The Search bar appears, as shown in Figure 4-1.

2. **Pick a search service.**

   If you're new to Internet searching, just go with the service Internet Explorer suggests. As you gain experience with the Internet, try each of the search services and decide for yourself which one you like best.

Search bar

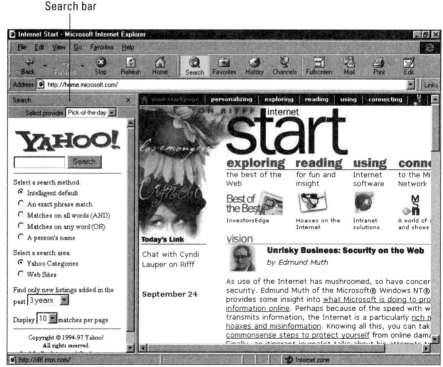

Figure 4-1:
The Search
bar.

3. **Type the word or phrase you're looking for in the text box next to the Search button.**

   For example, type the word **arachnid** in the text box. (Note that in some services, the button may have a different name, such as *submit* or *seek*.)

4. **Click the Search button.**

   Your search request is submitted to the search service.

   A Security Alert dialog box with the following message may appear, warning you that other people may be able to see what you are sending. This annoying dialog box appears every time you try to send any information over the Internet until you check the In the Future, Do Not Show This Warning check box that appears in the Security Alert dialog box. I suggest you go ahead and check this check box and then click the Yes button.

5. **Whistle "Dixie."**

   You'll probably be able to make it through the song at least once before the results of the search appear. The format in which the search results are displayed depends on which search service you are using. Figure 4-2 shows how Yahoo! displays the results of a search for the word *arachnid*. The results for other search services are similar.

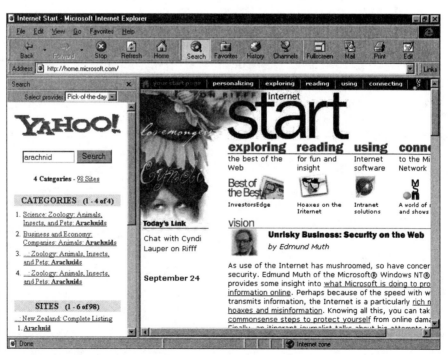

Figure 4-2:
Eureka!

6. If you find something that looks promising, click it.

Internet Explorer displays the page you selected on the right side of the Internet Explorer window. Meanwhile, the Search bar remains visible in the left side of the window so you can choose a different link.

7. If nothing looks promising, click the link for the next set of entries.

Each search service displays only a certain number of *hits* (found Web pages) at a time, typically 10 or 15. If none of the hits at the top part of Search bar looks promising, scroll to the bottom of the Search bar and locate a link that says something along the lines of <u>Next 10 Entries</u>. Clicking this link displays additional results for the search.

Here are some thoughts to keep in mind when searching:

✔ If the search comes up empty, try again using a different search word or phrase. For example, try *spider* instead of *arachnid*.

✔ When picking search words, try to think of words that are specific enough that you don't end up with thousands of hits, but general enough to encompass the topic you're trying to find.

✔ Most of the search services list results in sorted order, with the pages that most closely match your search criteria presented first. In particular, if you search with two words, the pages that contain both words are listed before pages in which just one of the words appears.

✔ Each of the search services available from the Search bar has its own set of options for customizing your search. For example, you may be able to indicate whether the search should be case-sensitive (so that *RAM* is not the same as *ram*) or whether to search for pages that contain all the words you type or pages that contain any of the words you type.

An even faster way to search

Internet Explorer 4 offers a fast way to quickly search the Internet for specific information. Simply type the word **Find** or type a question mark in the Address box, followed by the word or words you want to look up. For example, to search for *arachnid*, type **find arachnid** or **?arachnid** in the Address box. Internet Explorer picks a search service to look up the word or phrase you typed and displays the results in the main Internet Explorer window.

Using Popular Search Services

Internet Explorer uses one of seven different search services to look up information on the Internet. By default, Internet Explorer picks a different search service each day. You can tell Internet Explorer which search service to use by choosing the service you want from the Select Provider drop-down list that appears at the top of the Search bar.

The following sections describe the search services. To access one of the services directly and work with it in the entire Internet Explorer window, type the service's Internet address in the Address box and press Enter.

Each of these services has its own peculiar approach to categorizing information and searching its database in response to your queries. As a result, you should experiment with the various services to determine which one best suits your needs.

AltaVista

`www.altavista.digital.com`

AltaVista is a project of Digital Equipment Corporation, one of the world's major computer companies. AltaVista is a large and fast catalog of individual Web pages and Usenet discussion groups found throughout the Internet. The search network uses a special program called a *spider,* which automatically reads and catalogs three million Web pages every day. The AltaVista catalog lists tens of millions of Web pages. Figure 4-3 gives you a glimpse of the AltaVista home page.

One of the drawbacks of AltaVista is that many searches return literally thousands of Web pages, and the pages aren't sorted or categorized in any useful way. As a result, you have to plow through pages and pages of results looking for Web sites that might contain the information you're looking for.

However, AltaVista does offer very powerful advanced search capabilities. If you're a bit of a computer guru and want a powerful search tool, AltaVista is worth checking out.

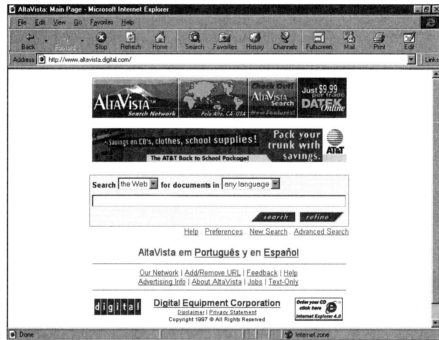

Excite

```
www.excite.com
```

Excite is a search service that catalogs more than 50 million Web pages. In addition to this huge index of Web pages, Excite also features thousands of reviews prepared by Excite's editorial staff; it also indexes Usenet newsgroup postings and classified ads. Excite's opening page appears in Figure 4-4.

AOL NetFind

```
www.netfind.com
```

AOL NetFind is sponsored by America Online, the most popular online service on the Net, and catalogs a wide variety of Internet information. NetFind borrows its basic Web searching capabilities from Excite. In addition, NetFind offers a kid-safe search section that doesn't include adult-only Web pages. NetFind is shown in Figure 4-5.

Figure 4-4:
Excite.

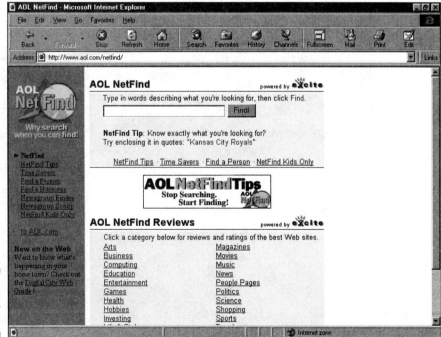

Figure 4-5:
AOL
NetFind.

HotBot

www.hotbot.com

HotBot, sponsored by *Wired* magazine, is a comprehensive index of more than 50 million Web pages with a powerful search interface, pictured in Figure 4-6. HotBot also offers a feature called the Wired Cybrarian which contains links to the very best Internet information sources, neatly arranged into categories to make searching easier.

Infoseek

www.infoseek.com

Infoseek is a large database that indexes millions of Web pages. It also enables you to browse through category listings or search by keywords. Infoseek is not just limited to the Web; it also allows you to search Usenet newsgroups, e-mail addresses, news stories from Reuters News, and a catalog of Frequently Asked Question (FAQ) files from popular newsgroups. Infoseek's main page appears in Figure 4-7.

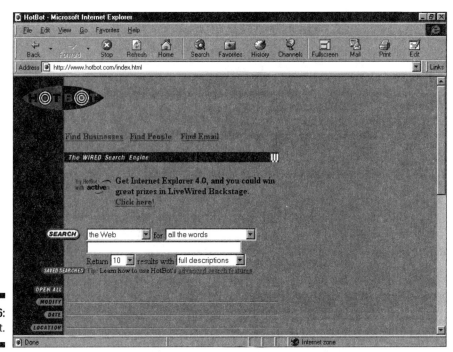

Figure 4-6:
HotBot.

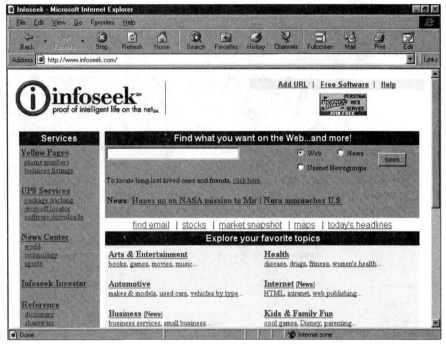

Figure 4-7:
Infoseek.

Lycos

www.lycos.com

Lycos is a huge Web index compiled by the computer nerds at Carnegie Mellon University. Lycos is primarily a keyword search tool, but it also includes categories you can browse. It's my personal favorite when I'm looking for obscure information. Figure 4-8 shows the Lycos opening page.

Lycos includes such features as CityGuide, which lists the best regional Web sites around the world; PeopleFind, which looks up names, phone numbers, and addresses; and RoadMaps, which enables you to print a map for just about any location in the USA. I tried it for my own house, and — lo and behold — it worked!

Figure 4-8:
Lycos.

Yahoo!

www.yahoo.com

Yahoo! is tops in popularity among search services. It contains tens of thousands of listings, organized into categories such as Art, Business and Economy, Computers and Internet, Education, and so on. You can browse through Yahoo!'s categories or search for specific pages by keyword. Yahoo!'s opening page appears in Figure 4-9.

Yahoo! is excellent for searching categorized information, but its keyword search abilities aren't as strong as other services such as Lycos or AltaVista.

Yahoo! was founded by two college students at Stanford University. Rumor has it that Yahoo! stands for Yet Another Hierarchical Officious Oracle, but the two student founders deny the allegation.

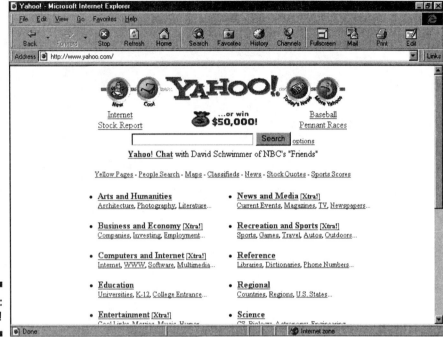

Figure 4-9:
Yahoo!

Chapter 5

Using Favorites and the Links Toolbar to Get Around Quickly

• •

• •

*T*he World Wide Web offers millions of interesting destinations. Exploring them all just to see what's available would be fun, assuming you could live long enough. But after you see a few hundred or a few thousand Web pages, you probably come to realize that not all Web pages are created equal. You soon settle on a few Web sites that are your personal favorites. This chapter shows you how to use two features of Internet Explorer 4 that are designed to make it easier to access frequently visited pages: Favorites and the Links toolbar.

Playing Favorites

The Internet Explorer Favorites feature is designed to expedite travel to your favorite Web sites without you having to remember a bunch of Web addresses or navigate your way through link after link. The Favorites feature is basically a menu on the Internet Explorer menu bar that lists links to your favorite Web sites. You can add links to and remove links from the Favorites menu whenever you want. The following sections describe how to use Internet Explorer's Favorites feature.

Adding a Web page to the Favorites menu

To designate a Web page as one of your Favorites so that you can later find it fast, follow these steps:

1. **Browse your way to the page you want to add to your list of favorite pages.**

2. **Choose the Favorites⇨Add to Favorites command.**

   The Add Favorite dialog box appears, as shown in Figure 5-1. The Name text box displays the name of the Web site that you want to add to your Favorites menu.

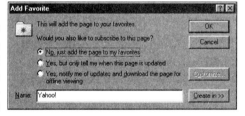

Figure 5-1:
The Add
Favorite
dialog box.

3. **Click OK.**

   Internet Explorer adds the Web page to your Favorites menu.

Notice the three options beneath the question, "Would you also like to subscribe to this page?" in the Add Favorite dialog box. These options let you *subscribe* to a Web page so that you are automatically notified whenever the Web page changes. For now, leave the No, Just Add the Page to My Favorites option chosen. I show you how to use the other two options in Chapter 6.

If you're on a Web page that contains a link to another Web page that you want to add to your Favorites menu, you can right-click the link you want to add, and then choose Add Favorite from the pop-up menu that appears. This trick adds the link to your Favorites menu without actually taking you to that Web site.

Going to one of your favorite places

After you add your favorite Web pages to your Favorites menu, you can open the menu to jet away to any of the pages it contains. Here's how:

1. **Choose Favorites from the menu bar.**

   The Favorites menu reveals your list of favorite places, as shown in Figure 5-2. Your Favorites menu undoubtedly contains a different collection of links than mine, so don't panic if your Favorites menu doesn't resemble the one shown in Figure 5-2.

2. **Select the Web page you want to view, and off you go.**

   Notice that the Favorites menu in Figure 5-2 includes several submenus that contain my favorite Web pages organized into categories. You can find instructions for setting up submenus like these in the next section, "Using Favorites folders."

Using Favorites folders

If you keep adding pages to it, pretty soon the Favorites menu becomes so full of links to your favorite sites that you can't find anything. To ease crowding on the Favorites menu, and to help you organize your favorite links, Internet Explorer enables you to create separate folders in which you can categorize your favorite sites.

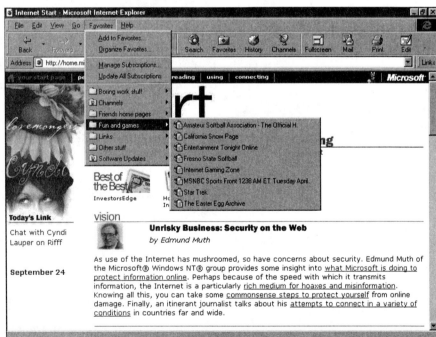

Figure 5-2:
The Favorites menu contains your list of favorite places.

To create a Favorites folder in which to place a link to the Web page you're
viewing, follow these steps:

1. **Choose Favorites⇨Add to Favorites.**

   The Add Favorite dialog box appears.

2. **Click Create In>>.**

   The Add Favorite dialog box expands, as shown in Figure 5-3.

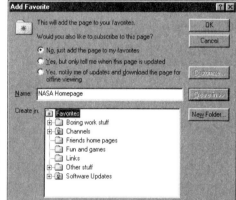

Figure 5-3:
Adding a
page to a
Favorites
folder.

3. **Click the New Folder button.**

4. **Type a name for the new folder.**

5. **Click OK.**

The folders within the Favorites menu appear as menu items with arrows
next to them. If you point the mouse to one of these menu items, a second
menu appears, listing the contents of the folder.

If you want to place a link to a Web page in an existing folder, follow these
steps:

1. **Choose Favorites⇨Add to Favorites.**

   The Add Favorite dialog box appears.

2. **Click Create In>>.**

   The Add Favorite dialog box expands.

3. **In the Create In list, select the folder in which you want to store the
   new link.**

4. **Click OK.**

Organizing your Favorites

Eventually, your Favorites menu becomes filled with Web links that no longer hold your interest, that are out of date, or that just need to be reorganized. When you reach this point, it's time to roll up your sleeves and reorganize your Favorites. Fortunately, Internet Explorer provides a command just for this purpose.

To organize your Favorites, choose the Favorites⇨Organize Favorites command. The Organize Favorites dialog box appears, as shown in Figure 5-4.

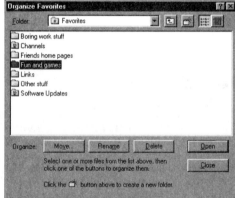

Figure 5-4:
The
Organize
Favorites
dialog box.

The buttons in the Organize Favorites dialog box enable you to delete, rename, or move items around in your Favorites folders.

- ✔ To move a page or folder, select the page or folder and click the Move button. Then select the folder to which you want move the item and click OK. Or, just drag the page or folder to its new location.

- ✔ To rename a page or folder, select the page or folder and click the Rename button. Type a new name for the page or folder and then click OK. If you prefer, you can simply click once on the page or folder you want to rename, wait a second or two, and then click again. You can then type a new name for the folder or page. (The purpose of waiting a second or two between clicks is to make sure Internet Explorer doesn't think you are attempting to double-click the folder or page.)

- ✔ To delete a page or folder, select the page or folder and then click the Delete button or press the Delete key. A dialog box appears asking if you are sure you want to delete the folder or page; click Yes.

Using the Favorites button on the Standard toolbar

The Favorites button on the Standard toolbar works a little differently from the Favorites menu. When you click the Favorites button, a separate Favorites bar appears on the left side of the Internet Explorer window, as shown in Figure 5-5. This bar enables you to view the list of your favorite Web pages while viewing a Web page at the same time in the right-hand portion of the Internet Explorer window.

To display any of the Web pages in your Favorites, just click the link for the page. To remove the Favorites bar so that the Web page once again occupies the entire window, just click the Favorites button on the Standard toolbar again.

Using the Links Toolbar

Internet Explorer Favorites are a great way to keep track of all the Web pages you visit periodically. However, Internet Explorer provides an even more convenient method of quickly visiting up to five of your absolute favorite Web sites: the Links toolbar. The Links toolbar enables you to place links to your very favorite Web pages on a toolbar that's always available at the click of a mouse.

When you first install Internet Explorer, the Links toolbar is configured with the following five default links:

- ✔ **Best of the Web:** A listing of links to various pages throughout the Internet that Microsoft deems to be "tops."
- ✔ **Channel Guide:** A listing of Internet channels you can subscribe to. For more information about channels, see Chapter 6.
- ✔ **Customize Links:** Takes you to a help page that displays information about how you can customize the Links toolbar.
- ✔ **Internet Explorer News:** A page that keeps you up-to-date about the latest Internet Explorer developments.
- ✔ **Internet Start:** Takes you to Microsoft's Internet Start page (which is also the default home page displayed when you click the Home button).

Accessing the Links toolbar

Ordinarily, the Links toolbar is covered up by the Address toolbar. To reveal the Links toolbar, double-click the word *Links* near the top right of the Internet Explorer window. The Links toolbar appears, as shown in Figure 5-6.

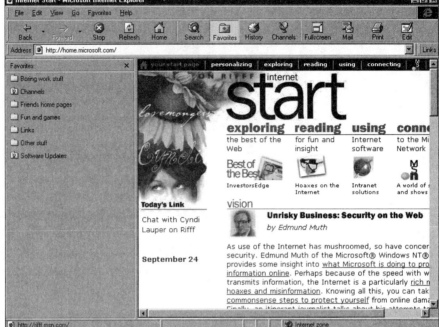

Figure 5-5:
The
Favorites
bar in
action.

Figure 5-6:
The Links
toolbar.

Links toolbar

To display one of the pages on the Links toolbar, just click its button. To show the Address toolbar again, double-click the word *Address* to the left of the Links toolbar.

Adding a link

Internet Explorer enables you to customize the Links toolbar: by removing any or all of the five default links with links of your own, and by adding additional links. To add a link of your own to the Links toolbar, follow these steps:

1. **Browse your way to the Web page that you want to add to the Links toolbar.**

2. **Choose the F̲avorites⇨A̲dd to Favorites command.**

   The Add Favorite dialog box appears. (It was shown back in Figure 5-2.)

3. **Click the C̲reate In>> button.**

   The Add Favorite dialog box expands to show your Favorites folders. (The expanded version of the dialog box was shown back in Figure 5-3.)

4. **Click the Links folder.**

5. **Click OK.**

The page that you displayed in Step 1 is added to the Links toolbar. If the page doesn't appear on the Links toolbar, try clicking the small right-pointing arrow that appears at the right edge of the toolbar. This scrolls the toolbar to the right so that the link you just added comes into view. (To scroll back to the beginning of the toolbar, click the small left arrow at the left of the Links toolbar.)

You can quickly add the currently displayed page to the Links toolbar by dragging the page icon from the Address bar to the Links toolbar.

Removing a link

To remove a link from the Links toolbar, follow these steps:

1. **Call up the F̲avorites⇨O̲rganize Favorites command.**

   The Organize Favorites dialog box appears. (It was shown back in Figure 5-4.)

2. **Double-click the Links folder.**

   The Links folder appears, showing all the links that are on your Links toolbar.

3. **Select the link you want to remove.**

4. **Click the D̲elete button.**

   A dialog box appears, asking if you really want to delete the link.

5. **Click Y̲es.**

You're done! The link you deleted is removed from the Links toolbar.

Another way to delete a link is to right-click the link in the Links toolbar, and then choose the Delete command from the pop-up menu that appears. A dialog box appears asking if you are sure that you want to delete the link. Click Yes and the link is deleted.

EASY INTERNET

Adobe Acrobat Reader 3.0 {Reads Adobe Acrobat format – mostly used for manuals}

CommNet {Communications program CUSTOMERS SHOULD NOT NEED THIS}

Domain Name Searcher {Utility for DNS Lookups}

EudoraLight {E-mail Program}

Graphics Work Shop {Graphic designer}

Hotdog Web Editor {Web page editor, used for creating web pages}

Internet Phone {Voice chat program}

Kali {Online Gaming and Chat}

*MS Explorer 3.02a {Browser}

*MS Explorer 4.0 {Web browser}

*Netscape Navigator 3.01 {Web browser}

*Netscape Communicator 4.04 {Browser}

NewsXpress {News group reader}

Net Nanny {Blocks out XXX sites}

Pegasus Mail {Used to track time online}

PowWow {Chat}

Thumbs Plus {Graphic Viewer}

Win Telnet & FTP {Telnet & FTP}

Win Weather {Weather Info}

Win Zip {Compression – Needed for downloading .zip files}

WS_FTP LE {FTP – transfers files to server for web pages}

Chapter 6

Tune In to the Web with Channels and Subscriptions

In This Chapter

▶ Subscribing to a Web page

▶ Changing or canceling a subscription

▶ Subscribing to channels

*O*ne of the big annoyances of wandering around the Web is that after you find a Web site you like, you have to keep going back to it over and over again to make sure you don't miss anything new. The Internet Explorer Favorites feature makes it easier to find your favorite Web sites quickly, but you still have to click your way from page to page, carefully checking to see if any new information has been added to each page.

With Internet Explorer 4, there's a simpler way. The new subscriptions feature offers you the opportunity to *subscribe* to any Web page. After you have subscribed, Internet Explorer automatically checks the Web page on a daily basis and downloads any pages that have changed. If you want, you can schedule this automatic download so that it happens in the wee hours of the morning. Then, the next day, you can instantly access the changed pages without having to wait for the pages to download.

Although you can subscribe to any page on the Web, the subscription feature works even better for Web sites that have designated themselves as channels. A *channel* is a Web site that knows that people will be subscribing to it. As a result, the channel can ease the process of finding new information. This chapter explains how to subscribe to ordinary Web sites and how to work with channels.

Subscribing to a Web Page

Say you discover a Web site that you want to visit often, and you're interested in having Internet Explorer 4 notify you whenever there is new information available on the site. All you have to do is subscribe to the site. Subscribing to a Web page doesn't cost you any money. It just means that Internet Explorer will regularly check the Web site for new information.

Here is the procedure for subscribing to a Web site:

1. **Browse your way to the site you want to subscribe to.**

   For example, I like to follow the antics of the Fresno State Softball team, whose home page can be found at `www.fresnostatesoftball.com`.

2. **Choose the F̲avorites⇨A̲dd to Favorites command.**

   This command summons the Add Favorite dialog box, shown in Figure 6-1.

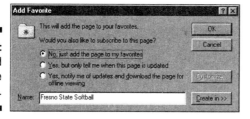

Figure 6-1:
The Add
Favorite
dialog box.

3. **If you don't like the name provided in the N̲ame field, change it.**

   Most of the time, the name is acceptable, so you can usually skip this step.

4. **Choose one of the two subscription options in the Add Favorite dialog box.**

   The two choices are:

   • **Yes, but only tell me when the page is updated:** This option checks the Web page for changes on a daily basis. If the page changes, the page's icon in your Favorites menu shows a special red gleam to notify you of the change.

   • **Yes, notify me of updates and download the page for offline viewing:** This option not only checks for updates but also automatically downloads the page whenever the page has changed. That way, you can view the page later without connecting to the Internet.

5. **Click OK.**

   The Add Favorite dialog box vanishes; you have now successfully subscribed to the Web site.

6. **If you have not already added the site to your F̲avorites menu, do so now.**

   Choose the F̲avorites⇨A̲dd to Favorites command to add the site to your Favorites menu.

Internet Explorer will automatically check the Web site on a daily basis. If the site has changed, a special red gleam is added to the site's icon in the Favorites menu to alert you that new information is available.

The Customize button in the Add Favorite dialog box calls up a Web Site Subscription Wizard that enables you to control how the subscription works — in particular, the following aspects:

- ✔ You can download not only the page you have subscribed to, but also any pages that are linked to it. You can also specify how many "levels" of links to download.

- ✔ You can have Internet Explorer send you an e-mail message whenever new information becomes available on the Web page.

- ✔ You can specify how often and at what time the site should be checked for changes.

- ✔ If the site requires you to enter a user ID and password, you can supply that information.

Canceling a Subscription

If you subscribe to a Web page and then lose interest, you can cancel your subscription. To do so, follow these steps:

1. **Choose the F̲avorites⇨S̲ubscriptions⇨M̲anage Subscriptions command.**

   This command brings up the Subscriptions window, shown in Figure 6-2.

2. **Click the subscription you want to cancel to select it.**

3. **Press the Delete key.**

   Or, if you prefer, right-click the subscription you want to cancel and choose the Delete command from the pop-up menu that appears. Either way, the confirmation dialog box shown in Figure 6-3 appears.

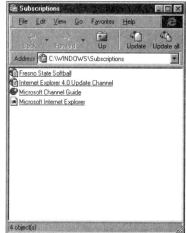

Figure 6-2:
The
Subscriptions
window.

Figure 6-3:
Canceling a
subscription.

4. Click Yes.

The subscription is canceled.

Changing Subscription Information

You can easily change a subscription — for example, to add e-mail notification or to change how often Internet Explorer checks for updates — by following these steps:

1. Choose the Favorites➪Subscriptions➪Manage Subscriptions command.

This command summons the Subscriptions window, which was shown back in Figure 6-2.

2. Right-click the subscription you want to change, and then choose the Properties command from the pop-up menu that appears.

This command brings up the subscription Properties dialog box shown in Figure 6-4.

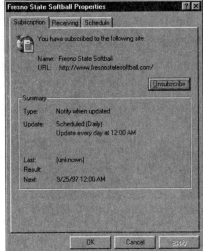

3. **Change the subscription settings as you see fit.**

The subscription Properties dialog box has three tabs — Subscription, Receiving, and Schedule — that contain the buttons and check boxes you need to use to set any of the subscriptions settings you want to change. Poke around in this dialog box for a moment and change anything that strikes your fancy.

4. **When the settings are just right, click OK.**

The subscription is changed per your orders.

Subscribing to a Channel

A *channel* is a special type of Web site that is automatically delivered to your computer on a regular basis. Subscribing to a channel is similar to subscribing to a regular Web site, except that channels are designed specifically with subscriptions in mind. As a result, information from channels is downloaded to your computer more efficiently than information from regular Web sites.

To view channels, click the Channels button in the Internet Explorer Standard toolbar (pictured in the margin). Clicking this button activates the Channels bar in the left portion of the Internet Explorer window, as shown in Figure 6-5. The Channels bar is similar to your television's remote control: It enables you to flip through the various channels you have subscribed to. You can view any channel you have subscribed to simply by clicking the channel's icon in the Channels bar.

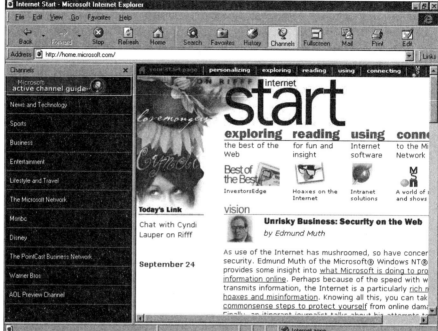

Figure 6-5:
The
Channels
bar.

If you installed Internet Explorer 4 with the Active Desktop option, a special version of the Channels bar appears directly on your desktop. You can access channels without first starting Internet Explorer.

The Channels bar groups channels according to the following categories:

- ✔ News and Technology
- ✔ Sports
- ✔ Business
- ✔ Entertainment
- ✔ Lifestyle and Travel

You can click any of these categories to reveal a list of channels related to the category's theme.

In addition to categories, the Channels bar lists six of the most popular channels:

✔ The Microsoft Network

✔ MSNBC

✔ Disney

✔ The PointCast Business Network

✔ Warner Bros.

✔ AOL Preview Channel

To subscribe to a channel, first click the channel you want to subscribe to, either directly in the Channels bar or from one of the Channels bar's category lists. You see a preview of the channel that may include a lengthy if not stunning animated presentation that you must watch. Eventually, the channel preview settles down and displays a page such as the one shown in Figure 6-6, which includes a button labeled Add Active Channel. Click this button to subscribe to the channel.

When you click the Add to Active Channel button, your computer grinds and whirs for a moment while it downloads important information about the channel. Then, the Modify Channel Usage dialog box shown in Figure 6-7 appears. Click OK to subscribe to the channel.

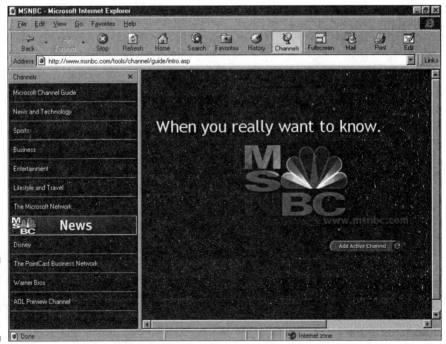

Figure 6-6:
The
Channel
Guide.

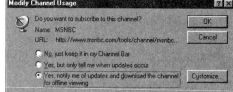

Figure 6-7:
The Modify
Channel
Usage
dialog box.

Push-me pull-you

Subscriptions and channels are part of a new Internet craze called *push technology*.

Most of the World Wide Web relies on what is now known as *pull technology*, which means that your computer "pulls" information off the Internet whenever you request it. Simply put, push technology doesn't wait for you to request information. Instead, it anticipates the information you need and "pushes" it down to your computer without you having to ask.

The advantage of push over pull is that you don't have to sift through Web page after Web page to find new information. With push, new information is automatically sent to your computer and brought to your attention.

The drawback of push is that before you know it, you can collect more information than you ever need (or want), and you end up spending precious time staring into your computer as if it were a TV set.

The proponents of push technology believe that push is destined to revolutionize the Internet, and that within two years (an eon in computer time), Web-surfing will yield to the power and convenience of channels. The naysayers argue that computer users don't want information crammed down their throats and prefer to tour the Web at their leisure.

Only time will tell which earns the popular vote: push or pull.

Chapter 7

Getting Help While You Explore

● ●

In This Chapter

▶ Getting assistance with Internet Explorer's Help features

▶ Using Windows 95 troubleshooters

▶ Finding help on the Internet

● ●

*I*magine that you have a pet Internet guru who sits at your side while you surf the Web, ready and willing to answer your questions with straight-forward responses spoken in plain English, gently but firmly correcting you when you make silly mistakes, never giggling at you behind your back? All you have to do is supply a steady stream of pizza and Diet Coke, let him or her out twice a day, and absorb the wisdom of the master.

The next best thing to having your own personal Internet guide is using Internet Explorer built-in Help features. No matter how lost you become while exploring the Internet, help is but a few keystrokes or mouse clicks away.

Summoning Help

Internet Explorer comes with an excellent built-in Help system that can probably answer your most burning questions about the Web and Internet Explorer. You can summon this help in any of the following ways:

✔ **Press F1.** This action catapults you into Internet Explorer's Help system.

✔ **Choose Help⇨Help Topics.** This menu command is the mouse lover's equivalent to pressing F1.

✔ **Click the Question Mark icon.** Dialog boxes often have a question mark icon near the upper-right corner. Click this icon to transform the mouse pointer into a big question mark. You can then click any field in the dialog box to call up specific help for that field.

Getting to Know the Help Window

When you call up Internet Explorer's Help system, a separate window, like the one shown in Figure 7-1, appears. The Help window is divided into three main areas: a toolbar at the top, a contents area at the left, and the actual Help text on the right. As you can see, the contents portion of the Help window has three tabs across the top labeled Contents, Index, and Search. All three tabs access the same Help information, but in a different fashion. The Contents tab groups Help topics by category, whereas the Index tab lists all Help topics in alphabetical order. And the Search tab lets you look up Help information based on the word you type.

Figure 7-1:
The Internet
Explorer
Help
window.

Scanning the Contents

Clicking the Contents tab of the Help window displays a window that lists Internet Explorer Help topics by category. As Figure 7-1 shows, each category has a closed-book icon next to it. To expand a category, double-click the book icon. The Help topics associated with that category appear and the closed book icon changes to an open book. In addition, a category may include subcategories, which may themselves have additional subcategories.

Notice that individual Help topics (as compared with categories that contain several topics) are represented by an icon resembling a page with a big question mark. To display an individual Help topic, click the icon for the topic you want to display. The Help information for the topic appears on the right side of the Help window, and the Contents remain visible on the left. For example, Figure 7-2 shows the Help Contents after you open the Exploring the Web category and click the topic titled *Change your home page.*

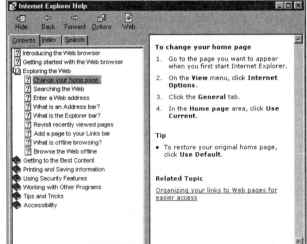

Figure 7-2: Help Contents with a category expanded.

Many Help topics include links to other Help topics. For example, the Help topic that was shown in Figure 7-2 includes a link to another related topic: <u>Organizing your links to Web pages for easier access</u>. This link works just like the links in a Web document: Click once to follow the link.

Scanning the Index

The Help Index, shown in Figure 7-3, lists all the Internet Explorer Help topics in alphabetical order. To get help on a particular Help topic, type the word you want to look for in the first text box. Then locate and double-click the appropriate Help topic in the list that appears below, in the second text box.

Searching for Help Topics

You can also search for Help topics by clicking the Search tab in the Help dialog box and then typing a word or phrase and clicking the List Topics button. This displays a list of all the Help topics that contain the word or phrase you typed. For example, Figure 7-4 shows the results of a search for the word *favorites*. Double-click any of the topics listed to display the Help topic.

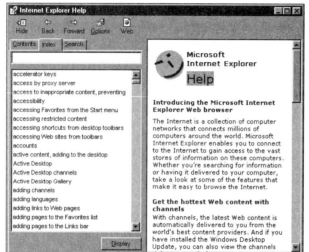

Figure 7-3:
The Help
Index.

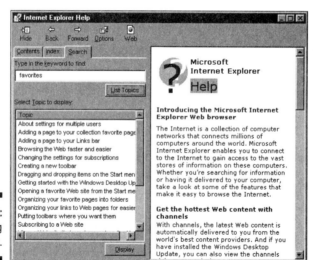

Figure 7-4:
Searching
for Help.

Troubleshooting at Your Fingertips

If you don't find the clue you're looking for in the Internet Explorer Help feature, you may find the answer buried within the Help files that come with Windows 95 itself. In fact, the Windows 95 Help system includes several special troubleshooting features that can walk you through typical causes of common problems.

To conjure up one of the Windows 95 troubleshooters, follow these steps:

1. **Click the Start button located on the taskbar and then choose Help.**

   The Windows 95 Help screen appears, as shown in Figure 7-5.

Figure 7-5:
The
Windows 95
Help
screen.

2. **Double-click Troubleshooting under the Contents tab.**

   A list of several troubleshooting topics appears.

3. **Double-click the troubleshooting topic that interests you.**

   For solving Internet Explorer problems, the two troubleshooters you're most likely to find useful are the topics labeled If you have trouble using your modem and If you have trouble using Dial-Up Networking. Figure 7-6 shows the Modem Troubleshooter.

4. **To use the troubleshooter, double-click the icon to open the topic and then answer each of the troubleshooter's questions by clicking the appropriate button.**

   With luck, the troubleshooter leads you to the solution you seek.

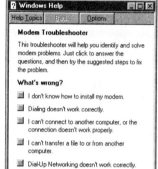

Figure 7-6:
The Modem
Trouble-
shooter.

Getting Help Online

If you can't find help for a specific problem in the Internet Explorer Help files, you can always turn to your online comrades on the Internet. The first place to check for online help is Microsoft's own Web page that's devoted to Internet Explorer technical support. You can call up this Web page by starting Internet Explorer and then choosing Help⇨Online Support. Or, you can manually navigate to the Internet Explorer technical support Web site at www.microsoft.com/iesupport.

The Internet Explorer Support Home page, shown in Figure 7-7, provides up-to-date information about the latest releases of Internet Explorer. This Web page also includes links to pages that list frequently asked questions (FAQs), known problems with Internet Explorer, a troubleshooting guide, and other helpful information.

You can also locate help for specific Internet Explorer problems by visiting Microsoft's support newsgroups. Microsoft operates more than a dozen newsgroups that are devoted to Internet Explorer support. To access the newsgroups, click the Peer to Peer Newsgroups link on the Internet Explorer support page. This option brings up a page that lists the various Internet Explorer newsgroups. Click the newsgroup that seems most relevant to your problem. You can then post a question about the problem you're having with Internet Explorer, and odds are, by the following day you'll have half a dozen responses. For more information about using newsgroups, see Chapter 9.

Figure 7-7:
The Internet
Explorer
online
support
page.

Part III
Outlook Express and Other Ways to Talk

The 5th Wave

By Rich Tennant

"It's a letter from the company that installed our in-ground sprinkler system. They're offering Internet access now."

In this part . . .

Internet Explorer comes with several companion programs that are designed to let you communicate with other Internet users. The most important of these programs is Outlook Express, which lets you access the other two commonly used portions of the Internet besides the World Wide Web: newsgroups and e-mail.

Besides Outlook Express, Internet Explorer 4 also comes with a pair of programs that, although they don't work directly with the Internet Explorer browser, complement Internet Explorer's functions. The first of these programs, Microsoft Chat, lets you access one of the more popular areas of the Internet: Internet Relay Chat (or IRC), which allows you to engage in live conversations with other Internet users throughout the planet. The second program, NetMeeting, is sort of like IRC on steroids. NetMeeting gives you more than mere chatting; you can usher in voice communication and the ability to actually share a program running on your computer with other Internet users.

You can download all these extra features when you first acquire Internet Explorer, or you can add them later from the Internet Explorer 4 download page at www.microsoft.com/ie/ie40/download.

Chapter 8

Keeping in Touch with Outlook Express

*O*ne big reason many people set foot on the Internet is to use electronic mail — *e-mail,* as it's called. You can think of e-mail as the high-tech equivalent of Mr. McFeeley, the friendly, bespectacled mailman on *Mr. Rogers' Neighborhood.*

Sending an e-mail message is much like sending a letter through regular mail. In both cases, you write your message, put an address on it, and send it off through an established mail system. Eventually, the recipient of the message receives your note, opens it, reads it, and (if you're lucky) answers by sending a message back.

But e-mail offers certain advantages over regular mail. For example, e-mail arrives at its destination in a matter of minutes, not days. E-mail can be delivered any day of the week, including Sundays. And, as a special bonus, no way yet exists for your great-aunt to send you a fruitcake through e-mail.

About the only thing that keeps the post office in business anymore, other than transporting fruitcake, is that e-mail only works when both the sender and the receiver have computers that are connected to the Internet. In other words, you can't send e-mail to someone who isn't on the Internet.

Internet Explorer 4 comes with a handy e-mail program called Outlook Express, which is actually a scaled-back version of the more powerful Outlook program that's incorporated into Microsoft Office 97. Outlook Express handles not only Internet e-mail, but also Usenet newsgroups. (You find out about newsgroups in Chapter 9.) In this chapter, I focus on using Outlook Express for reading and sending e-mail.

Starting Outlook Express

Like all Windows 95 programs, you can start Outlook Express a few different ways. Here are some of the more popular methods:

- ✔ On the Windows 95 taskbar, click the Launch Outlook Express button (shown in the margin).
- ✔ On the Windows 95 taskbar, click the Start button and choose Programs➪Internet Explorer➪Outlook Express.
- ✔ In Internet Explorer, choose Go➪Mail.
- ✔ In Internet Explorer, click the Mail button and then choose Read Mail from the pop-up menu that appears.

However you open it, Outlook Express springs to life, displaying the window shown in Figure 8-1.

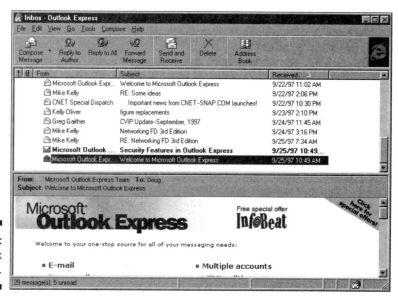

Figure 8-1:
Outlook
Express.

As Figure 8-1 shows, Outlook Express has a similar user interface to Internet Explorer. For example, you use the Outlook Express toolbars the same way you use the Internet Explorer toolbars. Notice that the Outlook Express window is divided into two major sections, called *panes*. The top pane, called the *Inbox*, is a list of all the e-mail you have received. The bottom pane shows the text of the currently selected message.

Each time you start Outlook Express, the program automatically checks to see whether you have any new mail. Provided that you leave Outlook Express open (you can minimize it if you want), Outlook Express periodically checks to see whether new mail has arrived. Any new messages that you haven't yet read appear in boldface in the Inbox pane.

When you first install Outlook Express, you automatically receive two messages in your Inbox: one welcoming you to Outlook Express, the other describing the security features that are available in Outlook Express. Be sure to read both of these messages.

Sending Electronic Mail

To send electronic mail, all you have to do is follow these steps:

1. **Click the Compose Message button on the left side of the toolbar.**

   Or choose Compose⇨New Message, or use the keyboard shortcut Ctrl+N. Whichever option you choose, the New Message dialog box shown in Figure 8-2 appears.

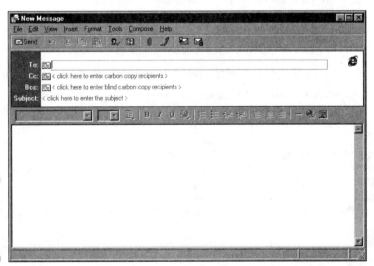

Figure 8-2: The New Message dialog box.

2. Type the Internet address of the person to whom you want to send the message.

The To: field is automatically selected when the New Message dialog box appears, so you can just start typing the recipient's address.

Note that you can send mail to more than one recipient by typing more than one name or address in the To: field. Type a semicolon between each name.

For examples of different kinds of Internet addresses, check out the sidebar, "Addressing your e-mail." Also, see the section "Using the Address Book," later in this chapter, for information about retrieving e-mail addresses from your Address Book.

3. If you want to send a copy of the message to another user, type that person's address in the Cc: field.

Click where you see the words `<click here to enter carbon copy recipients>` and then type the address or addresses of anyone to whom you want to send a copy of the message.

If you want to send a copy of a message to someone else but you don't want the other recipients to know about it, use the Bcc: field instead of the Cc: field. A copy of the message is sent to each person listed in the Bcc: field, but the people listed in the To: and Cc: fields aren't notified of the Bcc: recipients.

4. Type a succinct but clear title for the message in the Subject field.

Click where you see the words `<click here to enter the subject>` and then type the subject of your message. For example, type **Let's Do Lunch** or **Jetson, You're Fired!**

5. Type your message in the message area of the New Message dialog box.

Figure 8-3 shows what a message looks like with all this information typed in and ready to go.

6. When you finish typing your message, click the Send button.

Outlook Express dismisses the New Message dialog box and places the message in your Outbox — a folder that contains messages that are ready and waiting to be sent to their intended recipients.

If you're working in Internet Explorer and you want to send some quick e-mail without starting up Outlook Express, just click the Mail button in the toolbar and choose New Message from the pop-up menu that appears. This command takes you straight to a New Document window, where you can compose and deliver your message without starting Outlook Express.

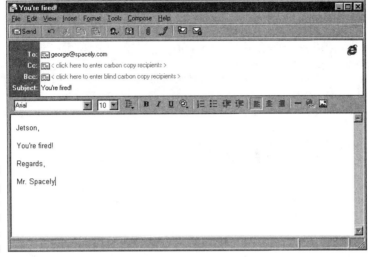

Figure 8-3:
A message
ready to
be sent.

Instead of typing a full Internet address, you can simply type the person's name if you already created an entry for that person in your Address Book. For more information, see the section "Using the Address Book," later in this chapter.

Addressing your e-mail

Before you send electronic mail, you need to know the address of the person to whom the message is intended (just like that pesky post office expects with paper mail). The easiest way to find out someone's e-mail address is simply to ask for it.

To send e-mail to a user of one of the major online services, compose the user's e-mail address as follows:

✔ For America Online users, type the user name followed by @aol.com. For example, Lurch@aol.com.

✔ For CompuServe users, type the numeric user ID followed by @compuserve.com. Be sure to use a period rather than a comma to separate the two parts of the numeric user ID. For example: 12345.6789@compuserve.com.

✔ For users of The Microsoft Network, type the user name followed by @msn.com. For example, BillG@msn.com. (No, that's not really Bill Gates's e-mail address. So please don't flood The Microsoft Network with hate mail — or love mail — for Bill!)

If you're not sure whether you typed the names and addresses correctly, click the Check Names button. This feature checks the names you typed against the Address Book to reveal any errors. (Outlook Express assumes that any name typed in the form of an Internet address — rather than bounced off the Address Book — is correct.) The Check Names feature checks to make sure that the address is in the correct format, but does not check to make sure that the address actually exists.

Using the Address Book

Most Internet users have a relatively small number of people with whom they exchange e-mail on a regular basis. Rather than retype their addresses every time you send e-mail to these people, you can store your most commonly used addresses in Outlook Express's Address Book. As an added benefit, the Address Book enables you to refer to your e-mail friends by name (for example, George Jetson), rather than by address (george@spacely.com).

Adding a name to the Address Book

Before you can use the Address Book, you must add the names of your e-mail correspondents to it. The best time to add someone to the Address Book is after you receive e-mail from that person. Here's the procedure:

1. **Open an e-mail message from someone you want to add to the Address Book.**

   The message is displayed. For more information about reading e-mail, see the section "Receiving Electronic Mail," later in this chapter.

2. **Right-click the user's name and then choose A**dd **to Address Book.**

   The address is added to the Address Book.

3. **Close the message.**

   Thereafter, you can access the person's address in the Address Book.

 You can configure Outlook Express to automatically add to your Address Book the address of anyone who sends you a message to which you reply to by choosing Tools➪Options, checking the Automatically Put People I Reply to in My Address Book option, and then clicking OK.

To add someone from whom you have not yet received e-mail to your Address Book, follow these steps:

1. **In Outlook Express, choose Tools⇨Address Book.**

   The Address Book window appears, as shown in Figure 8-4.

2. **Click the New Contact button.**

   The Properties dialog box appears, as shown in Figure 8-5.

3. **Type the information for the new Address Book entry.**

   At a minimum, type the person's first and last name and e-mail address. If you want, you can include additional information such as phone numbers and addresses under the Home, Business, and Notes tabs.

4. **Click OK.**

   The Address Book entry is created.

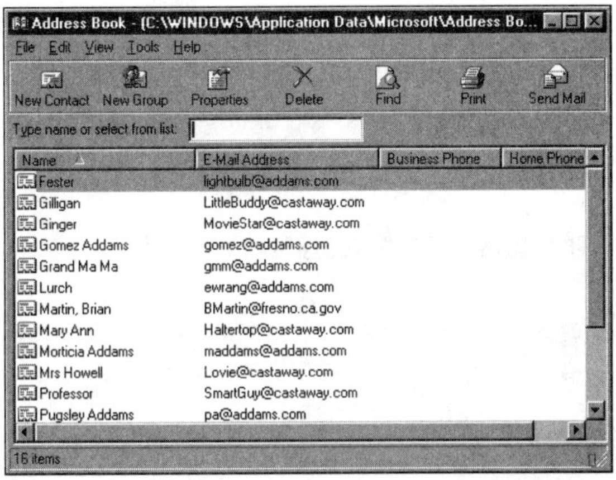

Figure 8-4: The Address Book main window.

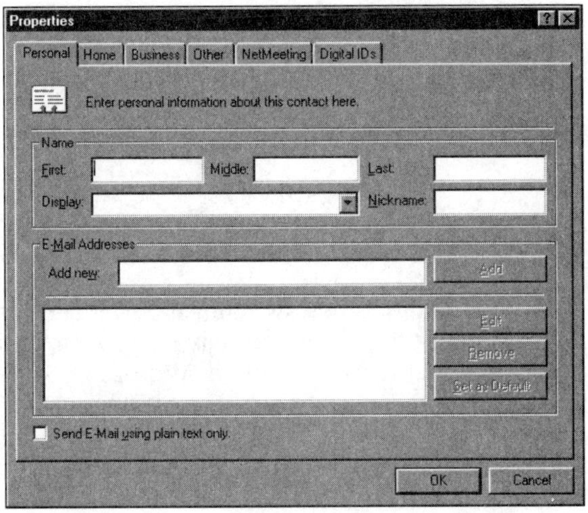

Figure 8-5: The Properties dialog box for a new Address Book entry.

Using an address from the Address Book

To send a message to a user who's already in the Address Book, follow
these steps:

 1. **In the New Message window, click the little Rolodex-card icon next to
the To: field.**

The Select Recipients dialog box appears, as shown in Figure 8-6.

2. **Double-click the name of the person to whom you want to send e-mail.**

The person's name is added to the To: list on the right side of the dialog
box. If double-clicking is against your religion, just click once on the
person's name and then click the To button.

Note: You can add more than one name to the To: list. You can also add
names to the Cc: or Bcc: lists by clicking the Cc: or Bcc: buttons.

3. **After you have selected all the names you want, click OK.**

Poof! You're back at the New Message dialog box, and the names you
selected appear in the To:, Cc:, and Bcc: fields.

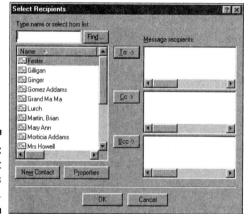

Figure 8-6:
The Select
Recipients
dialog box.

Changing or deleting Address Book entries

On occasion, one of your e-mail buddies switches Internet service providers
and gives you a new Internet address. Or you may lose touch with someone
and decide to remove his or her name from your Address Book. Either way,
the following steps guide you through the process of keeping your Address
Book up to date:

1. **From Outlook Express, choose Tools⇨Address Book.**

   The Address Book dialog box appears (refer to Figure 8-4).

2. **Click the address you want to change or delete.**

3. **To delete the address, click the Delete button.**

4. **To change the address, click the Properties button.**

   When the Properties dialog box appears, make any necessary changes and then click OK.

5. **Click OK when you're finished.**

Looking Up an E-Mail Address

Outlook Express includes a built-in link to several Internet search services that can help you find an e-mail address for an individual or business. To use this feature, call up the Edit⇨Find People command. The Find People dialog box, shown in Figure 8-7, appears.

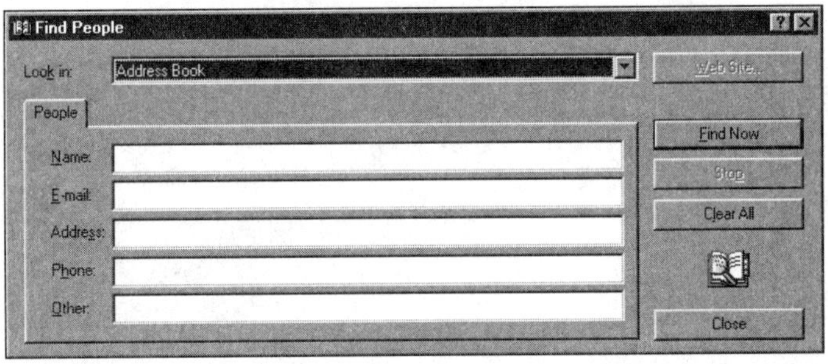

Figure 8-7: The Find People dialog box.

This dialog box enables you to access the following address databases and services:

- ✔ Windows Address Book (that's your address book)
- ✔ MSN (only if you are a member of The Microsoft Network)
- ✔ Switchboard (with more than 100 million residential listings and 11 million business listings)
- ✔ Four11 (featuring a phone directory with over 100 million numbers and an e-mail directory with over 10 million e-mail addresses)
- ✔ InfoSpace (business, residential, and government listings)

 ✔ Bigfoot (yet another directory with 100 million residential listings and 8 million e-mail addresses)

 ✔ WhoWhere (with huge directories of individual phone numbers, companies, toll-free numbers, and much more)

To search for a person's e-mail address, first select the search service you want to use from the drop-down list. Then, type the person's name and click the Find Now button. After a brief delay, the Find People dialog box expands to show a list of all those who match the name you typed, as shown in Figure 8-8.

If the name you're looking for doesn't appear in the list, try again with a different search service. If the name does appear, select it, and then click the Add to Address Book command.

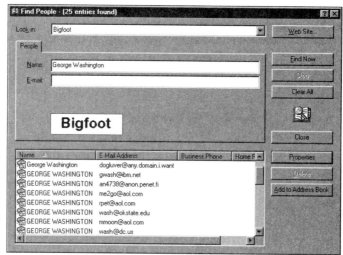

Figure 8-8: There are a lot of George Washingtons.

Checking Your Message for Spelling Errors

If you have Microsoft Office or any of its programs (Word, Excel, or PowerPoint), Outlook Express includes a bonus feature: a spell checker that is capable of catching those embarrassing spelling errors before they go out to the Internet. The spell checker checks the spelling of every word in your message, looking up the words in its massive dictionary. Any misspelling is brought to your attention, and the spell checker is under strict orders from

Bill Gates himself not to giggle or snicker at any of your misspellings, even if you insist on putting an *e* at the end of *potato*. The spell checker even gives you the opportunity to tell it that you are right and it is wrong — and that it should learn how to spell the way you do.

To spell check your messages, follow these steps:

1. **In the New Message window, choose Tools⇨Spelling after you have finished composing your message.**

   The spell checker comes to life, looking up your words in hopes of finding a mistake.

2. **Try not to be annoyed if the spell checker finds a spelling error.**

   Hey, you're the one who told it to look for spelling mistakes; don't get mad if it finds some. When the spell checker finds an error, it highlights the offending word and displays the misspelled word along with a suggested correction, as in Figure 8-9.

Figure 8-9:
The spell checker can be very annoying.

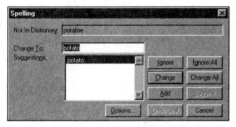

3. **Choose the correct spelling and then click Change, or click Ignore to skip to the next word the spell checker doesn't recognize.**

   If you agree that the word is misspelled, scan the list of suggested corrections and click the one you like. Then click the Change button.

   If, on the other hand, you prefer your own spelling, click Ignore. To prevent the spell checker from asking you over and over again about a particular word that it doesn't recognize (such as someone's name), click Ignore All.

4. **Repeat Steps 2 and 3 until the spell checker gives up.**

   When you see the message `The spelling check is complete,` your work is done.

Sending Attachments

An *attachment* is a file that you send along with your message. Sending an attachment is kind of like paper-clipping a separate document to a letter. In fact, Outlook Express uses a paperclip icon to indicate that a message has an attachment, and the button you click to add an attachment sports a paperclip design as well.

Be aware that sending large attachments can sometimes cause e-mail troubles, especially for attachments that approach a megabyte or more in size. If possible, you should mail several smaller attachments instead of one large one.

Here is the procedure for adding an attachment to an outgoing message:

1. Click the Insert File button.

The Insert Attachment dialog box shown in Figure 8-10 appears.

Figure 8-10:
Inserting an attachment.

2. Rummage through the folders on your hard drive until you find the file you want to insert.

When you find the file you want to attach, click the filename to select it.

3. Click <u>A</u>ttach.

The file is inserted into the message as an attachment. An icon appears in a separate pane in the New Message dialog box, as you see in Figure 8-11. The icon represents the program with which the attachment is associated.

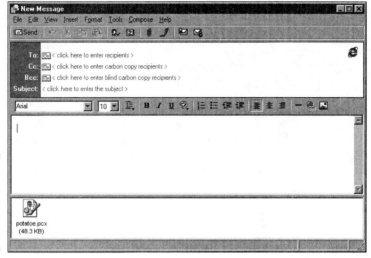

Figure 8-11:
Any e-mail
attachment
is shown as
an icon.

4. **Finish the message and then click the Send button.**

Complete the rest of the fields in the New Message dialog box, and type a message to go along with the attachment. When your message is complete, send it on its way.

Using Stationery

Outlook Express lets you attractively format your e-mail messages using what it calls *stationery.* Stationery consists of the following elements that you can automatically apply to all the messages you compose:

- ✔ **A background image.** Outlook Express comes with about a dozen images you can use.

- ✔ **A signature.** A *signature* is nothing more than a bit of text that's inserted at the end of all your e-mail messages.

- ✔ **A vCard.** A *vCard* is an electronic business card that contains your personal contact information.

Follow these simple steps to set up your stationery:

1. **Choose the Tools⇨Stationery command.**

The Stationery dialog box appears, as shown in Figure 8-12.

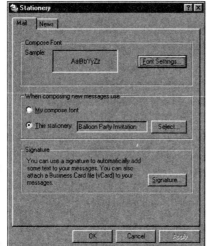

Figure 8-12:
The
Stationery
dialog box.

2. **Click the This Stationery option button, and then click the Select button.**

   The Select Stationery dialog box appears, as shown in Figure 8-13.

3. **Select the stationery you want to use, and then click OK.**

   You return to the Stationery dialog box.

   If you don't like any of the stationery samples that appear in the Select Stationery dialog box, click the Get More button. Clicking this button connects you to a page at the Microsoft Web site that provides additional stationery to download.

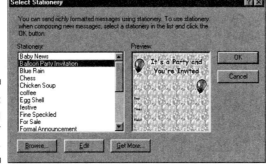

Figure 8-13:
Selecting
your
stationery.

4. **If you want to include a signature, click the Signature button.**

   A Signature dialog box appears, in which you can set the signature options.

5. **Type the text you want to use for your signature.**

   Figure 8-14 shows an example.

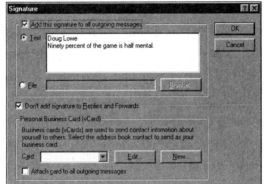

Figure 8-14:
A typical
signature.

6. **Check the Add This Signature to All Outgoing Messages option if you want the message to appear at the tail end of all your e-mail.**

7. **If you want to include an electronic business card with your e-mail (a vCard), select the Address Book entry you want the card's information to be taken from in the Card drop-down list, and then check the Attach Card to All Outgoing Messages option.**

8. **Click OK.**

   You return to the Stationery dialog box.

9. **Click OK again.**

   The Stationery dialog box disappears. From now on, all your e-mail messages will utilize the stationery you just created.

Receiving Electronic Mail

Electronic mail wouldn't be much good if it worked like a send-only set, sending out messages but not receiving them. (I once had an aunt who worked that way.) Fortunately, you can receive e-mail as well as send it — assuming, of course, that you have friends who write.

To read electronic mail that other users have sent you, follow these steps:

1. Start Outlook Express.

Refer back to the section "Starting Outlook Express," at the beginning of this chapter, if you're not sure how.

After Outlook Express starts, it immediately checks to see whether you have any new messages. If you do, your computer beeps and the subject line and sender name for the new messages are displayed in boldface in the Outlook Express window.

2. Double-click a new message to read it.

The message is displayed in its own window.

3. Read the message.

4. After you read the message, dispense with it in one of the following ways:

- If the message is worthy of reply, click the Reply to Author button. A new message window appears, allowing you to compose a reply. The To: field is automatically set to the user who sent you the message, the subject is automatically set to `RE: (whatever the original subject was)`, and the complete text of the original message is inserted at the bottom of the new message. Compose your reply and then click the Send button.

- If the message was originally sent to several people, you can click the Reply to All button send a reply to all of the original recipients.

- If the message was intended for someone else, or if you think someone else should see it (maybe it contains a juicy bit of gossip!), click the Forward button. A new message window appears, allowing you to select the user or users to whom the message should be forwarded. The original message is inserted at the bottom of the new message, with space left at the top for you to type an explanation of why you think the message qualifies for more audience (`Hey Mr. Spacely, get a load of this!`).

- To print the message, click the Print button.

- To save the message to a separate disk file, click the Save button.

- If the message is unworthy even of filing, click the Delete button. Poof!

5. If you have additional messages to read, click the Next or Previous buttons to continue reading messages.

Click the Next button to read the next message in sequence.

Click the Previous button to read the previous message.

Saving an Attachment as a File

If someone is kind enough to send you a message that includes an attached file, you can save the attachment as a separate file by following these steps:

1. **Open the message that has the attachment.**

   You can tell which messages have attachments by looking for the paperclip icon next to the message in the message list.

2. **Right-click the attachment icon and then choose the Save As command from the pop-up menu.**

   A Save As dialog box appears.

3. **Choose the location where you want to save the file.**

   You can use the controls on the standard Save As dialog box to navigate to a different drive or folder.

4. **Type a filename for the file.**

   Outlook Express, always trying to help out, proposes a filename. You need type a new filename only if you don't like the filename that Outlook Express suggests.

5. **Click Save.**

   The attachment is saved as a file.

If the attachment is a graphic image, Outlook Express displays the image directly in the message when you open the message. As a result, you don't have to do anything special to view images your friends send to you via e-mail.

Beware of attachments from unfamiliar sources: They may contain a virus that could infect your computer. Unfortunately, Outlook Express doesn't have any built-in virus protection. So if you are concerned about viruses (and you should be), purchase and install separate virus protection software.

Using HTML Formatting

Outlook Express has a nifty feature that enables you to add formatting to your e-mail messages. To accomplish this feat, Outlook Express employs the same HTML formatting codes used to create pages on the World Wide Web. Of course, when you send an HTML-formatted message to another Internet user, that user must have a mail program that's capable of reading messages formatted with HTML. Otherwise, your beautiful formats will be for naught.

To apply HTML formatting, you use the special HTML formatting toolbar that appears in the New Message window. If your New Message window doesn't have this toolbar, summon the Format➪Rich Text (HTML) command.

Table 8-1 shows how you can use the various buttons and controls on the HTML formatting toolbar to enhance the text in your e-mail messages.

Table 8-1	Controls on the HTML Formatting Toolbar
Control	*Format*
Arial ▼	Changes the font
10 ▼	Sets the size of the text font
≣	Selects a heading style or other style for the text
B	Makes the text bold
I	Makes the text italic
U	Underlines the text
🎨	Changes the text color
≔	Creates a bullet list
≔	Creates a numbered list
≣	Left-aligns the text
≣	Centers the text
≣	Right-aligns the text
—	Inserts a horizontal line
🌐	Creates a hyperlink
🖼	Inserts a picture

Outlook Express Keyboard Shortcuts

Several keyboard shortcuts are available to you as you compose an e-mail message. Many of these shortcuts, summarized in Table 8-2, are pretty much standard throughout Windows.

Table 8-2	Keyboard Shortcuts for Editing E-Mail Messages
Keyboard Shortcut	*What It Does*
Moving and Selecting	
Ctrl+Left arrow	Moves cursor left one word
Ctrl+Right arrow	Moves cursor right one word
Home	Moves cursor to the beginning of the line
End	Moves cursor to the end of the line
Ctrl+Home	Moves cursor to the beginning of the message
Ctrl+End	Moves cursor to the end of the message
Ctrl+A	Selects the entire message
Editing	
Ctrl+X	Cuts the selection to the Clipboard so you can paste it in another location
Ctrl+C	Copies the selection to the Clipboard
Ctrl+V	Pastes the contents of the Clipboard to the location of the insertion point
Ctrl+Delete	Deletes to the end of the word
Ctrl+Z	Undoes the last action you did (not available for some actions, such as sending a message)
Shortcuts for Reading Mail	
Ctrl+F	Forwards the message to another user
Ctrl+R	Replies to the sender of a message
Ctrl+Shift+R	Replies to the sender of a message and all the message's recipients
Ctrl+U	Reads the next unread message
Ctrl+>	Skips to next message
Ctrl+<	Returns to previous message

(continued)

Table 8-2 *(continued)*

Keyboard Shortcut	What It Does
Other Shortcuts	
Alt+S	Sends the message
F7	Checks the spelling of the message
Ctrl+N	Composes yet another message
Ctrl+K	Checks the names listed in the To: and Cc: fields against the Address Book
Ctrl+M	Sends and receives e-mail

Using Outlook Express Folders

The icons that run down the left side of the Outlook Express window enable you to access any of the four message folders that are available in Outlook Express. Normally, only the Inbox folder is displayed. You can display other folders by clicking the icon for the folder you want to view.

The four message folders are

- ✔ **Inbox:** Where your incoming messages are stored
- ✔ **Outbox:** Where messages are stored until they're sent to their intended recipients
- ✔ **Sent items:** Where messages are placed after they're sent
- ✔ **Deleted items:** Where deleted messages are stored. (This folder enables you to undelete a deleted message if you later decide you want the message back.)

Outlook Express also enables you to create your own message folders. For example, you may want to create separate folders for different categories of messages, such as work-related, friends and family, and so on. Or you may want to create date-related folders for storing older messages. For example, you can create a 1997 folder to save all the messages you received in 1997.

The following sections explain how to work with message folders.

Creating a new folder

Before you start saving important messages, it's wise to create one or more folders in which to save the messages. I use just a single folder, named Saved Items, but you may want to create several folders for saving messages according to their content. For example, you may create a Personal Items folder for personal messages and a Business Items folder for business messages. You have to come up with a good scheme for organizing saved messages, but my advice is to keep your method simple. If you create 40 folders for storing saved messages, you run the risk of forgetting which message is in which folder.

To create a new folder, follow these steps:

1. **From Outlook Express's main window, choose File⇨Folder⇨ New Folder.**

   The Create Folder dialog box appears, as shown in Figure 8-15.

Figure 8-15:
The Create
Folder
dialog box.

2. **Type a name for the new folder.**

   For example, type **Work Related**.

3. **Click OK.**

Moving messages to another folder

After you create a folder for your messages, moving a message to the folder is easy. Just follow these steps:

1. **From the Inbox, select the message you want to save.**

2. **Right-click the message, and then choose Move To from the pop-up menu that appears.**

   A dialog box listing all the available folders appears.

3. **Click the folder to which you want to move the message.**

   The message moves to the folder you selected and is deleted from the Inbox folder.

If you prefer, you can make a copy of the message rather than move the message. Just choose Copy to instead of Move to after you right-click the message.

Chapter 9

Staying Informed with Outlook Express

*B*esides handling Internet e-mail, the Outlook Express program that comes with Internet Explorer 4 can also access *newsgroups,* the Internet equivalent of a bulletin board. This chapter explains the ins and outs of using Outlook Express to access newsgroups.

Introducing Newsgroups

A *newsgroup* is a place where you can post messages (called *articles*) about a particular topic and read messages that others have posted about the same topic. People with similar interests visit a newsgroup to share news and information, find out what others are thinking, ask questions, get answers, and generally shoot the breeze.

The Internet has thousands of newsgroups — yea, *tens* of thousands — on topics ranging from astronomy to the Civil War. You can find a newsgroup for virtually any subject that interests you.

Newsgroups come in two basic types:

✔ **Moderated newsgroup:** In a moderated newsgroup, one person is designated as a moderator, and has complete control over what appears in the newsgroup. All new articles are submitted to the moderator for his or her review. Nothing is actually posted to the newsgroup until the moderator approves it.

The moderator establishes the criteria for which articles get posted to the newsgroup. For some newsgroups, the criterion is nothing more than that the article must be somehow related to the subject of the newsgroup. Other newsgroups use more stringent criteria, enabling the moderator to be more selective about what's posted. As a result, only the best postings actually make it into the newsgroup. This supervision may seem stifling, but in most cases, the overseeing dramatically improves the quality of the newsgroup articles.

✔ **Unmoderated newsgroup:** In an unmoderated newsgroup, anyone and everyone can post an article. Unmoderated newsgroups are free from censorship, but they're also often filled with blatant solicitations, chain letters, and all sorts of noise such as articles that have nothing to do with the newsgroup topic.

Using Usenet

The term *Usenet* refers to a collection of newsgroups that are distributed together to computers that run special software called *news servers*. Each Internet service provider (ISP) provides its own news server so that you can access the newsgroups that are part of Usenet. For example, my ISP, California State University Fresno, has a news server named `news.csufresno.edu`.

In theory, Usenet servers share their new postings with one another, so all the servers contain the most recent postings. In practice, Usenet servers are never really quite up-to-date, nor are they always in sync with one another. When you post an article to a newsgroup, a day or so may pass before your article propagates through the Usenet and appears on all servers. Likewise, replies to your articles may take awhile to show up on your server.

Each Usenet site decides on its own which of the Usenet newsgroups to carry. As a result, you may find that a particular newsgroup isn't available from your Internet service provider.

Because the content of newsgroups, particularly the renegade `alt` newsgroups, is sometimes a bit offensive, your Internet service provider may not automatically grant you access to all newsgroups. If you find yourself locked out of these groups, consult your ISP to find out how to gain access.

The Microsoft news server

Usenet is the most popular source of Internet newsgroups, but it's not the only source. For example, Microsoft itself has its own news server that contains several dozen newsgroups related to Microsoft products. Through the Microsoft news server, you can find official online support for Microsoft products.

Understanding Usenet newsgroup names

Usenet boasts thousands of newsgroups. Each newsgroup has a unique name that consists of one or more parts separated by periods. For example, soc.culture.assyrian is a newsgroup that discusses Assyrian culture, sci.polymers contains information on the scientific field of polymers, and rec.food.drink.beer is a place to discuss your favorite brew.

The first part of a newsgroup name identifies one of several broad categories of newsgroups, as described in the following list:

✔ comp: Newsgroups that start with comp contain discussions about computers. Many of the participants in the comp newsgroups wear pocket protectors and glasses held together by tape.

✔ news: These newsgroups contain discussions about the Usenet itself, such as help for new Usenet users, announcements of new newsgroups, and statistics about which newsgroups are most popular.

✔ rec: Recreational topics, such as sports, fishing, basket weaving, model railroading, and so on, are discussed in rec newsgroups.

✔ sci: Look to the sci newsgroups for discussions about science.

✔ soc: In the soc newsgroups, people gather to shoot the breeze or to discuss social issues.

✔ talk: These newsgroups favor long-winded discussions of topics such as politics and religion.

✔ misc: These newsgroups are for topics that don't fit in any of the other categories.

✔ bit: Bitnet is the network that supports Internet mailing lists (a *mailing list* is like a newsgroup, except that all messages are exchanged via e-mail). The bit newsgroups are the bitnet mailing lists presented in newsgroup form.

✔ biz: This prefix denotes a business-related newsgroup.

✔ bionet: Newsgroups with this prefix discuss topics related to biology.

✔ Regional newsgroups: Newsgroups that share regional interests are indicated by a short prefix (usually two or three letters), such as aus (Australia) or can (Canada). Most states have regional newsgroups designated by the state's two-letter abbreviation (CA for California, WA for Washington, and so on).

✔ alt: Hundreds of newsgroups using this prefix discuss topics that range from bizarre to X-rated to paranoid. These newsgroups are not officially sanctioned by Usenet, but some of the more popular newsgroups fall into the alt category. The most visited of the alt newsgroups are those with an alt.binaries designation. These newsgroups contain binary files (such as pictures, sounds, and actual programs) that are specially encoded to be sent via Usenet's text-only messages. Fortunately, Internet Explorer is able to automatically decode these attachments, so you don't have to worry about using a separate program to do so.

All the support newsgroups on the Microsoft news server begin with the words `microsoft.public`, followed by the name of a Microsoft product (or an abbreviation of it). Here are some of the Microsoft newsgroups that are dedicated to supporting users of Internet Explorer 4 and related products:

- `microsoft.public.inetexplorer.ie4`
- `microsoft.public.inetexplorer.ie4.browser`
- `microsoft.public.inetexplorer.ie4.outlookexpress`
- `microsoft.public.inetexplorer.ie4.netmeeting`

These newsgroups are not distributed on Usenet, so you can't find them in your Internet service provider's list of newsgroups. Instead, you have to sign directly in to the Microsoft news server to access them. (Unless, of course, your Internet service provider happens to use the Microsoft news server as its default news server. That's unlikely, though.)

Checking the Internet news

Outlook Express can handle Internet news just as easily as it can handle e-mail. You can start Outlook Express several ways:

- Click the Start button in the Windows 95 taskbar and then choose Programs⇨Internet Explorer⇨Outlook Express.
- Click the Launch Outlook Express button in the Windows 95 taskbar (shown in the margin).
- In Internet Explorer, click the Mail icon and select the Read News command from the pop-up menu that appears.
- In Internet Explorer, choose Go⇨News.
- In Internet Explorer, click a link to a newsgroup. (Newsgroup addresses begin with `news:`. For example, `news:rec.backcountry` refers to the newsgroup named `rec.backcountry`.)

After you're in Outlook Express, you can switch from e-mail to Internet news by choosing the Go⇨News command. Outlook Express complies by displaying a list of newsgroups that you have subscribed to, as shown in Figure 9-1. Note that if you haven't worked with newsgroups before, you won't see any subscriptions when you switch to news.

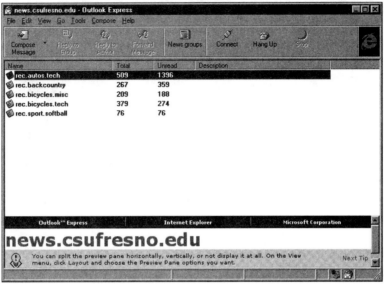

Figure 9-1:
Outlook
Express
displays
your
subscribed
newsgroups.

Accessing Newsgroups

When you start Outlook Express, a list of the newsgroups you have subscribed to appears. (For more information about subscriptions, see the
section "Subscribing to a Newsgroup," later in this chapter.) To access one
of these newsgroups, double-click it.

If you haven't subscribed to any newsgroups or if you want to access a
newsgroup you haven't subscribed to, you can follow these steps:

1. **Click the Newsgroups button (or choose Tools⇨Newsgroups).**

   The Newsgroups dialog box appears, as shown in Figure 9-2.

2. **Scroll through the list to find the newsgroup you want to read.**

   The newsgroups are arranged in alphabetical order.

3. **Click the newsgroup you want to read and then click the Go To button.**

   The newsgroup opens. You may have to wait a few moments as Outlook
   Express downloads the subject headers for the newsgroup.

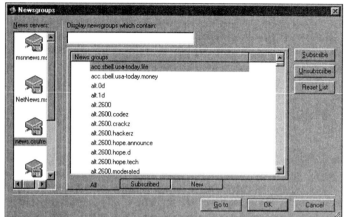

Figure 9-2:
The
Newsgroups
dialog box.

You can type a word or phrase in the Display Newsgroups Which Contain text box to display only those newsgroups whose names contain the word or phrase you type. For example, Figure 9-3 shows a list of all newsgroups that contain the word *startrek*. (As you can see, Usenet plays host to some pretty strange *Star Trek* fans.)

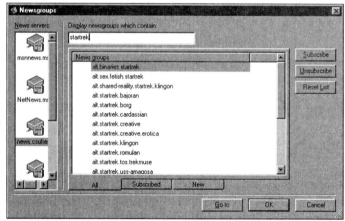

Figure 9-3:
A list of
newsgroups
that contain
startrek.

When you arrive at a newsgroup, Outlook Express displays a list of the messages that are currently available on the newsgroup, as shown in Figure 9-4. You can sort this list by subject, author, or date by clicking on the appropriate header above each column.

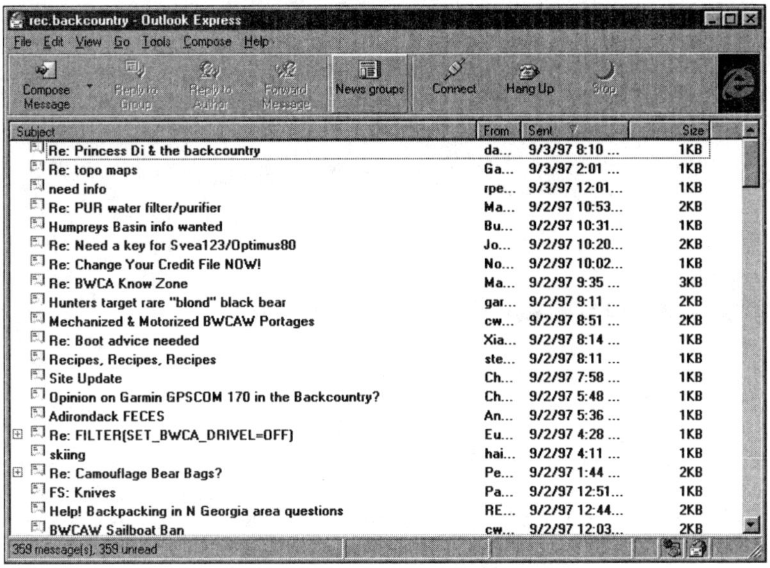

Figure 9-4:
Accessing
a news-
group.

Subscribing to a Newsgroup

If you find a newsgroup that you want to visit frequently, you should subscribe to it. Subscribing to a newsgroup adds the newsgroup to the list of
newsgroups that appears in the main Outlook Express window in the
Newsgroups drop-down list box (where your current newsgroup is listed).

To subscribe to a newsgroup, click the Newsgroups button to bring up the
Newsgroups dialog box pictured in Figure 9-2. Then select the newsgroup
you want to subscribe to and click the Subscribe button. To remove a
newsgroup from your subscription list, select the newsgroup and click the
Unsubscribe button.

First come, first server

If you use more than one news server, the
servers appear at the left of the Newsgroups
dialog box. To switch to another news server,
just click its icon. Each news server has a
different set of newsgroups, so some newsgroups may not be available on your server.

If you need to configure Outlook Express to
work with a different news server, choose
Tools⇨Accounts and click the News tab. You
can find buttons that enable you to add a new
server, delete a server, or change the properties of a server.

Don't confuse newsgroup subscriptions with the subscriptions feature in Internet Explorer 4. As explained in Chapter 6, the Internet Explorer 4 subscriptions feature automatically checks Web sites and channels for new content. Outlook Express does not automatically check your subscribed newsgroups for new articles. Newsgroup subscriptions are more like the Internet Explorer favorites; they simply provide a quick way to access the newsgroups you use most.

Reading Threads

A *thread* is a newsgroup article plus any articles that were posted as replies to the original article, articles posted as replies to the replies, and so on. Outlook Express groups together all of the articles that belong to a thread. A plus sign next to a message title indicates that the article has replies.

To expand a thread, click the plus sign that appears next to the article. You see all the replies to the articles, as well as replies to the replies, replies to the reply replies, and so on. The plus sign on the original message will turn into a minus sign.

To collapse the thread — that is, to hide all replies and list only the original message, click the minus sign.

Reading an Article

To read an article, double-click the article's title. The article appears in a separate window, as shown in Figure 9-5. After you finish reading the article, click the article window's Close button to close the window.

To save an article to your computer, choose File⇨Save As or click the Save button.

 To print an article, choose File⇨Print or click the Print button.

You can go to the next or previous articles by clicking the following buttons:

 ✔ Read the next article

 ✔ Read the previous article

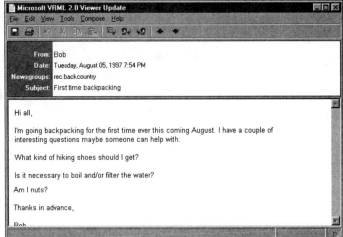

Figure 9-5:
A news-
group
article.

Replying to an Article

To reply to a newsgroup posting, follow these steps:

1. **Count to ten and then reconsider your reply.**

   Keep in mind that replying to a newsgroup is not like replying to e-mail. Only the intended recipient can read an e-mail reply. Anyone on the planet can read your newsgroup postings. If you don't really have anything to add to the discussion, why waste your time?

2. **After reading the article you want to reply to, click the Reply to Group button in the toolbar.**

   A new message window appears, with the subject line already filled in.

3. **Type your reply.**

4. **Click the Post Message button.**

   Your article is sent to the newsgroup.

5. **You're about to become a published writer.**

By default, the complete text of the original message is added to the end of your reply. If the message is long, you may want to delete some or all of the original text. If you don't want the original message text to be automatically added to your replies, choose Tools⇨Options, click the Send tab, and deselect the Include Message in Reply option.

If you want to reply to several specific points of an article, you can inter-mingle your responses with the original message. The original message appears after greater-than signs, setting it off from your insightful responses.

Hold the spam

No, I'm not referring to that canned meat product that was the butt of many jokes in the old TV series, *M*A*S*H*. I'm talking about a particular type of annoying newsgroup message. A *spam* is a bogus message that's posted to more than one — perhaps dozens — of newsgroups, all at the same time, in an effort to generate hundreds of responses. Spams often have subject headers such as "Make money fast" or "Free X-rated pictures in your mailbox!"

You can spot a spam right away by looking at the newsgroups listed in the Newsgroups field at the top of the message window. If more than one or two newsgroups are listed, you're probably looking at a spam.

The best way to deal with spams is to ignore them. You see, the main problem with spams is that they generate hundreds of responses, which may themselves generate hundreds of responses. Most of the responses are along the lines of "Quit spamming us, you idiot," but the responders don't realize that they themselves are helping the spammer by keeping his or her bogus thread alive. Better to ignore the spam altogether so it will go away.

Writing a New Article

When you have finally mustered the courage to post an article of your own to a newsgroup, follow these steps:

1. **Open the newsgroup in which you want to post a new article.**

2. **Click the Compose Message button.**

   A new message window appears.

3. **Type a subject for the article in the Subject box.**

   Make sure that the subject you type accurately reflects the topic of the article — or prepare to get flamed. (Being *flamed* doesn't mean that your computer screen actually emits a ball of fire in your direction, singeing the hair off your forearm. It refers to getting an angry — even vitriolic — response from a reader.) If your subject line is misleading, at least one Internet user is sure to chew you out for it.

4. **Type your message in the message area.**

5. **If you're worried about your vice-presidential prospects, choose Tools⇨Spelling.**

   The spell checker gives you the option to correct any misspelled words. (For more information about spell checking in Outlook Express, refer to Chapter 8.)

    6. **Click the Post Message button when you're satisfied with your response.**

Using Stationery

Just as it does with e-mail, Outlook Express allows you to create fancy stationery for your newsgroup postings. The stationery can include a background design, a choice of fonts for your text, a signature that appears at the end of each message, and an optional electronic business card attachment.

The procedure for creating stationery for newsgroup articles is the same as it is for e-mail messages, so I humbly refer you back to Chapter 8 for the steps required to do so.

Dealing with Attachments

Internet Newsgroups are text only; you cannot attach binary files (such as program, picture, and sound files) to newsgroup messages. Internet users are very resourceful, however, and they long ago figured out a way to get around this dilemma. They invented a technique, called *encoding,* that converts a nontext file into a series of text codes that you can post as a newsgroup article. Such an article looks completely scrambled when you see it. However, you can save the article to a file on your hard disk and then run the saved file through a special decoding program that converts it back to its original form, whether it's a program, picture, or sound file.

With Outlook Express, the decoding routine is built in, so you don't need a separate program. To save a binary file that has been attached to a newsgroup article, all you have to do is follow these steps:

1. **Open the article that has the attachment.**

   Unlike for e-mail, Outlook Express does not indicate which newsgroup messages contain attachments by displaying a paper clip next to the subject line. The only way to tell whether a message has an attachment is to open the message.

2. **Click the attachment icon with the right mouse button.**

   A pop-up menu appears.

3. **Choose the Save <u>A</u>s command from the pop-up menu.**

   A standard Save As dialog box appears.

4. **Select the location where you want to save the file.**

   The controls in the Save As dialog box allow you to navigate to any drive or folder.

5. Check the filename that is proposed for the file.

If you don't like it, change it.

6. Click Save.

The file is saved.

You can view an attachment without saving it to disk by double-clicking the attachment.

Adding Formatting to Your Messages

Outlook Express gives you the option of adding fancy formatting such as **bold** or *italic* type to your newsgroup articles. To accommodate this special formatting, Outlook Express posts its articles in HTML format, using the same formatting codes that Web pages use.

To enable HTML formatting while composing a message, choose Format⇨ Rich Text (HTML). An additional formatting toolbar appears in the New Message window, sporting buttons that enable you to apply various types of formatting to your text. The formatting toolbar is identical to the one you use to compose e-mail messages. To figure out how to use it, check out Chapter 8.

Keep in mind that if you use HTML formatting in your newsgroup articles, many newsgroup users won't be able to see or appreciate your formatting. Sooner or later, though, most everyone will enjoy an advanced news-reader program (such as Outlook Express) that's capable of displaying HTML-formatted newsgroup articles. Until then, consider yourself on the cutting edge.

Chapter 10

See You in the Funny Papers: Microsoft Chat

● ●

In This Chapter

▶ Installing Microsoft Chat

▶ Chatting with other users using comic-book-style characters

▶ Configuring Microsoft Chat

● ●

*O*nline chatting is one of the more talked-about features of the Internet. Chatting enables you to communicate live with other Internet users throughout the world. Whereas e-mail and newsgroups have built-in communication delays, chatting gives you immediate feedback on your messages.

On the Internet, people chat using a special service called *Internet Relay Chat* (or IRC for short). IRC offers thousands of different *chat rooms* where people gather to discuss whatever's on their minds. Some chat rooms have just a few participants; others may have dozens or even hundreds of participants.

Although Internet Explorer does not provide a built-in method for accessing IRC, Microsoft offers a free companion program called Microsoft Chat so that you can participate in Internet chats. As this chapter explains, Microsoft Chat is a bit unusual. Whereas most IRC programs are text-based, Microsoft Chat presents IRC chats in a goofy comic-book format. Microsoft Chat uses a cartoon character to represent each Internet user participating in the chat. If this sounds weird, that's because it *is* weird.

Setting Up Microsoft Chat

The first step to using Microsoft Chat is to obtain a copy of the Microsoft Chat program and install it on your computer. If you got Internet Explorer 4 on a CD-ROM, you already have Microsoft Chat. But if you downloaded Internet Explorer 4 from Microsoft's Web site, you may not have chosen the complete download that includes Microsoft Chat. If not, you have to return to the Internet Explorer 4 download page to download Microsoft Chat. The Web address for this download is

```
www.microsoft.com/ie/ie40/download
```

After you get to the download page, you can click your way to the Microsoft Chat download option. The Chat program file is about 875KB in size. With a 28.8 bps modem, it should take only about four minutes to download.

When you download Microsoft Chat, Internet Explorer 4 offers two options for handling the downloaded program file:

- ✔ **Open:** Installs Microsoft Chat on your hard disk immediately after the download is complete.

- ✔ **Save It to Disk:** Saves the file on your hard disk in a folder you specify. You have to manually install Microsoft Chat later if you choose this option. To do so, open My Computer, find the folder where you saved the downloaded Microsoft Chat file, and then double-click the file's icon.

After the Microsoft Chat Setup program starts, just follow the instructions that appear on your screen to install Microsoft Chat. It takes only a minute or two.

Connecting to a Chat Server

After you download and install Microsoft Chat, the fun begins. Start Microsoft Chat by clicking the Start button on the Windows 95 taskbar and choosing Programs➪Microsoft Chat. The first time you run Microsoft Chat, a dialog box appears asking you for a nickname that other chat participants will know you by. Type any name you want, and then click OK. After your computer grinds and whirls for a moment, the dialog box shown in Figure 10-1 greets you.

In the Connect dialog box, you specify important information required to initiate a chat with other Internet users. Here's the lowdown on the fields in the Connect dialog box:

Figure 10-1:
The
Microsoft
Chat
Connect
dialog box.

✔ **Favorites:** As you use Microsoft Chat, you can add the chat rooms you visit most frequently to a list of favorite chat rooms. Initially, though, this list is empty. Microsoft doesn't presume to know what your favorite chat rooms are. (Kind of surprising, isn't it?)

✔ **Server:** Hundreds of chat servers exist throughout the world. Most are a part of the IRC system of chat servers. Microsoft sponsors five chat servers, named `chat.microsoft.com`, `chat1.microsoft.com`, and so on up to `chat4.microsoft.com`. You can connect any of these chat servers if your Internet service provider doesn't have its own chat server.

Microsoft Chat isn't limited to working with Microsoft's chat servers. You can connect to any IRC chat server you have access to. To connect to a different chat server, just type the name of the server in the Server field.

✔ **Go to chat room:** If everyone on the Internet chatted in the same place, the conversations would be incomprehensible. To keep conversations more manageable, chatting occurs in *chat rooms,* which are gathering places where people with common interests can meet to chat. If you know the name of a chat room you want to visit, select this option and type the name of the chat room in this field. Otherwise, select the next option.

✔ **Show all available chat rooms:** Select this option if you don't know the name of the chat room you want to visit, or if you aren't sure which chat rooms are available on the server to which you're about to connect.

After you set all the Microsoft Chat Connect options, click OK to connect to the chat server.

Selecting a Chat Room

If you select Show all available chat rooms from the Connect dialog box, you're greeted with a list of all the chat rooms available on the server you connected to, as shown in Figure 10-2.

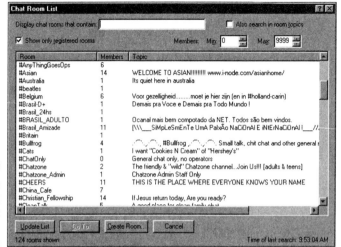

Figure 10-2:
The Chat
Room List
dialog box.

As you see in Figure 10-2, you can find a wide variety of chat rooms on the Internet. Notice that the descriptions for some of the chat rooms are in languages other than English, illustrating the international flavor of Internet chatting.

Plenty of sleazy chat rooms appear on just about any chat server, including Microsoft's own servers. Beware of such hangouts.

If you find a chat room you like, you can add it to your Favorites by choosing Favorites⇨Add to Favorites.

Chatting in Microsoft Chat

After you have selected a chat room, Microsoft Chat connects you to the room and displays a screen similar to the one shown in Figure 10-3. This screen displays the conversation occurring within the chat room as a never-ending stream of text.

When you first see the Microsoft Chat window, you may be bewildered — especially if you jump into a busy chat room and messages fly by so fast you can't read them. After you become familiar with the chat window and how chatting works, you won't be so overwhelmed.

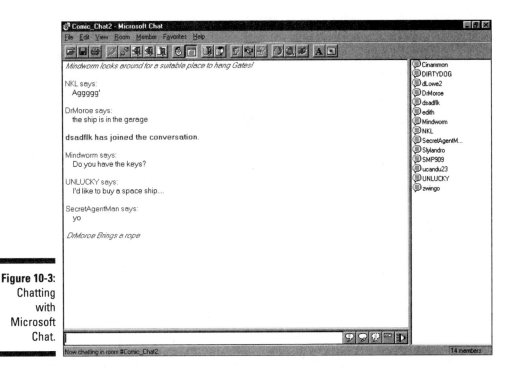

Figure 10-3:
Chatting
with
Microsoft
Chat.

The chat window is divided into three areas:

✔ **Viewing pane:** The chat itself is in the middle portion of the screen, called the viewing pane. Here you see messages sent by you and others who are chatting. The viewing pane has scroll bars, so you can scroll up to read messages that flew off the screen. (When you scroll up to see past messages, you won't be able to see new messages that are added to the conversation. To return to following the conversation as it occurs, just scroll back all the way to the bottom of the chat viewing pane.)

✔ **Member list pane:** Down the right edge of the screen is a member list pane, which lists all of the participants who are currently in the chat room. Each participant is identified with one of three icons:

A regular participant, who can listen and speak.

A spectator, who can listen to the conversation, but cannot speak.

A host, who moderates the chat. The host tries to keep the conversation on track and makes sure no one crosses the bounds of decorum. Cross the line and you may find yourself made a spectator.

✔ **Compose pane:** At the bottom of the screen is the compose pane, where you compose messages that you want to contribute to the chat.

The first frame of any chat shows the chat's title and lists the active chat participants (by nicknames) and their character names. At the bottom of the screen is the *message box,* where you type messages to be sent to the chat.

Sending a message

When you first enter a chat room, your best bet is to eavesdrop for a while to figure out what is happening. When you get up the nerve to contribute your own messages to a chat, follow these simple steps:

1. **Compose a brilliant message in the message box.**

   The message box is at the bottom of the screen, in the compose pane.

   If you just entered a chat room, it's customary to send a greeting before jumping into the chat. Type **Hello, Howdy Doody,** or whatever suits your fancy.

   If you're addressing a comment to a specific person, preface your comment with the person's name. For example

   Hawkeye: Ever heard of the second amendment?

   To create a line break in a message, press Ctrl+Enter. If you press only the Enter key, your message is sent as it is.

2. **When you're ready to send your message, click one of the Send buttons that appears next to the message box.**

   The four Send buttons determine how your message is conveyed to the group:

   • **Say button:** Sends a normal message. Microsoft Chat prefaces your message with *so-and-so says. . . .*

   • **Think button:** Used as an aside. Microsoft Chat prefaces your message with *so-and-so thinks. . . .*

   • **Whisper button:** Used to send a private message to a single user. First, select the user from the list of chat participants on the right side of the screen. Then click the Whisper button.

   • **Action button:** Used to send a descriptive message, often to suggest body language. For example, *Billy-Bob shrugs and wipes his forehead.*

When you compose an action message, keep in mind that Microsoft Chat always adds your name before the message. For example, if your name is John and you send the action message "sits back and enjoys a cold one," Microsoft Chat displays the message "John sits back and enjoys a cold one."

Leaving the conversation

When you're tired of chatting, you can leave Microsoft Chat by choosing the File➪Exit command or clicking the Chat window's Close button. If you've been actively participating in the chat, proper chat etiquette is to say good-bye first. But if you haven't participated in the chat, you can leave without saying good-bye and no one will be offended.

See You in the Funny Papers

Microsoft Chat, like most chat programs, displays a chat room conversation as a never-ending stream of text. However, Microsoft Chat offers a unique alternative to plain text: a comic-strip version of the chat, as shown in Figure 10-4.

Figure 10-4:
Chatting in
Comics
View.

To switch to Comics View, click the Comics View button in the toolbar, or choose the <u>V</u>iew⇨<u>C</u>omic Strip command.

 To return to normal text view, click the Text View button or choose the <u>V</u>iew ⇨Plain Te<u>x</u>t command.

In Comics View, each person in the chat room is represented by one of several comic-strip characters that come with Microsoft Chat. You can choose the character you want to represent you, but if you don't pick a preference, Microsoft selects one for you (free of charge, of course).

When you switch to Comics View, the text mode viewing pane is changed to a series of comic-strip panels. In addition, a portion of the member list pane is replaced by an image representing your own character and a gizmo called the Emotion Wheel, which enables you to control your character's facial expressions.

Microsoft has indicated that, in a future release of Microsoft Chat, you will be able to create your own characters. For now, you're limited to the characters that come with Microsoft Chat. Figure 10-5 shows the stock characters. Read "Having It Your Way," later in this chapter, to find out how to choose a character.

Each time you send a message in the chat room, Microsoft Chat adds your character to the comic strip and includes your message in a bubble. If possible, Microsoft Chat adds your character to the current comic-strip frame, zooming back if necessary so that all the characters in the frame are visible. Whenever the frame becomes too crowded, Microsoft Chat creates a new frame and scrolls the entire comic strip so you can see the new frame.

Figure 10-5:
The characters that come with Microsoft Chat.

Expressing Emotions

Perhaps Microsoft Chat's most surprising feature is that it examines the text of each message and attempts to draw the characters accordingly. Here are some of the inferences Microsoft Chat makes about your messages:

- ✔ If you **SHOUT** something in all capital letters, Microsoft Chat draws your character with a wide-open mouth.

- ✔ When your message begins with the word **You** or contains a phrase such as **are you**, **will you**, or **did you**, your character points to the other person.

- ✔ If you type **LOL** or **ROTFL,** your character laughs. *LOL* stands for "Laughing Out Loud," and *ROTFL* stands for "Rolling On The Floor Laughing."

- ✔ If you type a facial expression such as **:), :-), :(, or :-(,** Microsoft Chat draws your character smiling or frowning. (In Internet lingo, facial expressions constructed from keyboard symbols like this are called *smileys*.)

- ✔ If you type **Hi**, **Howdy**, **Hello**, **Welcome**, or **Bye**, your character waves.

You can also set your own emotion when you send a message by using the Emotion Wheel. To pick an emotion, just click somewhere in the Emotion Wheel. The sample character above the Emotion Wheel changes to show how your character's expression appears when you send your message. To return to a neutral expression, click in the exact center of the Emotion Wheel.

Note that any emotion from the Emotion Wheel overrides any facial expression that would have been selected based on your message text.

Getting Personal

In Microsoft Chat, each user can fill out a Personal Information profile, which includes the user's real name and a description of the user. You compose your own description, which can include your interests, hobbies, home-town, gender, age, or anything else that may be interesting. (Of course, you should limit the amount of personal information you give out here. Most importantly, don't list your phone number or address.) In the following sections, I show you how to set your own Personal Information profile and how to display the profile for other users.

Setting your Personal Information profile

To set your Personal Information profile, follow these steps:

1. Choose View⇨Options.

The Microsoft Chat Options dialog box appears, as shown in Figure 10-6. (If the Personal Information options are not displayed, click the Personal Info tab.)

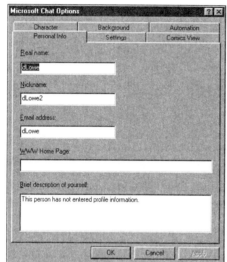

Figure 10-6:
Setting the
Personal
Information
options.

2. Type your name in the Real Name text box.

Of course, there's nothing to stop you from typing **Elvis Presley** or **Jimmy Hoffa**.

3. Type the name you want to use in the chat rooms in the Nickname text box.

Use your first name if you want, or choose something more interesting, such as **Snoopy** or **Baby Cakes**.

4. Type your e-mail address in the E-mail Address text box.

If they have your e-mail address, people will be able to send you e-mail directly from within Chat. This is useful, for example, if someone wants to send you a file as an e-mail attachment.

5. If you have your own home page on the Internet's World Wide Web, type the URL in the WWW Home Page text box.

This enables people to visit your home page from within Chat.

6. **Type a description of yourself in the Brief Description of Yourself text box.**

   Type something interesting about yourself here if you want others to know something about you. You might include information such as what city you live in, what line of work you're in, and so on.

7. **Click OK.**

   Your personal information is updated so that other users can view it.

Finding a member's profile

Microsoft Chat enables you to find out information about the other users who are in a chat room with you, provided that those users have filled out the Personal Information dialog box. To display a chat user's personal information, follow one of these procedures:

- ✔ Right-click the user's nickname in the member list that appears at the right side of the Microsoft Chat window, and then select Get Profile from the pop-up menu that appears.
- ✔ Select the user's nickname in the member list, and then choose Member➪Get Profile from the main menu.

Microsoft Chat draws a new frame showing the user's character, with the user's personal information displayed at the top.

Ignoring Obnoxious Users

Every once in a while, you get into a chat room with someone who insists on dominating the conversation with a constant stream of obnoxious remarks. Or, you may be pestered by a couple of chat users who go on and on about a topic that's far from interesting to you.

Fortunately, Microsoft Chat gives you a way to tune these people out. Just follow these steps:

1. **Select the nickname of the person you want to ignore from the nickname list that appears at the right of the Microsoft Chat window.**

2. **Choose Member➪Ignore.**

   Don't expect any messages from the user you silenced to show up on your computer. The ignored user can still participate in the chat, and other users can see the ignored user's messages as if nothing happened.

Alternatively, you can right-click the member's name in the member list and select Ignore from the pop-up menu that appears.

To reinstate someone you have ignored, repeat the procedure. Select the member in the member list, and then choose the Ignore command again.

The person you tune out has no clue what you did. He or she will keep babbling on, wondering why you never seem to answer. Of course, if no one ever seems to answer you, it could be that *you* are the one who is being ignored!

Having It Your Way

Microsoft Chat enables you to customize the appearance of the chat comic strip in several ways by using the View➪Options command.

✔ You can select one of the 12 comic characters to represent you in Microsoft Chat.

✔ You can change the background scenery.

✔ You can change the arrangement of comic strip frames used in the Microsoft Chat window.

Changing your image

Wouldn't it be nice if you could just snap your fingers to instantly change your appearance? Politicians are deft at manipulating their images, but most of us are not. Microsoft Chat offers a welcome chance to change the way you look, merely by following this procedure:

1. **Choose View➪Options.**

   The Options dialog box appears.

2. **Click the Character tab.**

   The Character options appears, as shown in Figure 10-7.

3. **Select the character you want to represent you.**

   As you click on each character name, a picture of the character appears in the Preview window of the dialog box. If you want to see how the character appears with various expressions, you can click in the Emotion Wheel at the bottom right corner of the Options dialog box.

4. **Click OK.**

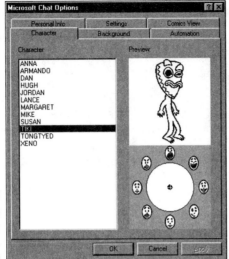

Figure 10-7:
Overhauling
your image.

Unfortunately, you're limited to the 12 characters provided with Microsoft Chat. Microsoft has hinted that, in a future release, you'll be able to create your own characters. But until then, you just have to be content with the stock characters.

Enjoying a change of scenery

You can change the background scenery that Microsoft Chat uses. The scenery change applies only to your computer. You cannot change the background scenery that other users see on their screens. To change the comic-strip background, follow these steps:

1. Choose View▷Options.

The Options dialog box appears.

2. Click the Background tab.

The Background options appears, as shown in Figure 10-8.

3. Select the background you want to use.

Microsoft provides three backgrounds with Microsoft Chat: FIELD, PASTORAL, and ROOM.

4. Click OK.

The new background is put in place.

Figure 10-8:
Changing
the
scenery.

Although you can't draw your own characters, Microsoft Chat does enable you to create your own backgrounds. In fact, you can use any graphics file stored in bitmap format (.BMP) file as a background for Microsoft Chat. All you have to do is copy the file you want to use as a background to the folder `c:\Program Files\CChat\ComicArt`. Any bitmap files that appear in this folder are displayed when you call up the Background options.

Changing Rooms

When you get tired of chatting in a room, you can always leave and wander into another room. Just follow this procedure:

1. **Say good-bye.**

   It's rude to leave without saying good-bye, especially if you've been active in the conversation. Send a parting message. And, if you're in a silly mood, type an action message such as **exits stage right**, or **leaves with a bang.**

2. **Choose Room⇨Room List.**

   The Chat Room List dialog box appears, listing all the chat rooms on your chat server. Refer back to Figure 10-2 for a look at this dialog box.

3. **Double-click the chat room you want to join.**

   Off you go to the chat room you selected.

Unfortunately, Microsoft Chat won't let you visit two chat rooms at one time. However, you can chat in two or more rooms at one time simply by running multiple copies of Microsoft Chat.

Using Macros

If you're a chat-a-holic, Microsoft sports a handy feature called *macros* that enables you to summon up your most common responses or messages with a single keystroke. For example, suppose you frequently find yourself typing **What is the meaning of life?** Rather than type this entire question every time you want to ask it in a chat, you can create a macro for the question. You can then ask the question by pressing the keyboard shortcut that you assigned to the macro.

Creating a macro

Microsoft Chat enables you to create and store up to ten different macros. Each macro is assigned to a combination of the Alt key plus one of the numeric digit keys: Alt+0 through Alt+9. Here's the procedure for creating a macro:

1. **Choose the View⇨Options command, and then click the Automation tab.**

   The dialog box shown in Figure 10-9 appears.

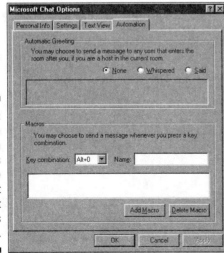

Figure 10-9: The Automation options in the Microsoft Chat Options dialog box.

2. **In the Key Combination list box, choose the key combination you want the macro assigned to.**

   The possible combinations are Alt+0 through Alt+9.

3. **Type a name for the macro in the Name field.**

   Use a simple name that suggests the content of your macro. For example, type **Life.**

4. **Type the text for your macro in the large text box.**

   For example, type **What is the meaning of life?**

5. **Click the Add Macro button.**

   The macro is created.

6. **Repeat Steps 2 through 5 if you want to create additional macros.**

   Note that you can have only one macro assigned to a keyboard short-cut at a time. For example, if you create a macro for Alt+1 and then create another macro that also uses Alt+1, the original Alt+1 macro is deleted.

7. **Click OK.**

   The Options dialog box is dismissed.

Using a macro

Here are two ways to use a macro you create:

✔ Press the keyboard shortcut assigned to the macro.

✔ Choose the View⇨Macros command to display a list of your macros, and then select the macro from the list.

Either way, the complete text of your macro is instantly sent to the chat for all to see.

Chapter 11

Microsoft NetMeeting: Feel the Synergy

● ●

In This Chapter

▶ Downloading and installing NetMeeting

▶ Placing a call to another NetMeeting user

▶ Drawing on the Whiteboard

▶ Resorting to NetMeeting's Chat feature

▶ Sending files to NetMeeting participants

▶ Sharing your programs across the Internet

● ●

*M*icrosoft NetMeeting is a highly touted new program that Microsoft says will revolutionize the way you communicate on the Internet. NetMeeting is a *computer telephony* program, which means that it turns your computer into a $3,000 telephone. Computer telephony is still in its infancy, with many glitches yet to be worked out. Still, NetMeeting is a cool program, one you should definitely look into if you're at all interested in cutting-edge Internet technology.

NetMeeting offers the following features in addition to voice communication:

- ✔ **Whiteboard:** This feature is similar to Windows Paint. Whiteboard displays a drawing area in which all the participants in a conference can doodle.

- ✔ **Chat:** This feature works similarly to Internet Relay Chat. NetMeeting chat enables more than two users to join together in a conference and type messages to one another. (Only two users can use voice communications.)

- ✔ **File transfer:** You guessed it — file transfer enables you to send files to other NetMeeting users.

- ✔ **Application sharing:** This feature enables other NetMeeting users to see on their screens an application that you're running on your computer. You can also share applications so that several NetMeeting users can work together on a single document over the Internet.

NetMeeting is included on the Internet Explorer 4 CD-ROM disk. However, if you downloaded Internet Explorer 4 from Microsoft's Web site, you may not have chosen to download NetMeeting. If not, you need to return to the Internet Explorer download page (www.microsoft.com/ie/ie40/download) to download NetMeeting.

Using NetMeeting

At its core, NetMeeting is an Internet telephone. NetMeeting enables you to conduct voice conversations with another Internet user.

The voice features of NetMeeting won't work unless your computer is equipped with all of the following:

- ✔ A sound card (any sound card that is compatible with Windows 95)
- ✔ Speakers
- ✔ A microphone

If you don't have these components, or if you aren't sure how to use them, pick up a copy of *Multimedia & CD-ROMs For Dummies,* 2nd Edition by Andy Rathbone (published by IDG Books Worldwide, Inc.).

NetMeeting allows voice conversations between only two users at a time. If you want to start a conference call with more than two users, you have to limit yourself to NetMeeting's nonvoice features.

Configuring NetMeeting

To start NetMeeting, click the Start button and then choose <u>P</u>rograms⇨ Internet Explorer⇨Microsoft NetMeeting. The first time you start NetMeeting, you have to wade through a sea of dialog boxes to configure the program for yourself and your computer. The first dialog box (shown in Figure 11-1) lists some of NetMeeting's nifty features. Reading about all the cool stuff you can do with NetMeeting takes the sting out of all the dialog boxes you have to fill out to configure the program!

When you click Next>, NetMeeting asks for the name of the directory server to which you want to connect, as shown in Figure 11-2. A directory server is a computer that keeps track of people who are using NetMeeting. In order to have a NetMeeting conference with another user, you both must be logged on to the same directory server. The default directory server is ils.microsoft.com, which should work just fine.

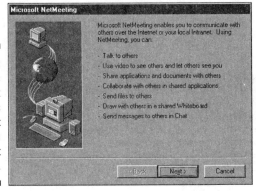

Figure 11-1:
This
dialog box
welcomes
you the first
time you
start
NetMeeting.

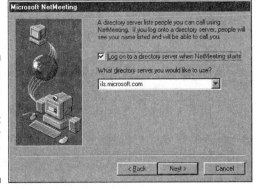

Figure 11-2:
NetMeeting
wants to
know what
directory
server to
connect to.

Click Next> to display the next dialog box, shown in Figure 11-3. This dialog box asks you for information it can use to identify you to other NetMeeting users. You must enter at least your first and last name and your e-mail address. (You don't have to enter your real name here; Queen Victoria or Snow White will do.)

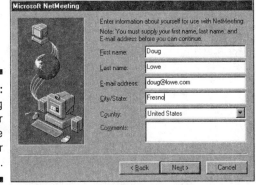

Figure 11-3:
NetMeeting
asks for
your name
and other
information.

When you click Next>, NetMeeting asks how you would like to categorize your information: personal, business, or adult-only. See Figure 11-4. Check the appropriate option, and then click Next> again.

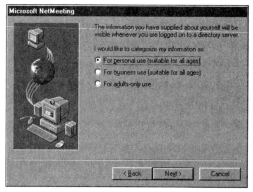

Figure 11-4:
Tell
NetMeeting
whether
your
information
is personal,
business, or
adult-only.

At this point, NetMeeting continues with a series of dialog boxes that automatically configures your sound card and modem. Follow the instructions on-screen to complete NetMeeting's configuration procedure.

Rest assured that all these configuration steps are required only the first time you run NetMeeting. After you install and configure NetMeeting, it starts right up whenever you click Start and choose Programs⇨ Internet Explorer⇨Microsoft NetMeeting.

Reaching Out and Touching Someone

To call up another NetMeeting user for a voice conversation, connect to the Internet via your Internet service provider (if you haven't done so already) and then follow these steps:

1. **Click the Start button on the Windows 95 taskbar and then choose Programs⇨Microsoft NetMeeting.**

   NetMeeting comes to life, connects to the directory server, and — after a few moments — displays a list of everyone who's connected to the server. Figure 11-5 shows the main NetMeeting window after the connection to the server is established.

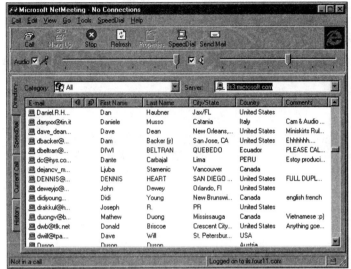

Figure 11-5:
NetMeeting
is
connected.

2. **Double-click the name of the person you want to call.**

   NetMeeting attempts to contact the user you selected. This process may take a few moments, so be patient. Messages appear at the bottom of the NetMeeting window to let you know the status of your call. If the person you're trying to call is already in another conference, NetMeeting extends the offer to barge in on the conference. However, the members in that conference may decide not to let you in, so don't be surprised if your call goes unanswered.

   When the connection is finally established, your name and the name of the person you're calling appear in the NetMeeting window.

3. **Talk into your microphone.**

   NetMeeting works just like a telephone. You talk into the microphone, and you can hear the person on the other end of the line through your computer's speakers.

4. **When you're done, say good-bye and choose Call⇨Hang Up.**

   That's all there is to it!

Drawing on the Whiteboard

Another way to communicate in NetMeeting is with Whiteboard, which is sort of like an Internet version of the venerable Paint accessory that comes with Windows 95. The difference between the two programs is that both you and your friend on the other end of the call can doodle on the Whiteboard, and you can instantly see each other's artistic endeavors.

To use Whiteboard, follow these steps:

1. **Establish a call to another NetMeeting user.**

2. **Click the Whiteboard button (or choose Tools➪Whiteboard or press Ctrl+W).**

   Whiteboard appears, as shown in Figure 11-6.

Figure 11-6:
Whiteboard
looks a lot
like Paint.

3. **Draw something.**

   If you know how to use Microsoft Paint, you already know how to use Whiteboard. Just select one of the drawing tools in the toolbar on the left edge of the Whiteboard window and then doodle something in the drawing area.

4. **Gasp in amazement when Whiteboard appears to draw stuff all by itself.**

   Actually, Whiteboard isn't drawing that stuff, your counterpart on the other end of the NetMeeting call is. The whole point of Whiteboard is that any of the NetMeeting participants can draw on the Whiteboard at the same time. Anything one person draws on NetMeeting's Whiteboard automatically shows up on every participant's computer.

5. **If the drawing is worth hanging on to, choose File➪Save to save the drawing or File➪Print to print it.**

6. **When you're done, close Whiteboard by clicking the standard Windows 95 Close button (you know, the one with the X on it that's in the upper-right corner of the window).**

   Alternatively, you can choose File➪Exit.

Although Whiteboard is similar to Paint, it has several features that are especially useful when working on the Internet:

 ✔ **Highlighter:** Quickly highlight any region of the Whiteboard by clicking this button and then dragging it over the region you want to highlight. You can change the color of the highlighter by clicking one of the colors at the bottom-left corner of the Whiteboard window.

 ✔ **Select Window:** Copy the contents of another window into the Whiteboard by clicking this button and then clicking anywhere in the window you want to include. As soon as you click the mouse, the contents of the window you clicked are automatically pasted into the Whiteboard.

 ✔ **Select Area:** You can copy a selected area from anywhere on your screen into the Whiteboard by clicking this button and then dragging a rectangle over the area you want copied. When you release the mouse button, the area you selected is automatically pasted into the Whiteboard.

 ✔ **Lock Contents:** Click this button to prevent other users from modifying the contents of the Whiteboard. Click it again to unlock it. Note that any user in a conference can lock the Whiteboard.

 ✔ **Remote Pointer:** Click this button to activate a special pointer that appears on everyone else's NetMeeting screen. You move the remote pointer around by dragging it with your mouse.

Using the NetMeeting Chat Feature

Although NetMeeting's voice features are interesting, voice communication is possible only between two users. For a conference with more than two users, you must resort to NetMeeting's Chat feature. You may even want to use Chat for two-way conversations, if you find that the sound quality of voice communications is less than adequate. (Sound quality is often a problem when using NetMeeting, depending on the speed of your Internet connection, the load on the server, and the quality of your sound card.)

To use Chat, follow this procedure:

1. **Call up another NetMeeting user.**

2. **Click the Chat button (or choose Tools⇨Chat or press Ctrl+T).**

   Up springs the Chat window, shown in Figure 11-7.

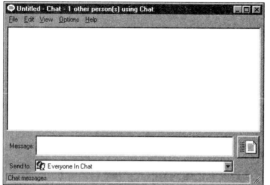

Figure 11-7:
The
NetMeeting
Chat
window.

3. **Type something in the text box at the bottom of the Chat window.**

4. **Press Enter to send your message.**

   Or click the Send button shown in Figure 11-7. Messages that other NetMeeting users send are displayed automatically.

5. **When you're finished chatting, choose File⇨Exit.**

   You can also close Chat by clicking the Close button in the upper-right corner of the Chat window.

Don't confuse NetMeeting's Chat feature with IRC (Internet Relay Chat). Although the two programs serve the same purpose, they're not compatible with one another. Thus, you can't use Microsoft Chat in a NetMeeting Chat session. Likewise, you can't use NetMeeting Chat for IRC chatting.

Sending a File

You can send a file to another NetMeeting user by following these steps:

1. **Call up another NetMeeting user.**

2. **Choose Tools⇨File Transfer⇨Send File command.**

   A dialog box appears, allowing you to select the file you want to send.

3. **Select the file you want to send.**

4. **Click OK.**

   That's all there is to it!

If you're in a conference with more than one other person, following the preceding steps sends a file to *all* the members of the conference. If you want to send a file to *just one* of the participants, right-click the icon for that person and select Send File from the pop-up menu that appears.

Sharing an Application

One of the cool features of NetMeeting is that it enables you to share programs over the Internet with other NetMeeting users. For example, if you are discussing your marketing budget in a NetMeeting conference, you can call up Microsoft Excel, open the budget spreadsheet, and let everyone in the conference see and even edit the spreadsheet.

To share an application, just follow these steps:

1. **Start the application you want to share.**

   If you want to share a particular document, open the document you want to share, too.

2. **Click the Share button or choose Tools➪Share Application.**

3. **Select the application you want to share from the list of applications that appears.**

4. **Use the application as you normally would.**

   Anything you do in the application is visible to the other members of the NetMeeting conference. However, other conference participants cannot take over and use the application until you complete the next step.

5. **Choose Tools➪Start Collaborating.**

   This command enables other users to take over and use the application you have shared. When another user takes over your application, you see your mouse pointer move magically by itself, with the other user's initials tacked onto the bottom of the mouse pointer so you can tell who's driving. You can wrest control away from the other user at any time by simply clicking the mouse.

6. **To stop the collaboration, choose Tools➪Stop Collaborating.**

   This command toggles on and off each time you use it.

7. **To stop sharing the application, click the Share button and select the application again.**

   The Share Application button also acts like a toggle, switching from On to Off each time you click it.

Beware of security problems when you share an application, especially when you enable Collaboration. When you give someone access to your application from across the Internet, that person can delete files, open sensitive documents, and even plant macro viruses on your computer. You should enable the Collaboration feature in NetMeeting only with users you trust. And never leave your computer unattended — even for a moment — with Collaboration enabled.

Saving Time with SpeedDial

The SpeedDial feature enables you to store the addresses of frequently called NetMeeting users for quick access. With the SpeedDial feature, you can call your best friend in San Diego without having to log in to a ULS server and wait for the directory to appear on your computer.

- To add a someone to your SpeedDial list, call up the user and then choose SpeedDial⇨Add SpeedDial. From then on, the user's name appears right on the SpeedDial menu.

- To call someone from your SpeedDial list, click the SpeedDial tab in the main NetMeeting window and then select the person's name from the list of names that appears.

- To remove a name from your SpeedDial list, select the name you want to remove and press the Delete key.

Part IV
Customizing Your Explorations

The 5th Wave   By Rich Tennant

PSYCHIC NETWORK

DOWNLOADING FILE...
ALTHOUGH IT WON'T
MAKE ANY DIFFERENCE
SINCE YOU WON'T BE
WORKING HERE NEXT
MONTH.

In this part . . .

This is the part to turn to when you're tired of working with Internet Explorer the way it runs out-of-the-box, and you want to customize it to more closely suit your working style. These chapters show you how to set up your own customized start page, how to set up parental controls to ensure that your kids have a safe and sane Internet experience, how to set the many Internet Explorer options, and how to create a Dial-Up Networking script so that you won't have to type your user ID and password every time you connect to the Internet.

Chapter 12

Personalizing Your Home Page

. . . .

In This Chapter

▶ Setting your own home page

▶ Customizing the home.microsoft.com home page

▶ Meeting two other customizable home pages

. . . .

*Y*our *home page* is the page that Internet Explorer automatically displays each time you begin an exploration of the World Wide Web. This chapter shows you how to designate any page of the Web as your home page and even how to create your own, customized home page.

Note: Your Internet Explorer home page is not the same as a home page that you can set up for other Web users to see. When you designate a page as your Internet Explorer home page or when you create a customized home page, only *you* can see the home page and the custom options that you selected. If you want to create a home page that other Web users can see, you must make arrangements with your Internet service provider to place your home page on their Web server.

Changing Your Home Page

Normally, Internet Explorer defaults to the page home.microsoft.com as its home page. If you obtained your copy of Internet Explorer from a company other than Microsoft — CompuServe, for example — Internet Explorer may be configured with a different home page. Whatever your home page currently is, Internet Explorer enables you to designate *any* page on the Web as the first one you see. For example, if the only Internet site you're interested in is David Letterman's Top Ten List, you can set the Top Ten List site to be your home page.

The home page is also the page that pops up whenever you click the Home button on the Standard toolbar.

To change your home page, follow these steps:

1. **Navigate your way to the page you want to use as your new home page.**

   See Chapter 3 for details about getting around on the Web.

2. **Choose the View⇨Internet Options command.**

   The Internet Options dialog box appears, as shown in Figure 12-1.

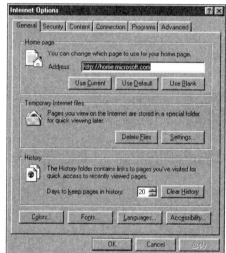

Figure 12-1:
The Internet
Options
dialog box.

3. **Click the Use Current button.**

   The home page is now set to the current page.

4. **Click OK to dismiss the Options dialog box.**

   You're done!

You can change back to the default home page by choosing View⇨Internet Options and clicking the Use Default button. And if you prefer to have no home page at all, click Use Blank. That way, Internet Explorer simply displays a blank page when you start it.

Customizing home.microsoft.com

One of the great things about the `home.microsoft.com` page is that you can customize it to include information you're interested in seeing every time you access the Internet. For example, you can add sports scores, daily news, links to your favorite Internet locations, weather reports, and other useful information.

Information you can add

The following is a list of the custom options that you can add to the `home.microsoft.com` customizable home page:

- **Headline News:** You can display headline news from MSNBC.

- **Microsoft News:** You can see stories from two Microsoft Web publications: Microsoft Internet News and 4.0 WebZine.

- **Technology:** Technology information can be provided by any of several sources, such as MSNBC and Forbes ASAP.

- **Money:** Market information and news can be extracted from MSNBC, Microsoft Investor, or Forbes.

- **Sports:** You can get sports news from MSNBC automatically placed on your home page.

- **Entertainment:** Slate, Cinemania, or Music Central are your choices for entertainment information.

- **Life:** Here you can select from MSNBC, Microsoft CarPoint, the Expedia travel service, Forbes FYI, and VinSight.

- **Default Search:** You can choose a default search engine from a list of 11 popular search services.

- **Stock Ticker:** You can have a stock ticker control added to your home page so that you can monitor the market.

- **Best of the Best:** Links to the leading sites on the Web.

- **Special Offers:** Offers up special promotions from Microsoft.

Customizing the home page

To customize the `home.microsoft.com` home page, just follow these steps:

1. **Display the home page.**

   The easiest way is to click the Home button.

2. **Click the <u>Personalizing</u> link.**

   The page illustrated in Figure 12-2 comes up. All the home page customization is done from this page.

3. **Specify the custom options that you want to include on your home page.**

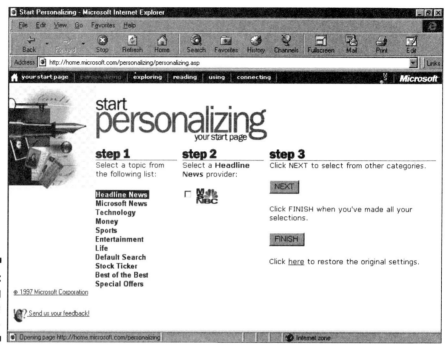

To get started, indicate whether you want headline news from MSNBC to be included on your home page. Then, click the Next button to move on to the next category: Microsoft News. Choose your options for this category, and then click Next again to move to the Technology category. Continue choosing options and clicking Next until you have completed all the categories.

4. **Click Finish.**

Your custom home page is built for you with the features you selected from the personalization page.

Other Home Pages You Can Customize

Not to be outdone by Microsoft, several other companies are jumping on the "customize your own home page" bandwagon. The following sections describe two alternatives to the home.microsoft.com personalized home page.

My Excite Channel

`home.excite.com/home`

Excite is a popular Internet search service. Besides offering an excellent Web search database, Excite provides a customizable home page called My Excite Channel, which offers more custom options than `home.microsoft.com`. Figure 12-3 shows My Excite Channel.

My Excite Channel enables you to add the following custom features to your home page:

✔ **News:** You can include headlines, business, sports, entertainment, technology, international, political, or odd news.

✔ **Information:** You can include stock quotes, weather reports, horoscopes, TV listings, movies, and cartoons.

✔ **Sports:** You can include sports scores as well as news about several sports, including football, baseball, basketball, hockey, golf, and even track.

✔ **Event Reminders:** Warns you a day, week, or month before an important birthday, anniversary, or other event (you can set as many as ten such reminders).

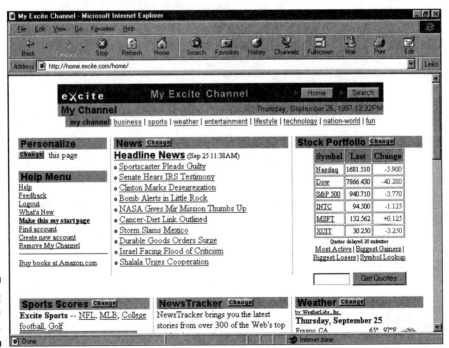

Figure 12-3:
My Excite
Channel.

Infoseek Personal

`personal.infoseek.com`

Infoseek, another popular search service, also offers a personalized home page. Its default setup, shown in Figure 12-4, provides quick access to Infoseek searches, plus a snippet of news, local TV, movies, weather, comics, and horoscope links.

One unique feature of Infoseek Personal is its Personal News, which works sort of like a news-clipping service. All you have to do is supply the keywords for news items you're interested in. For example, if you want to see news about Internet Explorer 4, you just type **Internet Explorer 4** as a keyword in the personalized news section.

Figure 12-4:
Infoseek
Personal.

Chapter 13

Exercising Your Parental Controls

● ●

In This Chapter

▶ Activating the Content Advisor feature of Internet Explorer

▶ Determining your blush threshold

▶ Picking a secret password

▶ Requiring password access to restricted sites

● ●

*A*lthough the Internet can be a great resource for kids, it's also a notoriously unsafe place for kids to hang out unsupervised. For every museum, library, and government agency that springs up on the Internet, a corresponding adult bookstore, sex shop, or smutty magazine seems to appear. What's a parent to do?

Fortunately, Internet Explorer has a built-in feature called *Content Advisor,* which enables you to restrict access to off-color Internet sites. Content Advisor uses a system of ratings similar to the ratings used for movies. Although this system isn't perfect, it goes a long way toward preventing your kids from stumbling into something they shouldn't.

About Internet Ratings

Internet ratings work much like motion picture ratings: They let you know what kind of content you can expect at a given Internet site. The ratings are assigned voluntarily by the publisher of each individual Internet site.

Although movie ratings give you an overall rating for a movie (G, PG, PG-13, R, or NC-17), the motion picture ratings system doesn't give you a clue about *why* a movie receives a particular rating. For example, does a PG-13 rating mean that a movie is filled with foul language, almost-explicit sex, or excessive violence? It could be any of these — or all of them.

By contrast, Internet ratings give specific information about several categories of potentially offensive material. Several different ratings systems are currently being developed. The system that Internet Explorer uses was created by a nonprofit organization called the Recreational Software Advisory Council, or RSAC. RSAC assigns a rating of 0 to 4 for each of the following four categories:

 ✔ Violence

 ✔ Nudity

 ✔ Language

 ✔ Sex

Table 13-1 shows the specific meaning for each rating number in an RSAC rating.

Table 13-1		What the RSAC Ratings Mean		
Rating	*Violence*	*Nudity*	*Language*	*Sex*
0	Harmless conflict; some damage to objects	No nudity or revealing attire	Inoffensive slang; no profanity	Romance; no sex
1	Creatures injured or killed; damage to objects; fighting	Revealing attire	Mild expletives	Passionate kissing
2	Humans injured or killed; small amount of blood	Partial nudity	Expletives; nonsexual anatomical references	Clothed sexual touching
3	Humans injured or killed; blood and gore	Nonsexual frontal nudity	Strong, vulgar language; obscene gestures; racial epithets	Nonexplicit sexual activity
4	Wanton and gratuitous violence; torture; rape	Provocative frontal nudity	Crude or explicit sexual references; extreme hate speech	Explicit sexual activity; sex crimes

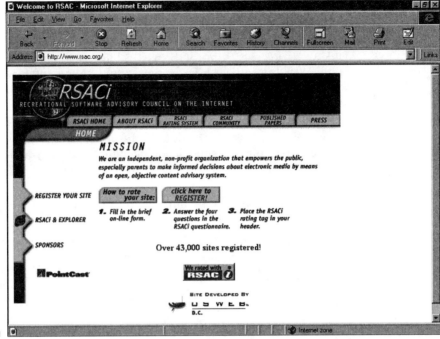

Figure 13-1:
The
Recreational
Software
Advisory
Council's
home page.

With Internet Explorer, you can set a threshold value for each of the four categories. If any attempt is made to access a Web site that has a rating higher than the threshold value, Internet Explorer blocks the user from viewing the Web site.

The RSAC rating system was developed by a group of recognized experts who study the effects of the media on children. For more information about RSAC, check out its Web site at www.rsac.org. Figure 13-1 shows the RSAC Web page, where you can learn more about RSAC; if you're a Web publisher, you can find out how to provide a rating for your site.

Limitations of Internet Ratings

Before I show you how to activate and configure the Internet Explorer Content Advisor, I want to be sure that I don't lull you into a false sense of security, thinking that after you activate the Ratings feature, you won't have to worry about your kids getting into trouble on the Internet. Just to be sure, here are a few of the limitations of the RSAC rating system:

✔ Ratings are voluntary. No one can guarantee that a Web site publisher will give his or her site an accurate rating.

✔ Currently, Internet Explorer's Ratings feature applies only to the World Wide Web. However, some of the nastiest Internet content is found not on the Web, but rather in Usenet newsgroups. Microsoft is working on a way to extend controls to newsgroups, but, as of now, RSAC ratings apply only to Web pages.

✔ Not all Web sites are rated. In fact, most are *not* rated. Internet Explorer allows you to either ban all unrated sites or allow full access to unrated sites. Neither option is good: If you ban unrated sites, you ban most of the Web. If you allow access to unrated sites, you let some garbage in. Sigh.

✔ Another area where kids get into trouble on the Internet is in Internet Relay Chats (IRCs). Ratings do not apply to IRCs.

✔ Kids are clever, and you can rest assured that some kids will figure out a way to bypass the ratings feature altogether. No security system is totally secure.

Activating Content Advisor

When you first install it, Internet Explorer does not check for Web site ratings. To screen out offensive Web sites, you must first activate the Content Advisor. Just follow these steps:

1. Choose View➪Internet Options.

The Internet Options dialog box appears.

2. Click the Content tab.

The Content options shown in Figure 13-2 appear.

3. Click the Enable button in the Ratings area of the dialog box.

Internet Explorer asks you to create a supervisor password in the dialog box shown in Figure 13-3.

4. Think up a good password.

Read the sidebar "Open sesame" for guidelines on creating a good password.

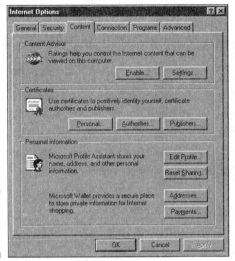

Figure 13-2:
The Content
options.

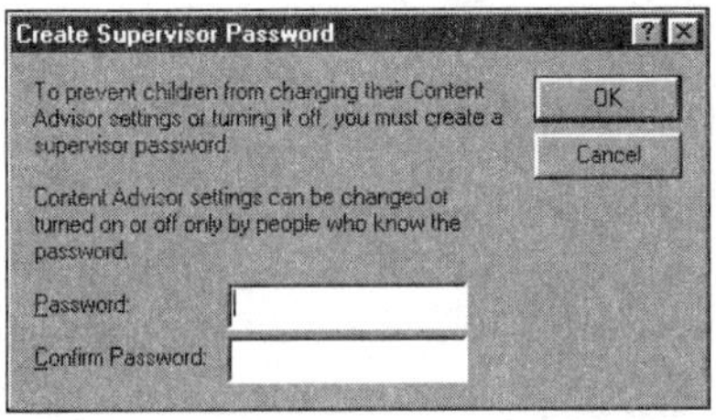

Figure 13-3:
Creating a
supervisor
password.

5. Type the password twice.

The password is not displayed on-screen as you type it. Therefore, Internet Explorer requires you to type your password twice, just to make sure that you don't make a typing mistake. Type the password once into the Password text box and then type it again into the Confirm Password text box.

6. Click OK.

The Content Advisor dialog box appears, as shown in Figure 13-4.

7. Set the rating for each category by clicking the category and then adjusting the slider bar for the rating that you want to use.

The slider bar magically appears after you click the category. For example, Figure 13-5 shows the slider bar that appears after you click the Language category. Notice also that a description of each rating level appears beneath the slider bar; this description changes as you move the slider bar.

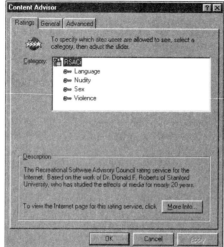

Figure 13-4:
The Content
Advisor
dialog box.

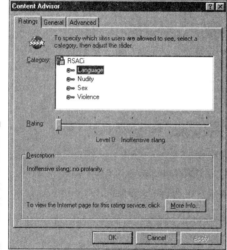

Figure 13-5:
Use the
slider bar to
figure out
what
ratings
mean.

8. After you have set the ratings to appropriate levels for your kids, click OK.

The following message appears in its own little dialog box:

Content Advisor has been turned on.

9. Click OK to dismiss the Internet Options dialog box.

The message dialog box disappears. Finally! You're finished!

After Content Advisor is in place, the dialog box shown in Figure 13-6 appears whenever someone attempts to access a site that your ratings do not allow.

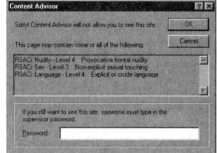

Figure 13-6:
Caught in
the act!

You can deactivate Content Advisor at any time by calling up the Content options (choose View⇨Internet Options and then click the Content tab) and clicking the Disable Ratings button. You are, of course, required to enter your password in the process.

If you turn off Content Advisor so that you (a consenting adult) can use Internet Explorer without restriction, don't forget to turn it back on after you're finished!

Open sesame

The Internet Ratings feature is only as good as the password you pick. Thus, you must make sure that you don't pick a password that your kids can easily figure out. Here are some passwords to avoid:

- Your name or your kid's name
- The names of your pets
- The name of your boat
- Your birthday or anniversary
- Your car license number
- The password you use to access the Internet

- Any other word or number that's important to you, and that your clever kids could come up with on their own

The best passwords are random combinations of letters and numbers. Of course, these are also the hardest to memorize. Next best passwords are randomly chosen words. Just flip open the dictionary to a random page, point to any word, and use it as your password.

Above all, do *not* write the password down on a sticky note attached to the computer monitor! If you must write the password down, put it in a secure place where only *you* can find it.

Dealing with Unrated Sites

Internet ratings are a great idea. Unfortunately, not all the sites on the Net have yet rated themselves. When you enable Content Advisor, Internet Explorer bans access not only to sites whose ratings are above the threshold you set, but also to any site that's not rated.

Unfortunately, many Internet sites are unrated. If you enable Content Advisor, your kids won't be able to visit any unrated sites.

Fortunately, Internet Explorer enables you to ease the ban on unrated sites. Here's the procedure:

1. **Choose View⇨Internet Options and click the Content tab.**

   The Content options appear. (Refer to Figure 13-2.)

2. **Click the Settings button.**

   You're asked for your password. Type the password and then click OK. The Content Advisor dialog box appears.

3. **Click the General tab.**

   You see the General Content Advisor options, as shown in Figure 13-7.

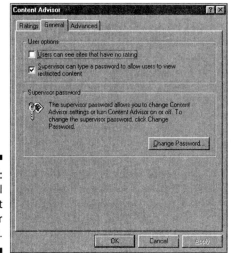

Figure 13-7:
The General
Content
Advisor
options.

4. **Check the Users Can See Sites That Have No Rating check box.**

5. **Click OK to dismiss the Content Advisor dialog box.**

   You return to the Internet Options dialog box.

6. **Click OK to dismiss the Internet Options dialog box.**

Now, you can view unrated sites without the constant `Sorry! Your ratings do not allow you to see this site` message.

To restrict access to unrated sites once again, repeat the procedure, but check (rather than uncheck) the Users Can See Sites That Have No Rating check box in Step 4.

Note that the General tab of the Content Advisor dialog box also enables you to change the supervisor password. Simply click the Change Password button. A dialog box appears, into which you can type a new password. (As before, you must type the password twice to make sure that you don't make any typing errors.)

You can disable the feature that allows the user to view restricted sites by entering the supervisor password. Just uncheck the Supervisor Can Type a Password to Allow Users to View Restricted Content option.

Chapter 14
Opting for Options

· ·

In This Chapter

▶ Getting to know Internet Explorer's options

▶ Changing option settings to suit your tastes

· ·

Selecting <u>V</u>iew⇨Internet <u>O</u>ptions opens the door to myriad options that affect the way Internet Explorer browses the World Wide Web. Of course, you can't use this command to pick your *real* preferences, such as playing golf instead of toiling with your computer. But you can do stuff that's almost as much fun, such as changing the colors used to display links you already visited or setting the default start page.

Read this chapter after you become comfortable with the out-of-the-box version of Internet Explorer and you're ready to find out what all those options really do. This chapter describes the most useful options, but what's more important, it tells you which options you can safely ignore so that you (unlike some people I know — me, for example) can catch up on your golf.

Note: I am aware, of course, that for some people golf is a more frustrating pastime than using your computer. And for some, golf is more boring than reading Internet Explorer's online help. If you're one of those poor, un-enlightened souls, feel free to substitute your favorite nongolf pastime — and may I recommend *Golf For Dummies,* by Gary McCord with John Huggan (published by IDG Books Worldwide, Inc.) ?

What's with All the Options?

Selecting <u>V</u>iew⇨Internet <u>O</u>ptions presents you with a killer dialog box that has tabs out the wazoo (whatever a *wazoo* is). Each of the tabs has its own set of controls. To switch from one tab to another, just click the tab label at the top of the dialog box.

Here's the lowdown on the six tabs that appear in the Internet Options dialog box:

- ✔ **General:** Contains options that affect the general operation of Internet Explorer.

- ✔ **Security:** Enables you to indicate whether you want to be warned before doing something that may jeopardize your security.

- ✔ **Content:** Enables you to filter out pages with questionable content (see Chapter 13).

- ✔ **Connection:** Indicates which dial-up connection to use to establish a connection to the Internet.

- ✔ **Programs:** Enables you to indicate which programs to use to read Internet mail and newsgroups and other necessary chores.

- ✔ **Advanced:** Holds a number of options that just didn't fit anywhere else.

To set any of the preceding options, follow this general procedure:

1. Choose View⇨Internet Options.

The Internet Options dialog box appears.

2. Click the tab that contains the option you want to set.

If you're not sure which tab to click, just cycle through them all until you find what you're looking for.

3. Set the options however you want.

Most of the options are simple check boxes that you click to check or uncheck. Some require that you select a choice from a drop-down list, and some have the audacity to require that you actually type something as proof of your keyboard proficiency.

4. Repeat Step 3 until you've exhausted your options (or yourself).

You can set more than one option with a single use of the View⇨Internet Options command.

5. Click OK.

You're done!

Saluting the General Options

Back in the days of Internet Explorer 1.0, the options on the General tab were lowly Private Options. But they re-enlisted for version 2.0, and eventually decided to become Career Options. Now, with Internet Explorer 4, they boast the rank of General. I suggest you snap-to whenever you call up these options, shown in Figure 14-1.

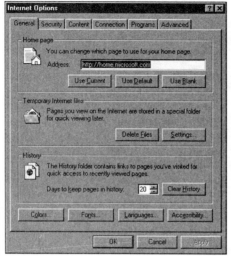

The General options comprise the following three categories:

- **Home Page:** Enables you to set the location of the page that's displayed when you click the Home button.

- **Temporary Internet Files:** This option enables you to manage the temporary files that Internet Explorer downloads to your hard disk. By default, Internet Explorer uses as much as 10 percent of your disk drive to store these files. The more disk space you allocate to Internet Explorer, the less often Internet Explorer is forced to download files that you've already seen. Of course, the tradeoff is that an increase in the amount of disk Internet Explorer can use decreases the amount of free disk space on your computer.

  You can empty the Temporary Internet files folder by clicking the Delete Files button. But be warned that deleting these files causes delays because Internet Explorer is forced to download files that were previously stored on your disk.

- **History:** Enables you to specify how many days of history information you want to retain. Also, you can click the Clear History button to remove all the files from the History folder.

Setting Security Options

Figure 14-2 shows the Security options, which are designed to protect you from Internet sites with offensive content, to protect your privacy, and to warn you about potential security problems. To call up these options, just click the Security tab at the top of the Internet Options dialog box.

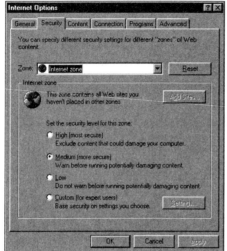

Figure 14-2:
The
Security
options.

Internet Explorer's security features divvies the entire Internet up into four *zones,* as follows:

- ✔ **Local intranet:** If your computer is connected to a local area network (LAN), this zone encompasses files or Web pages that reside on the local network, rather than on the Internet.

- ✔ **Trusted sites:** This zone involves sites that you're confident don't pose a security risk. Security for sites in this zone is relaxed.

- ✔ **Internet zone:** This zone contains the rest of the Internet.

- ✔ **Restricted sites:** This zone comprises sites that you think are not safe. Security for sites in this zone is beefed up.

For each of these zones, you can apply one of four levels of security: High, Medium, Low, and Custom. Custom security is designed for advanced users who want to tweak each little security option. For most of us, High, Medium, and Low are sufficient.

Cruising with the Content Options

The Content tab lets you fiddle with the Internet Explorer Content Advisor, which is designed to block access to offensive Web sites. Figure 14-3 shows the Content options.

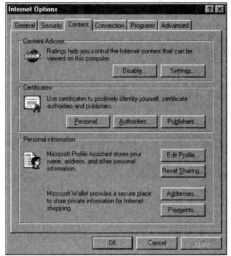

Figure 14-3:
The Content
options.

You can find a complete run-down on the Content Advisor in Chapter 13, so I won't discuss it further here.

Cajoling the Connection Options

The Connection options, shown in Figure 14-4, enable you to specify which dial-up connection you use to connect to the Internet. You may find yourself turning to this tab frequently if you have more than one Internet service provider and you often switch from one to another. You should also visit this tab if you decide to change providers.

If you've yet to create a dial-up connection for your Internet provider, click the Connect button. The Connection Wizard comes to life to create a connection for you after asking basic questions such as the phone number to dial and your user ID.

If you use a modem to connect to the Internet, the Connect to the Internet Using a Modem option should be set. If your computer is connected to the Internet via a local area network, the Access the Internet Via a Local Area Network option should be selected instead.

If you use a *proxy server,* the Connection tab is the place to set it. Click the Connect Using a Proxy Server check box, and then enter the proxy settings. (Your network manager can supply you with these settings.)

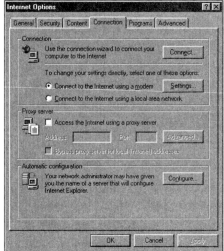

Figure 14-4:
The
Connection
options.

Perusing the Programs Options

The Programs tab, shown in Figure 14-5, contains options that enable you to tell Internet Explorer what programs you want to use to read your e-mail, access newsgroups, and handle Internet calls. The default settings are Outlook Express for e-mail and news and Microsoft NetMeeting for Internet calls.

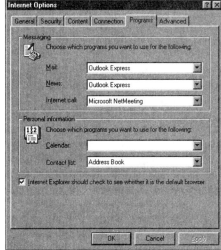

Figure 14-5:
The
Programs
settings.

Leave the default Programs settings as they are unless you have installed some other e-mail or newsgroup program that's designed to work with Internet Explorer.

The other settings on the Programs tab enable you to choose the program to use for your Calendar and Address Book. You should leave these settings well enough alone.

Achieving Advanced Options

The Advanced options, shown in Figure 14-6, enable you to set several features that govern Internet Explorer's operation. Wow, there are a lot of options in this dialog box. So many, in fact, that Microsoft uses an unusual method of enabling you to set them. Rather than spew a bunch of check boxes onto the Advanced options dialog box, all the options are shown in a big scrollable list box. To set any of the options, scroll down the list until you find the option you want to set, and then click the option.

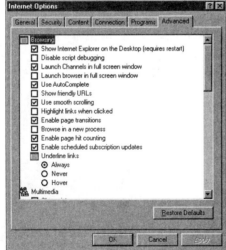

Figure 14-6:
The
Advanced
option
settings.

The Advanced options fall into the following categories:

✔ **Browsing:** These options control basic aspects of how the Internet Explorer browser works, such as whether to use the AutoComplete feature to finish typing Web addresses for you and whether to use fancy smooth scrolling. (If you have a slower computer, you may want to disable smooth scrolling.)

✔ **Multimedia:** You can indicate whether graphics, sounds, and video are downloaded automatically whenever you go to a Web page. Disabling any or all of these options improves Internet Explorer's performance.

✔ **Security:** Yep, there are still more security options that didn't fit in the Security tab. Fortunately, you don't have to worry about them.

✔ **Java VM:** If you're a Java guru, you may want to look at these options. Otherwise, try not to step in them.

✔ **Printing:** Enables you to include background colors and textures when you print a Web page. If you have a color printer, this option might be nice. But otherwise, you should leave it off. (In fact, you should probably leave it off even if you have a color printer, unless you want each page to be filled with the background color. Expect to go through a lot of ink cartridges if you turn this option on.)

✔ **Searching:** These options let you configure Internet Explorer so that if you type an Internet address that doesn't exist, Internet Explorer can look for other similar addresses using different domain suffixes. For example, if you type `www.whitehouse.com`, Internet Explorer can automatically find the White House for you by using the correct address, which is `www.whitehouse.gov`.

✔ **Toolbar:** This group includes a single option that enables you to use small icons with the Internet Explorer toolbars. When you activate this option, Internet Explorer's toolbars look more like the toolbars found in Microsoft Office.

✔ **HTTP 1.1 settings:** Steer clear of these options.

Chapter 15

Automating Your Log-In Procedures

● ●

In This Chapter

▶ Getting to know scripts

▶ Planning your own Dial-Up Script

▶ Creating a script file

▶ Using script commands

▶ Attaching a script to a connection

● ●

Dial-up Scripting is a feature of Windows 95 that I hope you don't have to use. It's the type of feature that requires you to don a pocket protector and assume the role of a computer geek. But after you have it set up, a Dial-Up Script can simplify your Internet sign-in procedures dramatically.

Dial-Up Scripting is designed for those users whose Internet service providers require them to go through a complicated log-in sequence whenever they access the Internet. If, when you dial up your ISP, a terminal window pops up and greets you with a message such as User-ID: and a cold, blinking cursor, then Dial-Up Scripting is for you.

If your Internet service provider launches you straight into Internet Explorer, you can fall down on your knees, give thanks, and skip this chapter.

What Is a Dial-Up Script?

A *Dial-Up Script* is a special file that contains text and commands that are automatically typed in for you when you log in to a computer network. If the computer system you use to connect to the Internet requires you to manually enter information before it sends you to the Net, you can create a Dial-Up Script to automate the process.

For example, my Internet service provider requires me to type in my user ID and password. Then it displays the text menu shown in Figure 15-1. From this menu, I must select item 4. Then I am prompted to enter an *IP address* (whatever that is), to which I must reply *Default.* Only then am I connected to the Internet so that I can use Internet Explorer.

By using a script, I can have the computer do all this typing for me. The script types in my name and password, waits for the menu to appear, chooses item 4, waits for the prompt, and then types *Default.* All I have to do is sit back and enjoy a sip of coffee while the script does all the work.

Unfortunately, you have to write the script yourself. The script is a simple text file that can be edited with ease, but it must contain certain commands, which I describe later in this chapter. In addition, you have to attach the script to the Dial-Up Connection so that Windows 95 knows to run your script when you dial in. I describe the procedure for attaching the script later in this chapter.

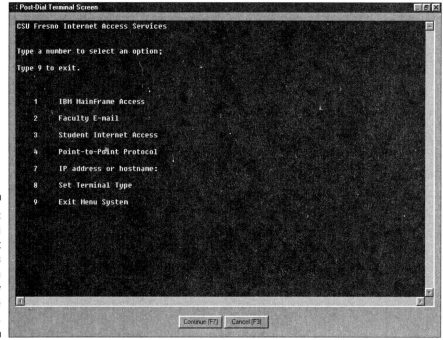

Figure 15-1:
The menu that appears when I sign into my service provider.

Installing Dial-Up Scripting

The first step in using Dial-Up Scripting is installing the Dial-Up Scripting tool. Dial-Up Scripting comes free with Windows 95, but many users don't have it installed on their computers. To find out whether you already have Dial-Up Scripting, click the Start button on the Windows 95 taskbar and select Programs⇨Accessories. If you see a Dial-Up Scripting Tool command, Dial-Up Scripting has been installed. If not, follow this procedure to install it:

1. **Insert your Windows 95 CD in your CD-ROM drive.**

   Wait a moment to see whether the CD opens by itself. If it doesn't, open it by double-clicking My Computer and then double-clicking the icon for the CD drive.

2. **Click the Add/Remove Software button.**

3. **Scroll through the list of Windows 95 components to find and select SLIP and Scripting for Dial-Up Networking.**

   See Figure 15-2. If this option doesn't appear on your list, click the Have Disk button and then click Browse and locate the folder \admin\apptools\dscript on your CD-ROM drive. Click OK and then check SLIP and Scripting for Dial-Up Networking.

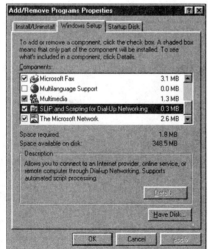

Figure 15-2:
Installing
Dial-Up
Scripting.

4. **Click OK.**

   Ta da! The Dial-Up Scripting tool is installed.

Planning a Script

The first step in creating a script file is to plan the contents of the script. Get a piece of paper and label two columns *Computer Types* and *I Type*. Then sit down at your computer and log in to your Internet service provider. As you do, carefully write down in the *I Type* column everything you must type. Also indicate when you must press the Enter key. In addition, enter in the *Computer Types* column the last thing displayed on-screen before anything you must type.

For example, here's what I wrote down to create the script for my provider:

Computer Types	I Type
Username:	user ID (Enter)
Password:	my password (Enter)
Exit Menu System:	4 (Enter not required)
hostname:	default (Enter)

You use the information as the basis for your script.

Creating a Script

To create a script, you must use a text editor such as Notepad. Here's the procedure for creating a script file:

1. **Click Start on the Windows 95 taskbar and choose Programs⇨Accessories⇨Notepad.**

   Notepad appears in its own window.

2. **Type whichever commands you need to type to establish your Internet connection.**

   The commands vary depending on your service provider's requirements. Figure 15-3 shows the script I use for my provider. I describe each of the commands in this script later in this chapter.

3. **Choose File⇨Save As to save the file.**

   Choose a filename that ends in .scp, and save the file in \Program Files\Accessories.

4. **Choose File⇨Exit to quit Notepad.**

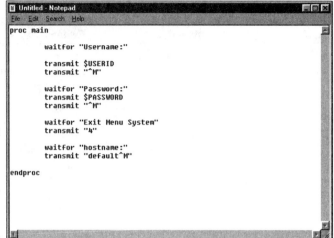

Figure 15-3:
The script I
wrote to log
in to my
service
provider.

Your script filename must end in .scp and reside in the \Program Files\
Accessories folder.

Script Commands

The hard part of creating a script is knowing which commands to include in
the script file. The following sections describe the commands that are used
in the script in Figure 15-3 (these are the most commonly used commands),
and Table 15-1 lists all the commands that you can use.

Table 15-1	Dial-Up Scripting Commands	
Command	*What It Does*	*Explanation*
`proc main`	Begins the script	The script begins running at the main procedure and stops at the end of the main procedure. (Every script must start with `proc main`.)
`endproc`	Marks the end of the script	When your computer reaches this command, Dial-Up Networking starts PPP or SLIP.

(continued)

Table 15-1 *(continued)*

Command	What It Does	Explanation
`delay <n seconds>`	Pauses the script for n seconds before executing the next command	For example, `delay 4` pauses for four seconds.
`waitfor "<string>"`	Waits until the computer you are connecting to has received the specified characters	Here, *string* refers to the words your Internet service provider uses to prompt you for information (from the *Computer Types* column). Note that the string is *case sensitive.* Thus, if your provider sends the text USERNAME (in all capital letters), you must type `waitfor "USERNAME"` (not `waitfor "Username"`) to wait for this string.
`transmit "<string>"`	Sends the specified characters to the computer to which you are connecting	Here, *string* refers to the words you type as you log in to your Internet service (from the *I Type* column).
`transmit $USERID`	Sends the user ID obtained from the Connect To dialog box	
`transmit $PASSWORD`	Sends the password obtained from the Connect To dialog box	
`set port databits <integer>`	Changes the number of bits in the bytes that are transmitted during the session, from 5 to 8	
`set port stopbits <integer>`	Changes the number of stop bits for the port during the session, either 1 or 2	
`set port parity none | odd | even | mark | space`	Changes the parity for the port during the session	

Command	What It Does	Explanation
set ipaddr	Sets the IP address for the session	
set screen keyboard on | off	Enables or disables keyboard input to the terminal window	
getip <optional index>	Reads an IP address and uses it as the workstation address	
halt	Causes Dial-Up Networking to stop running the script, but leaves the terminal window open so you can enter additional information manually	
;	Indicates a comment	All text after the semicolon is ignored — comments are for your reference only.

proc main *and* endproc

Every script must begin with a line that says proc main and end with a line that says endproc. It's a programming thing, required probably because the programmers at Microsoft who created the Dial-Up Scripting tool were in a bad mood that day and figured, hey, because we have to type stuff like proc main and endproc all day, everyone should have opportunity to enjoy the same wonderful experience.

So the first thing you do when creating a script is add these two lines, as follows:

```
proc main



endproc
```

Notice that I left a few blank rows between these two lines. This space is where the meat of the script goes.

Waiting for stuff: waitfor

Before your script can type anything to the computer, it must wait until the computer is ready to accept the information. To tell the script to wait, you must make note of the text that's displayed as a prompt and then use a waitfor command to tell the script to wait until that text appears on the screen.

For example, the following line tells the scripting tool to wait until the prompt Username: appears:

```
waitfor "Username:"
```

The only trick in using a waitfor command is to make sure that the text you specify is unique — it doesn't occur anywhere else during your log-in procedure.

The script in Figure 15-3 uses four waitfor commands. In each case, I used the text that I had written down in the *Computer Types* column when I planned the script.

Typing text: transmit

To send text to the computer, you use a transmit command. In the script in Figure 15-3, you can see several variations of this command:

✔ transmit $USERID: This command transmits the user ID that I enter into the Connect To dialog box. By using this command in your script, you don't have to actually type your user ID into the script.

✔ transmit $PASSWORD: This command sends the password I enter into the Connect To dialog box. Once again, typing your command this way enables you to send the password without actually having to type your top-secret password into the script.

✔ transmit "^M": This cryptic command is equivalent to pressing the Enter key.

✔ transmit "some text": This command transmits some text as if you had typed it at the keyboard. Note that if the text includes ^M, the Enter key is sent as well.

"^M" is but one example of several special characters that you can send as part of a text string. Table 15-2 lists all the special characters that can be included in strings.

Table 15-2	Special Characters for Strings
Character	*Explanation*
^M	Carriage return (Enter)
<cr>	Carriage return (Enter)
<lf>	Line feed
\"	Includes the quotation mark as part of the string
\'	Includes the apostrophe as part of the string
\^	Includes the caret (^) as part of the string
\<	Includes the less-than sign as part of the string
\\	Includes the back slash as part of the string

Attaching the Script to a Dial-Up Connection

After you create your script, you must attach it to a dial-up connection so
that the script plays automatically each time you start the connection.
Here's the procedure for attaching a script:

1. **Click Start on the Windows 95 taskbar and choose
   Programs➪Accessories➪Dial-Up Scripting Tool.**

   The Dial-Up Scripting Tool comes to life, as shown in Figure 15-4.

Figure 15-4:
The Dial-Up
Scripting
Tool.

If the Dial-Up Scripting Tool doesn't appear in the Start menu under
Programs➪Accessories, you can run the scripting tool by clicking Start,
choosing Run, and typing **C:\Program Files\Accessories\scripter.exe**
(where C is your hard drive).

2. **Select the connection to which you want to attach the script.**

3. **Click the Browse button.**

   An Open dialog box appears.

4. **Select the file you want to use as the script.**

   You may have to use the Open dialog box's navigation controls to find the correct drive and folder.

5. **Click the Open button.**

6. **Back in the Dial-Up Scripting Tool dialog box, click Apply.**

7. **Click Close to dismiss the Dial-Up Scripting Tool dialog box.**

You're almost there. You must make one more change in order for the script to work: You must turn off the terminal window that's displayed automatically after you start the connection. To suppress the terminal window, follow these steps:

1. **Click Start and Choose Programs⇨Accessories⇨Dial-Up Networking.**

   This command brings up a window that lists your connections.

2. **Right-click the icon for the connection you attached the script to and then choose Properties from the pop-up menu.**

   The dialog box shown in Figure 15-5 appears.

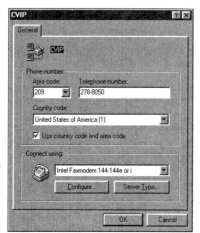

Figure 15-5:
The CVIP
dialog box.

3. Click the Configure button.

The dialog box shown in Figure 15-6 appears.

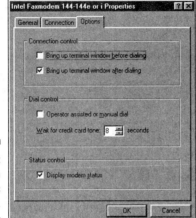

4. Click the Options tab.

5. Click to *uncheck* both Connection control options.

These options include bringing up the terminal window before and after dialing.

6. Click OK to dismiss the Modem Properties dialog box.

7. Click OK again to dismiss the Connection Properties dialog box.

8. Close the Dial-Up Networking window.

Now, at long last, you're ready to run the script. When you open the Dial-Up Network connection, the script should run automatically. As the script runs, watch it carefully to make sure that it appears to be running correctly. If it doesn't run properly, double-check the script to make sure that you're transmitting the correct information and, just as importantly, waiting for the correct text before transmitting information.

Part V
The Active Desktop

The 5th Wave — By Rich Tennant

In this part . . .

One of the highly touted features of Internet Explorer 4 is its capability to replace the standard Windows 95 desktop shell with its own integrated shell, called the *Active Desktop*. The shell enables you to work with the files and folders on your hard drive in the same way that you work with pages on the World Wide Web. In short, Internet Explorer 4 replaces your Windows desktop with a special Web-style desktop. Aren't you excited?

The two chapters in this part show you how to work with this new Active Desktop and how to customize it to your liking. If you like Windows 95 the way it is and have no desire to experiment with something different, you can tear out these pages and use them to line your bird cage.

Chapter 16

Using the Active Desktop

In This Chapter

▶ Activating the Active Desktop feature

▶ Browsing your computer as if it were a part of the Web

▶ Introducing some new features that appear on-screen

▶ Customizing the Active Desktop settings

Apparently, Microsoft isn't happy just building a superior browser. Those clever company folks believe that Internet Explorer 4 ought to come with a built-in overhaul of the Windows 95 desktop. This optional feature, called the *Active Desktop* (also called the *Windows Desktop Update*), is designed to make your Windows 95 desktop, as well as your files and folders, resemble the World Wide Web. When you turn on the Active Desktop, the folders on your hard drive begin to look suspiciously like Web pages, complete with links that represent the files contained in the folder. Instead of double-clicking an icon to open a folder or file, with the Active Desktop you just click once on the file or folder's link.

If you find it confusing that Windows 95 has one user interface for navigating the files and folders on your computer and a completely different interface for navigating pages on the Web, you'll appreciate the Active Desktop features described in this chapter. But even if you don't mind that you have to double-click file and folder icons and you only have to single-click Web links, you can still try out the Active Desktop. The Active Desktop adds a number of new and useful features to the Windows 95 desktop itself, to the taskbar, and to the Start menu.

In this chapter, I show you how to use the Web-like navigation features of the Active Desktop. Then, in Chapter 17, I show you how to use some of the more advanced features of the Active Desktop, including magic that enables you to customize your desktop in ways you never thought possible.

What Is the Active Desktop?

The basic idea behind the Active Desktop is to make your computer's desktop look and act just like the Internet Explorer Web browser. Before the Active Desktop, you were obligated to learn two completely different interfaces to use your computer and the Internet. To access the folders on your hard drive, you sought the Windows 95 My Computer or Explorer interface. But to access the Internet, you relied on Internet Explorer, which uses a completely different user interface.

To see the difference between the traditional Windows 95 way of navigating files and folders and the Active Desktop approach, look at Figure 16-1. This figure shows a typical Windows 95 desktop with two folders open: one for My Computer, the other for a folder that contains my daughter Bethany's files. To open any of the items within either of these folders, you double-click an icon.

Now have a look at Figure 16-2, which shows the same two folders after the Active Desktop is installed. The following differences may catch your eye:

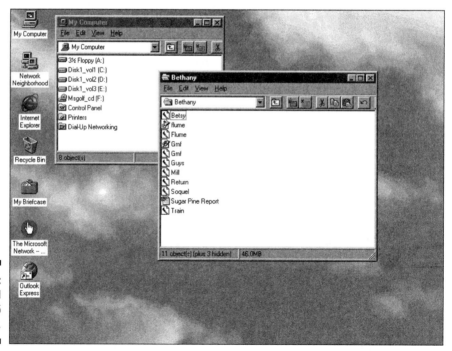

Figure 16-1:
A typical
Windows 95
desktop.

✔ The windows displaying the My Computer and Bethany folders have graphics and text in them. In the Active Desktop, each folder can have its own background that is displayed when you open the folder. You can also add custom messages, such as the message I added to Bethany's folder warning her sisters to keep out.

✔ The My Computer window includes a pie chart that shows the amount of free space available on the selected drive.

✔ The window for the folder named Bethany includes a preview area that shows the contents of the selected file (this preview area works for various types of graphic file formats and for HTML files).

✔ The names of the files and folders in each folder window are underlined in the same way that links are underlined in a Web page. That's because when you turn on the Active Desktop, file and folder icons actually become links that you can open by clicking just once rather than double-clicking.

✔ The names under the icons on the desktop are also underlined. Again, these icons are now links that you can open by single-clicking. Thus, you can open My Computer by clicking the icon once rather than double-clicking it.

✔ The toolbars in the folder windows contain buttons that are similar to the ones found in the Internet Explorer toolbar. You use the Back button to return to the last folder you viewed.

Figure 16-2:
Active
Desktop
changes
the
appearance
of the
Windows 95
desktop.

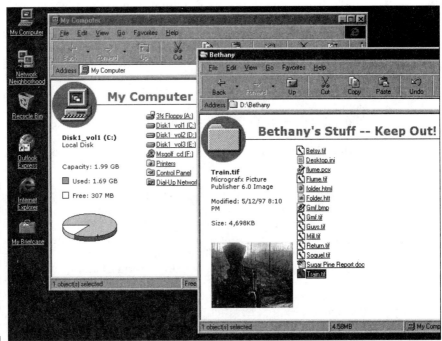

✔ The folder windows contain a Favorites menu that allows you to access your favorites from any folder. With Internet Explorer 4, you can add just about anything to your Favorites menu: a Web page, a folder on your hard drive, or a document that you use frequently. So it makes sense to be able to access the Favorites menu when you're exploring the files and folders on your hard disk.

All these differences make sense when you realize what the Active Desktop actually does. For starters, Active Desktop replaces Windows 95 wallpaper, which enables you to add a pretty graphic to the background of your desktop, but otherwise serves no useful purpose with an HTML document. In other words, Active Desktop replaces your Windows 95 wallpaper with a Web page.

Of course, the desktop HTML document is stored on your computer's own hard drive rather than out on the Internet, so you don't have to be connected to the Internet to display your desktop. And no one else out on the Internet can call up your computer and access your desktop HTML document.

The advantage of using an HTML document rather than plain wallpaper for your desktop is that anything you can do on a Web page also can be accomplished on your desktop. Your Active Desktop can include links to other pages, graphics, text, animations, and even programs written in the form of Java or Visual Basic scripts.

The Active Desktop doesn't stop at replacing your desktop wallpaper with an HTML document. The My Computer window also uses an HTML document for its background. That's how the My Computer window in Figure 16-2 is able to include text and graphics in addition to the icons for each of your disk drives. And that's why the icons themselves are actually links that you can open with a single click.

What's more, you can create an HTML document to display for *any* folder on your hard drive. In Figure 16-2, I create an HTML document for the Bethany folder. I customize Bethany's HTML document to display the message "Bethany's Stuff — Keep Out!" so that her sisters would know to leave Bethany's files alone. (Of course, my daughters still snoop in each others files, but at least they've been warned!)

The Active Desktop can display HTML documents for My Computer and your folders because the Active Desktop actually replaces the old Windows 95 Explorer program (which was responsible for displaying your files and folders in My Computer and Explorer view) with Internet Explorer 4. Thus, when you are browsing the files and folders on your hard drive using the Active Desktop, you're actually using Internet Explorer 4.

The good news is that you don't have to know anything about HTML to use the Active Desktop. For that matter, you don't even have to know any HTML to create a custom HTML document for a folder. In Chapter 17, I show you how to use the Active Desktop's Customize This Folder Wizard to automatically create an HTML document for a folder. And I show you how to customize the desktop itself.

Installing the Active Desktop

When you install Internet Explorer 4, you're offered the chance to include the Active Desktop. If you chose not to enable the Active Desktop when you installed Internet Explorer, you have to turn it on now if you want to use it. Here's how you do it:

1. **Click the Start button on the Windows 95 taskbar, and then choose Settings⇨Control Panel.**

    The Control Panel window appears.

2. **Double-click the Add/Remove Programs icon.**

    The Add/Remove Programs Properties dialog box appears.

3. **Select Microsoft Internet Explorer 4.0 from the list of programs, and then click Add/Remove.**

    The Internet Explorer 4.0 Active Setup dialog box appears, as shown in Figure 16-3.

Figure 16-3:
Adding the
Active
Desktop to
Internet
Explorer 4.0.

4. **Click the Add the Windows Desktop Update component from Web site option button.**

    Didn't I mention at the start of this chapter that Microsoft sometimes calls the Active Desktop the *Windows Desktop Update*? Go figure.

5. **Click OK.**

    Internet Explorer fires up. If necessary, Internet Explorer dials into your Internet service provider to connect you to the Internet. The Internet Explorer Active Setup program asks for permission to examine your system to determine which components of Internet Explorer are already installed. Click Yes, and then wait until the Internet Explorer Components Download page is displayed, as shown in Figure 16-4.

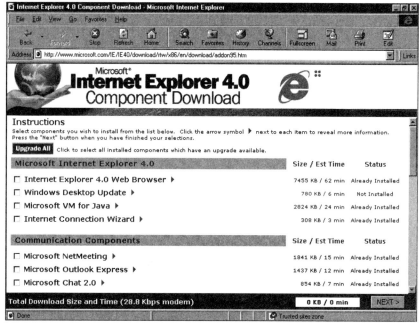

Figure 16-4:
The Internet
Explorer
Component
Download
page.

6. **Check the Windows Desktop Update option, and then click Next.**

The page shown in Figure 16-5 appears.

7. **Choose a download site that's near you, and then click the Install Now button.**

The drop-down list includes a bunch of download sites to choose from. Click the down-arrow on the drop-down list to see the choices and select one that's geographically near you.

8. **Wait while the Active components download.**

The download should take about five minutes if you have a 28.8 bps modem — just enough time for a few quick games of Solitaire.

When the download is finished, a dialog box appears to inform you that your computer must be restarted.

9. **Click Yes.**

Your computer restarts. When Windows comes back to life, the new desktop is active. Your desktop resembles Figure 16-6.

If you decide you don't like the Active Desktop and you prefer to go back to the original Windows 95 desktop, you can repeat the above procedure. In Step 6, instead of clicking the Windows Desktop Update option, check the Remove Windows Desktop Update but Keep the Internet Explorer 4.0 Web Browser option that appears in its place. Then click OK to restore the original Windows 95 desktop.

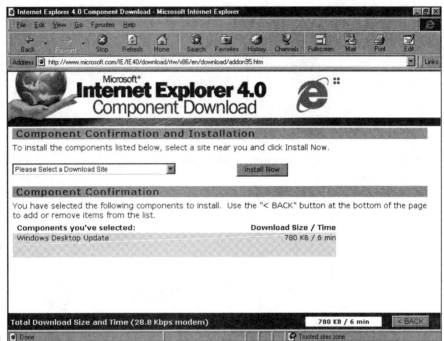

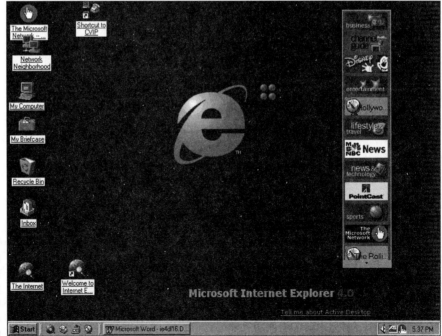

Working with the Active Desktop

The Active Desktop is a major change from the normal Windows 95 desktop. The following sections outline the most important changes you deal with when you switch to the Active Desktop.

Navigating with the Active Desktop

Navigating through the folders and files on your computer is a bit different when you turn on the Active Desktop. To dive into your files and folders, start by clicking (not double-clicking) the My Computer icon on the Active Desktop. This opens the My Computer window, which is pictured in Figure 16-7. As you can see, this window sports several new features that make browsing the drives and folders on your computer more like touring the Web with Internet Explorer.

Figure 16-7:
The new
My
Computer
window.

Notice that the left side of the My Computer window contains an information area. You can point to any of the drives listed in the My Computer window to see information about the drive. For example, Figure 16-8 shows information about my C drive in the My Computer window. To display this information, all I did was point the mouse at the C drive icon.

Each of the drives on your computer is shown as a link rather than a simple icon. To display the contents of a drive, just click once on the link. Figure 16-9 shows how the contents of my C drive is displayed by the Active Desktop.

Figure 16-8:
My
Computer
displays
information
about your
drives.

Figure 16-9:
How the
new My
Computer
window
displays the
contents of
a drive.

Again, each of the folders in the My Computer window is shown as a link rather than as a simple icon. To open any of the folders, just click the folder's link once. You don't have to double-click the folder to open it as you do with the standard Windows 95 desktop.

Using the Address toolbar

Notice that the My Computer window now includes an Address toolbar in which you can type a drive letter or the name of a folder. For example, to display the contents of drive D, just type **d:** and press Enter. Or, to display the contents of your Windows folder on drive C, type **c:\windows** and press Enter.

The Address toolbar works the same in a My Computer window as it does in Internet Explorer 4. In fact, you can display a page on the Web directly within a My Computer window by simply typing an Internet address in the Address toolbar. If you're not already connected to the Internet, Internet Explorer connects you automatically. Then, the Web page you specified is displayed in the My Computer window.

If Internet Explorer does not connect you automatically to the Internet when you type an Internet address in the Address toolbar, call up the View➪ Internet Options command and click the Connection tab. Click the Settings button to reveal a dialog box full of dial-up connection options. Check the Connect without User Intervention option in this dialog box, and then click OK once to dismiss the Dial-Up Settings dialog box and again to dismiss the Options dialog box.

Using the new toolbar buttons

The Standard toolbar in the Active Desktop My Computer window includes the following navigation buttons:

- ✔ **Back:** Takes you back to the folder you last viewed.

- ✔ **Forward:** Returns you to the folder you were viewing when you clicked the Back button.

- ✔ **Up:** Takes you up one level in the folder hierarchy. This button works the same as the Up button in standard Windows 95 My Computer windows.

Notice that both the Back and Forward buttons have small down-pointing arrows next to them, just as they do in Internet Explorer. You can click these arrows to reveal a list of all the folders you can return to via these buttons.

The Favorites menu

The Active Desktop My Computer menu bar includes a Favorites menu that displays your favorites, just as in Internet Explorer. Favorites can include not just Web pages, but drives, folders, or individual files as well. Thus, if you are working on a project and have stored all the project's files in a folder, you can add that folder to your Favorites. Then, you can access that folder from any My Computer window.

For more information about working with the Favorites menu, turn to Chapter 5.

Working with file and folder links

You use links for files and folders a little differently in the Active Desktop than you use the file and folder icons in standard Windows 95. I mentioned that you need to click a file or folder link just once to open the file or folder. There are other differences as well:

- ✔ To select a file or folder, just point the mouse at the link. The file or folder is automatically selected.

- ✔ To select a range of files or folders, point to the first one you want to select. Then, press and hold the Shift key and move the mouse to the last file or folder you want to select.

- ✔ To delete a file or folder, point to its link to select it. Then press the Delete key, choose the File⇨Delete command, or click the Delete button in the Standard toolbar. Or, right-click the link and choose Delete from the pop-up menu that appears.

- ✔ To rename a file or folder, point to its link to select it. Then choose the File⇨Rename command. Type a new name for the file, and then press Enter. Alternatively, you can right-click the link, choose Rename from the pop-up menu that appears, type a new name, and then press Enter.

- ✔ You can copy or move files the same as in standard Windows 95: by dragging the file's icons from one folder to another or by using the Edit⇨Copy, Edit⇨Cut, and Edit⇨Paste commands.

New Taskbar and Start Menu Features

In addition to changes in the way My Computer folders operate, the Active Desktop also sports several changes to the way the Windows 95 taskbar and the Start menu works. These new features don't dramatically change the way you work with the taskbar or the Start menu, but they do come in handy.

When you turn on the Active Desktop, four new buttons appear on the taskbar right next to the Start button. The following paragraphs describe the function of these buttons:

- ✔ **Launch Internet Explorer:** Starts Internet Explorer so that you can browse the Internet.

- ✔ **Launch Outlook Express:** Starts Outlook Express so that you can read your e-mail or access Internet newsgroups.

✔ **Show Desktop:** Minimizes all the currently open windows so that you can see your desktop. Click this button again to restore all windows to their original sizes and locations.

 ✔ **View Channels:** Starts the Channel Viewer so that you can view Internet channels. See Chapter 6 for more information about channels.

You also find two new commands on the Start menu when you install the Active Desktop:

✔ **Favorites:** Enables you to access your Favorites directly from the Start menu. That way, you can display one of your favorite Web sites without having to first launch Internet Explorer. Similarly, you can open a Word document you have added to your Favorites list without first having to start Word.

✔ **Log Off:** This command is used only if you have set up your computer to work with more than one user. It allows you to log off of Windows so that someone else can use the computer using his or her own settings. Before the Active Desktop came along, you had to do this by restarting Windows.

 The Log Off command is actually way beyond what I want to talk about in this book, but I had to at least mention it here because it shows up on your Start menu when you turn on the Active Desktop. Feel free to ignore the Log Off command unless your computer is already set up for multiple users and you are used to signing on and off of Windows 95.

Finally, you will find that the Start⇨Programs menu behaves a bit differently when you have loaded it up with more programs than can fit on the screen in a single column of program names. In standard Windows 95, the Start⇨ Programs menu simply expands to two or more columns to show all the programs the menu contains. When you install the Active Desktop, the Start Programs menu always uses a single column to display its programs. If there are more programs than can fit in the column, scroll arrow buttons appear at the top or bottom of the menu. You can view the additional program names by pointing at these arrows. (You don't have to actually click the arrow; just point at it.)

Changing the Active Desktop Settings

The Active Desktop enables you to customize many aspects of how the Web-like interface works. In Chapter 17, I share some of the more advanced options for customizing the desktop. Here, I show a few simple changes you can make to the way the desktop works. Based on your working style and personal preferences, you can decide whether you want to make these changes.

Reverting the My Computer window to classic Windows 95

If you don't like the Active Desktop's new My Computer window, you can revert to the classic Windows 95 My Computer window by following these steps:

1. Click the My Computer icon.

A My Computer window appears.

2. Choose the View⇨Folder Options command.

The Folder Options dialog box, shown in Figure 16-10, appears.

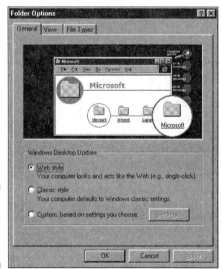

Figure 16-10: The Folder Options dialog box.

3. Check the Classic Style option.

4. Click OK.

Your My Computer window reverts back to the Windows 95 style. You have to double-click icons to open folders or launch programs, and each folder appears in a separate window.

Getting back to the double-click style

Personally, I really like most of Active Desktop's new features. However, one feature I don't particularly appreciate is the use of single clicks to open file and folder links. Fortunately, the Active Desktop enables you to turn off single-clicking but retain the rest of the new features. Just follow these steps:

1. Click the My Computer icon.

A My Computer window appears.

2. Choose the View➪Folder Options command.

The Folder Options dialog box appears. (This dialog box is shown back in Figure 16-10.)

3. Choose the Custom, Based on Settings You Choose option.

4. Click the Settings button.

The Custom Settings dialog box appears, as shown in Figure 16-11.

5. Choose the Double-Click to Open an Item (Single-Click to Select) option.

This allows you to select an icon by clicking it, but you must double-click an icon to open it — just like in the normal Windows 95 interface.

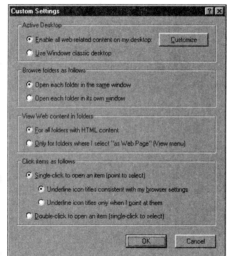

Figure 16-11:
The Custom
Settings
dialog box.

6. Click OK.

You return to the Folder Options dialog box.

7. Click OK again.

The Folder Options dialog box is dismissed, and the custom settings you chose are in effect.

There's also a bunch of other options from which to choose in the Custom Settings dialog box. I suggest you leave the rest of these settings alone.

Chapter 17

Fun Things to Do with the Active Desktop

. . . .

In This Chapter

▶ Adding toolbars to your desktop

▶ Adding special controls to your desktop

▶ Customizing a folder

. . . .

*T*he Active Desktop that comes with Internet Explorer 4 carries a generous gift: a means to customize your desktop in more ways than ever before. This chapter shows you how to customize your desktop by adding toolbars to the desktop, by adding special desktop controls that you can download from Microsoft's Web site, and by creating a Web page to customize a folder on your hard drive.

Adding a Desktop Toolbar

The standard Windows 95 desktop includes a taskbar that enables you to quickly access the Start menu and any other program that's running. You can position the taskbar on any of the four screen edges (top, bottom, left, or right). And, you can use the Auto Hide option to cause the taskbar to disappear when it's not being used; to summon the taskbar, you just move the mouse to the edge of the screen where the taskbar is hiding.

With the Active Desktop, the taskbar is even more useful. Instead of having just a single taskbar, you can have additional toolbars on your desktop. These additional toolbars can be placed right on the taskbar. Or you can detach them from the taskbar and place them anywhere on the desktop.

The Active Desktop comes with four built-in toolbars:

- **Address,** which adds an Address box to your desktop. When you type an Internet address, the Active Desktop launches Internet Explorer to view the Web page. You can also type a drive letter or folder name into the Address box.

- **Links,** which is the same as the Links toolbar that appears in Internet Explorer. This toolbar enables you to place the links to your favorite places on the desktop, where they are always accessible.

- **Desktop,** which features a button that corresponds to every icon on your desktop. Personally, I don't care for this toolbar. I'd just as soon click the Show Desktop button that lives in the taskbar to reveal the desktop whenever I need it.

- **Quick Launch,** which has four buttons for commonly used functions: launching Internet Explorer, launching Outlook Express, minimizing all desktop icons, and launching the Channel Viewer.

The four buttons that appear in the taskbar when you activate the Active Desktop are actually the Quick Launch toolbar.

To add one of the toolbars to your desktop, follow these steps:

1. **Right-click the Windows 95 taskbar, and then choose the Toolbars command.**

   A list of available toolbars appears.

2. **Click the toolbar you want to appear.**

   The choices are Address, Links, Desktop, and Quick Launch.

3. **Drag the toolbar to where you want it to appear.**

   To drag the toolbar, point the mouse right at the toolbar title. Then, press and hold the mouse button while moving the mouse to where you want the toolbar. When you drag the toolbar to any of the four edges of the screen, the toolbar "locks" onto the edge. (If the toolbar doesn't lock on, try again. You have to move the toolbar all the way to the edge to get it to lock.)

   Alternatively, you can leave the toolbar dangling in the middle of the screen.

4. **If necessary, resize the toolbar.**

   To change the size of the toolbar, drag any of its edges to increase or decrease the toolbar size.

Address toolbar   Links toolbar

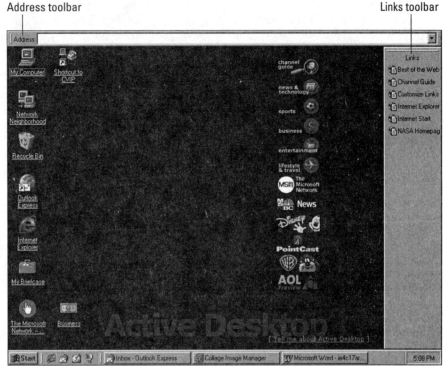

Figure 17-1:
The desktop
with the
Address
and Links
toolbars
enabled.

Figure 17-1 shows how the desktop appears with the Address toolbar enabled and locked on to the top of the screen and the Links toolbar placed at the right edge of the screen.

To remove a toolbar from your desktop, right-click the toolbar to bring up the pop-up menu and then choose the Toolbars command. The toolbar you right-clicked is checked in the pop-up menu; click the toolbar name to uncheck it. The toolbar disappears.

Using Auto Hide and Always on Top

The Auto Hide and Always on Top options enable you to control the appearance of toolbars. These options work the same for desktop toolbars as they do for the Windows 95 taskbar. The Auto Hide option causes the toolbar to disappear when you're not using it. To recall the toolbar, all you have to do is point to the edge of the screen where the toolbar is hiding.

The Always on Top option makes the toolbar always visible. If you leave Always on Top turned off and maximize a program window, the program window overlays the toolbar, and you can't see the toolbar. When you turn on the Always on Top option, the toolbar is always visible — even when other windows are maximized.

To enable the Auto Hide or Always on Top option for a toolbar, right-click the toolbar title, and then choose the Auto Hide or Always on Top command from the pop-up menu that appears. To turn either option off, right-click the toolbar title and choose the command again.

Creating a custom toolbar

The Active Desktop enables you to turn any folder on your hard drive into a desktop toolbar. For example, suppose you're working on a project and all the document files for the project are located in a folder. When you turn that folder into a desktop toolbar, all the documents for the project are available at the click of a mouse. Figure 17-2 shows how the folder I used to organize the files for this book appeared when I made the folder into a desktop toolbar and moved it over to the right edge of the screen.

The ie4 folder is its own toolbar.

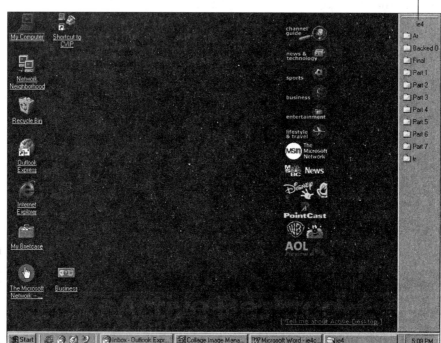

Figure 17-2:
Any folder can be made into a toolbar.

To create a custom toolbar like this, follow these steps:

1. **Identify a folder that you want to use as a toolbar.**

   You can use an existing folder as I did in Figure 17-2, or you can create a new folder that can contain any documents, programs, or folders you want to appear on your custom toolbar.

2. **Right-click the Windows 95 taskbar, and then choose** <u>T</u>**oolbars from the pop-up menu that appears.**

3. **Choose** <u>N</u>**ew Toolbar.**

   The New Toolbar dialog box appears, as shown in Figure 17-3.

Figure 17-3:
The New
Toolbar
dialog box.

4. **Select the folder you want to use as the toolbar.**

   You probably have to navigate through the drives and folders on your computer to find the one you're looking for.

5. **Click OK.**

   The toolbar is created.

6. **Drag and resize the toolbar as needed.**

   Move the toolbar to where you want it, and resize the toolbar if it's too large or too small.

7. **Apply the A**<u>u</u>**to Hide or Always On** <u>T</u>**op options if you want.**

   See the section "Using Auto Hide and Always on Top" earlier in this chapter for more information.

You're done! After you create a custom toolbar, you can delete it by right-clicking the toolbar, choosing Toolbars from the pop-up menu that appears, and clicking the custom toolbar you want to remove.

Adding an Active Desktop Control

The Active Desktop enables you to place fancy *active controls* right on your desktop. An active control is a special program that becomes a part of your desktop. The control may display its own window, or it may just take over a region of the desktop and display its information without the formality of a window.

One such control is already available on your desktop: the Channel Bar, which enables you to quickly access any Web channels you subscribe to. Microsoft provides several other desktop controls you can download from the Microsoft Web site and place on your desktop. These controls include

✔ **MSN Investment Ticker:** Displays stock quotes downloaded from the Microsoft Network.

✔ **MSN Custom Page:** Displays news on your desktop.

✔ **MSNBC Weather Map:** Displays an up-to-date map of weather across the United States right on your desktop.

✔ **Trip: Pictures from Around the World:** Displays a different set of pictures from around the world each day.

✔ **Movie News from Entertainment Drive:** Displays up-to-date information about movies.

✔ **Music News from *RollingStone:*** Displays news about the music industry.

Microsoft periodically adds new desktop controls to its Web site, so more controls will probably be available by the time you read this.

This section shows you how to add one such control — an online stock ticker — to your desktop. Here are the steps:

1. **Right-click any blank section of the desktop, and then choose <u>P</u>roperties from the pop-up menu that appears.**

   The Display Properties dialog box appears.

2. **Click the Web tab at the top of the Display Properties dialog box.**

   The Web settings appear, as shown in Figure 17-4.

3. **Click the <u>N</u>ew button.**

   The dialog box shown in Figure 17-5 appears. This dialog box asks if you want to connect to a Microsoft Web site called the Active Desktop gallery, where you can download desktop controls.

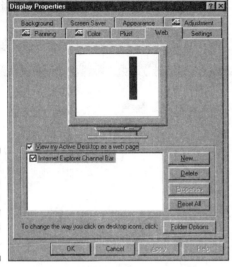

Figure 17-4:
The Web options on the Display Properties dialog box.

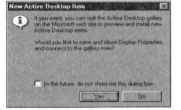

Figure 17-5:
Want to go online?

4. **Click Yes.**

   Internet Explorer comes to life and displays the Active Desktop Gallery page, as shown in Figure 17-6.

5. **Click the desktop item you want to install.**

   Clicking an item takes you to a page similar to the one in Figure 17-7, which is for the MSN Investor Ticker.

6. **Click the Add to my Desktop button.**

   You are asked if you want to add the item to your desktop.

7. **Click Yes.**

   Next, you see a dialog box similar to the one shown in Figure 17-8.

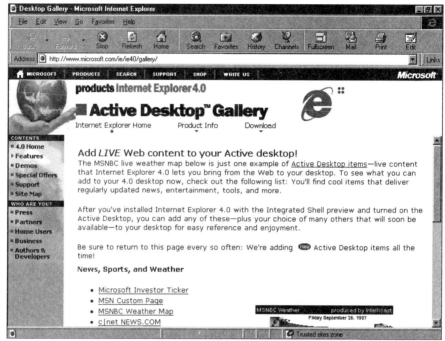

Figure 17-6:
The Active
Desktop
Gallery.

Figure 17-7:
The
download
page for
the MSN
Investor
Ticker
desktop
control.

Figure 17-8:
Adding an item to your desktop.

8. **Fiddle with the subscription settings if you want.**

   To change the subscription settings, click the Customize Subscription button. This brings up a Subscription Wizard dialog box that lets you specify how often the desktop item should be updated. For more information about subscriptions, refer to Chapter 6.

9. **Click OK.**

   The control is downloaded to your computer. A progress dialog box appears so you know how long the download will take.

10. **When the download progress dialog box disappears, close the Internet Explorer window.**

    The control you downloaded appears on your desktop, as shown in Figure 17-9.

Figure 17-9:
The MSN Investor Ticker control on the Active Desktop.

Here are a few thoughts to ponder as you lie awake tonight wondering about the marvels of the Active Desktop controls:

- ✔ If the control doesn't appear on your desktop after you download it, right-click a blank area of the desktop, and then choose the Refresh command.

- ✔ You can move and resize the desktop control by dragging it with the mouse.

- ✔ To remove a desktop control that you no longer want, call up the Display Properties dialog box (right-click anywhere in the desktop and choose Properties), click the Web tab, and then uncheck the check box that appears next to the control you want to remove.

Customizing a Folder

In the Active Desktop, each folder on your hard drive can have an HTML document associated with it. This HTML document will be displayed when you open the folder using a My Computer window. All the folders use a default HTML document that shows the contents of the folder plus information about the selected file. But you can customize the HTML document for any folder you want to create a unique appearance for.

With a little bit of effort, you can create a customized HTML document for a folder so that whenever you open the folder, background graphics, text messages, and images appear in the folder window. The following sections explain how to create a custom HTML document for a folder.

If the HTML information for a folder doesn't appear, choose the View⇨as Web Page command.

Adding a background to a folder

You can add a background image to any folder on your hard drive. For example, Figure 17-10 shows a folder on my hard drive that uses a background image.

To add a background image to a folder, follow these steps:

1. **Open the folder you want to add a background image to.**

2. **Choose the View⇨Customize This Folder command.**

   The Customize This Folder Wizard box appears, as shown in Figure 17-11.

Figure 17-10:
A folder
with a
background
image.

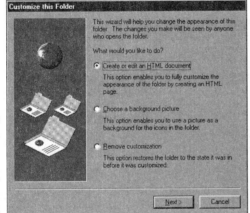

Figure 17-11:
The
Customize
This Folder
Wizard.

3. Click the Choose a Background Picture option, and then click Next>.

The Wizard asks you to select a picture to use for the background, as
shown in Figure 17-12.

4. Choose a picture from the list of background pictures supplied.

If you prefer, you can click the Browse button and then select a picture
from any of the folders on your hard drive.

5. Click Next>.

The Wizard congratulates you on your ingenuity, as Figure 17-13 shows.

6. Click Finish.

The Wizard applies the background image you selected to the folder.

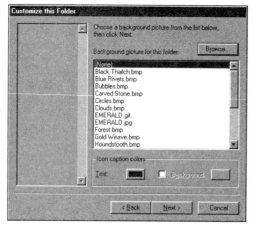

Figure 17-12:
Choose a
picture to
use for
the folder
background.

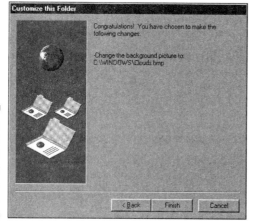

Figure 17-13:
The Wizard
is proud
of your
accom-
plishment.

That's all there is to it. If you later want to remove the background image, repeat the procedure, but choose the Remove Customization option in Step 3.

Customizing the Web page for a folder

The Active Desktop can display a customized HTML document for any folder that you open. The default HTML document for each folder resembles the My Computer window, with an information area at the left of the window that shows information about the currently selected file or folder and a preview area that shows the contents of the selected file if the file contains a graphic image or an HTML document, as shown in Figure 17-14. If your folders do not appear as shown in Figure 17-14, choose the View⇨as Web Document command to enable the HTML folder features.

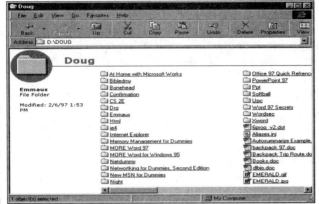

Figure 17-14:
A folder
viewed as
an HTML
document.

If you're adventuresome and you know a little about HTML, you can customize the HTML file that is used to display a folder. The following procedure shows you how to replace the name of the folder with a customized message of your choosing:

1. **Open the folder you want to add a message to.**

2. **Choose the View⯈Customize This Folder command.**

   The Customize This Folder Wizard box appears. This Wizard was shown back in Figure 17-11.

3. **Choose the Create or Edit an HTML Document option, and then click Next>.**

   The Wizard displays the dialog box shown in Figure 17-15.

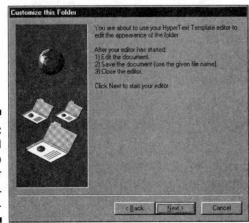

Figure 17-15:
The Wizard
is ready to
launch your
HTML
editor.

4. Click Ne_x_t>.

The Customize This Folder Wizard creates an HTML file to customize the folder, and then starts FrontPage Express to edit the HTML file as shown in Figure 17-16. (FrontPage Express is an HTML editor that comes with Internet Explorer 4.)

5. Stare at FrontPage Express for a few minutes and the HTML document.

The FrontPage Express window contains the HTML document that's used to display your customized folder. Although making extensive changes to this document requires some HTML savvy, you can easily change the text that appears in the folder. And if you have some HTML experience, you should have no trouble figuring out how to add additional elements to the HTML document, such as a graphic, a marquee (text that moves across the screen), or even a background sound that plays whenever the folder is opened.

6. Choose the _View_⇨_H_TML command.

A separate window containing the actual HTML codes used for the folder appears, as shown in Figure 17-17.

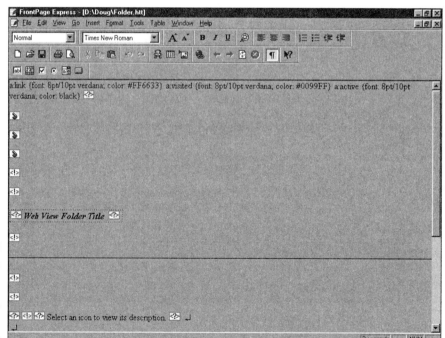

Figure 17-16:
FrontPage
Express
awaits your
command.

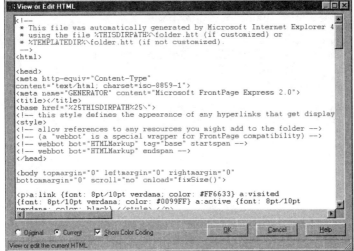

Figure 17-17:
The HTML
window.

7. **Scroll through the HTML window until you find a line containing only the word "%THISDIRNAME%".**

You have to scroll almost to the bottom of the HTML window. In Figure 17-18, the line you're looking for is highlighted.

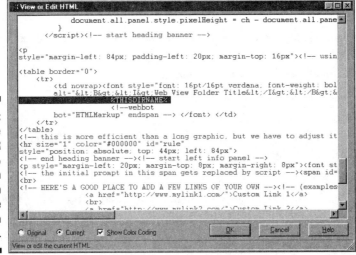

Figure 17-18:
The
%THISDIR
NAME%
line, which
you can
replace
with a
message.

8. Replace the word "%THISDIRNAME%" with the message you want to appear in place of the folder name.

For example, Figure 17-19 shows how the HTML file should appear when the %THISDIRNAME% line has been replaced by "This Is My Folder! Get Out!"

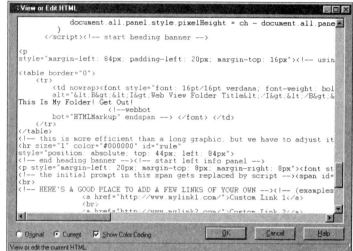

Figure 17-19:
The HTML file with a custom message.

9. Click OK.

The HTML window vanishes, and you return to the main FrontPage Express window.

10. Choose the File⇨Save command.

The HTML file is saved.

11. Choose the File⇨Exit command.

FrontPage Express quits. You return to the Customize This Folder Wizard dialog box shown in Figure 17-20.

12. Click Finish.

The HTML document you created is applied to the folder. Figure 17-21 shows how the folder appears when you open it.

To remove the HTML document (that is, to restore the folder to normal), repeat the entire procedure. When you get to Step 3, choose the Remove Customization option instead of Create or Edit an HTML Document. Then, skip ahead to Step 11.

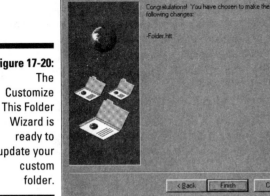

Figure 17-20:
The Customize This Folder Wizard is ready to update your custom folder.

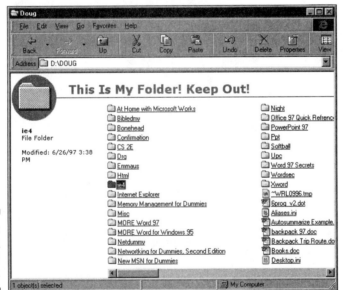

Figure 17-21:
A customized folder.

Part VI
Building Your Own Web Pages

In this part . . .

This part covers the ins and outs of creating Web pages that can be displayed with Internet Explorer 4. The first two chapters in this part show you how to use the simple tools that come with Internet Explorer 4 to create Web pages. In Chapter 18, you're introduced to FrontPage Express, a basic what-you-see-is-what-you-get HTML editor that you use to create HTML documents. Then, Chapter 19 shows you how to use the Web Publishing Wizard to post your Web pages on a Web server and how to set up a nifty little program called Personal Web Server, which can turn your own computer into a miniature Web server.

Chapter 20 is where the technical stuff comes out, including information about Microsoft's newest and greatest HTML feature called *Dynamic HTML,* which lets you create Web pages with more spit and polish than ever before. Chapter 20 is a bit on the technical side, however. You'll want to avoid it if you don't already have a fairly solid understanding of HTML.

Chapter 18

Creating Web Pages with FrontPage Express

. . . .

In This Chapter

▶ Using FrontPage Express to produce simple Web pages

▶ Using the Personal Home Page Wizard to create a home page

▶ Formatting your Web page

▶ Placing hyperlinks on your page

▶ Adding interesting items such as lines, graphics, and background pictures

▶ Viewing the HTML source code for a Web page

. . . .

*F*rontPage Express, which comes free with Internet Explorer 4, is a scaled-back version of the Microsoft FrontPage Web publishing program. With FrontPage Express, you can create your own Web pages, which you can publish on the Web for all the world to see. You can think of FrontPage Express as a word processor for Web pages: It enables you to create, edit, and save documents in the Web's special HTML document format.

The good news is that you don't have to learn a whit about HTML to use FrontPage Express. If you put off creating a home page because you hesitate to face the prospect of learning HTML, expect to fall head over heels in appreciation for FrontPage Express. What are you waiting for? Jump right in and get that home page started! Your friends will think you're a genius when they spot your home page on the Web.

If you don't have FrontPage Express, there's a good reason: You didn't elect to install it when you installed Internet Explorer 4. Fire up the CD again or, if you installed Internet Explorer 4 by downloading it from Microsoft's Web site, return to www.microsoft.com/ie/ie40/download. Then rerun the Internet Explorer 4 setup program, this time choosing to install FrontPage Express.

Starting FrontPage Express

There are two ways to start FrontPage Express:

- ✓ From the Windows 95 taskbar, click the Start button, and then choose Programs⇨Internet Explorer⇨FrontPage Express.

- ✓ From the Internet Explorer 4 browser, surf your way to a page you want to edit, and then choose the Edit⇨Page command or click the Edit button in the Standard toolbar (shown in the margin).

Either way, FrontPage Express springs to life. If you start FrontPage Express from the Start⇨Programs menu, FrontPage Express starts with a blank document, as shown in Figure 18-1. If you launch FrontPage Express from Internet Explorer 4, the Web page you were viewing is loaded into FrontPage Express.

If FrontPage Express starts up in a less-than-full-screen window, I suggest you maximize the FrontPage Express window by clicking the Maximize button (the button with the rectangle icon in the upper-right corner of the FrontPage Express window). That way, you have the entire screen on which to view and edit your Web pages.

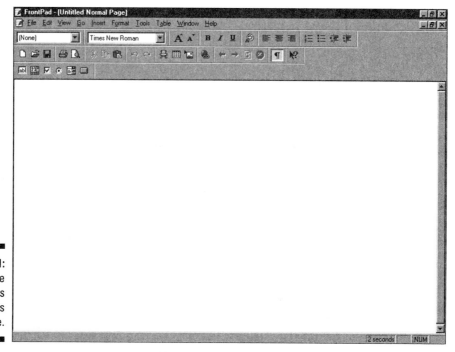

Figure 18-1:
FrontPage
Express
comes
to life.

Using the Personal Home Page Wizard

The easiest way to begin creating a Web page with FrontPage Express is to use the built-in Personal Home Page Wizard. This Wizard asks you a bunch of questions about what type of information you want to include in your home page, and then it automatically generates a sample home page for you. You can edit the page as you see fit, save it to your hard drive, and then use the Web Publishing Wizard (described in the next chapter) to upload the home page to your Internet service provider's Web server.

If you prefer, you can start from a blank Web page. When you start FrontPage Express from the Start⇨Programs menu, a blank page is automatically loaded for you, so you can just begin editing. If you started FrontPage Express from Internet Explorer, choose the File⇨Close command to close the current page. Then, choose the File⇨New command to create a new blank Web page. Either way, you can skip the rest of this section because you won't be using the Personal Home Page Wizard.

The following procedure shows you step-by-step how to use the Personal Home Page Wizard to create your own home page:

1. **Fire up FrontPage Express by clicking the Start button on the Windows 95 taskbar and then choosing the Programs⇨Internet Explorer⇨FrontPage Express command.**

   FrontPage Express comes to life.

2. **Choose the File⇨New command.**

   The New Page dialog box appears, as shown in Figure 18-2.

3. **Select Personal Home Page Wizard from the Template or Wizard list, and then click OK.**

   The Personal Home Page Wizard appears, as shown in Figure 18-3.

Figure 18-2: The New Page dialog box.

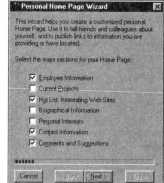

Figure 18-3:
The
Personal
Home Page
Wizard.

4. **Choose the major sections you want to include in your home page.**

   The Wizard offers seven choices for sections to include: Employee
   Information; Current Projects; Hot List: Interesting Web Sites; Biographical Information; Personal Interests; Contact Information; and Comments
   and Suggestions. You can select any or all of these sections to include
   in your own home page.

   Note: If you want to include a section that doesn't appear in this list,
   don't worry. You can always manually add the section when the Wizard
   is finished.

5. **Click Next>.**

   The Wizard displays the dialog box shown in Figure 18-4.

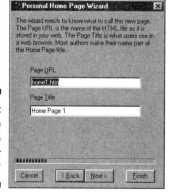

Figure 18-4:
What do
you want to
call your
home page?

6. Type the filename and title for your home page.

Type the filename in the Page URL text box; and then type the title in the Page Title text box. You can use any filename and title you want.

7. Click Next>.

The Wizard requests information about the first section of your home page, as shown in Figure 18-5.

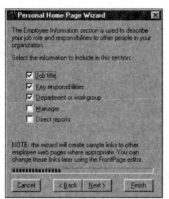

Figure 18-5: Tell the Wizard about the information you want to include in the Employee Information section.

8. Select the items you want to include in the first section of your home page, and then click Next>.

The Wizard displays a dialog box for the next section of your home page.

9. Repeat Step 8 for each section of your home page you selected back in Step 4.

For each section you choose to include in your home page, a slightly different dialog box appears and asks you what type of information you want to include in the section.

After you complete all the sections, the dialog box shown in Figure 18-6 appears.

10. Click Finish.

FrontPage Express whirs and spins for just a moment and then spits out a skeleton home page similar to the one shown in Figure 18-7.

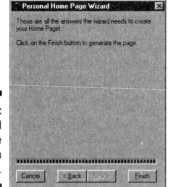

Figure 18-6:
The Wizard
has all the
information
it needs.

11. Make whatever changes you want to make to the document, filling in the blanks left by the Personal Home Page Wizard.

The page created by the Wizard includes text such as *My Job Description* and *Sample Site 3*. This text serves only as a placeholder for the actual text you want to appear on your Web page. You undoubtedly want to type some more meaningful text to replace these placeholders, and you want to add new information of your own. Later in this chapter, you find sections describing how to edit a Web page.

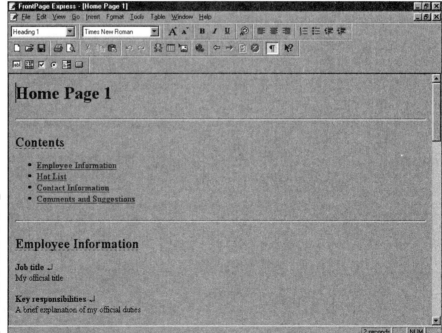

Figure 18-7:
A home
page
created
by the
Personal
Home Page
Wizard.

12. Save the document.

Use the File⇨Save command to save your work, or click the Save button found in the Standard toolbar.

After your home page is finished, you can use the Web Publishing Wizard to upload the page to your Web server. See Chapter 19 for more information about how to publish your Web page.

Formatting Text in a Web Document

FrontPage Express lets you apply formatting to the text in a Web page much the same as a word processor lets you format text in a document. FrontPage Express doesn't have all the text formatting abilities of an expensive word processing program such as Microsoft Word, but it offers enough text formatting to enable you to create good-looking Web pages.

Applying a style

Every paragraph of text in a FrontPage Express Web document must have a *style* that governs the basic formatting for the text. To apply a style to a paragraph, place the insertion point anywhere in the paragraph, and then choose a style from the Style drop-down list that appears in the toolbar.

Styles are most commonly used to create headings for a Web page. FrontPage Express enables you to create up to six levels of headings using Heading 1, Heading 2, and so on, up to Heading 6. The regular paragraph text of your document should be formatted using the Normal style.

Other styles enable you to create various types of lists (Bulleted List, Numbered List, Definition List, Directory List, and Menu List) or to create specially formatted paragraphs (Address and Formatted).

Applying text formatting

To change the font used for text, select the text you want to change, and then select the font of choice from the Font drop-down list that appears in the Standard toolbar next to the Style drop-down list.

You may wonder where the Font Size drop-down list is. Unfortunately, there isn't one. Instead, you control the size of your text by clicking one of the following two buttons:

✔ Increases the text size

   ✔ Decrease the text size

Only seven different point sizes are used in HTML documents. Your text can be 8, 10, 12, 14, 18, 24, or 36 points; no other sizes are allowed. Clicking the Increase or Decrease buttons increases or decreases the text size to the next allowable size.

You can apply bold, italic, and underline formats by using the following buttons or keyboard shortcuts:

Bold	**B**	Ctrl+B
Italic	*I*	Ctrl+I
Underline	**U**	Ctrl+U

You can also change the text color by clicking the Text Color button (shown in the margin). When you click this button, you see a dialog box that contains each of the standard colors that you can apply to text. Choose the color you want, and then click OK to apply the color.

Another way to apply text formatting is to summon the Format⇨Font command, which brings up the Font dialog box shown in Figure 18-8. This dialog box enables you to control all the font formatting options from one convenient place.

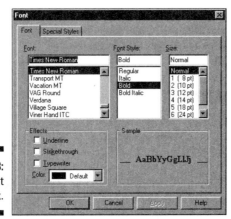

Figure 18-8:
The Font
dialog box.

As you can see, the Font dialog box has controls that enable you to set the Font, Font Style (Regular, Bold, Italic, or Bold Italic), Size, Underline, and Color. You can also apply two effects that are not available via toolbar buttons: Strikethrough and Typewriter.

If you click the Special Styles tab in the Font dialog box, the additional font controls shown in Figure 18-9 appears. These controls enable you to apply special text styles that are unique to HTML and to create subscripts and superscripts. You probably won't need to use these styles for most of your Web pages, but they're there if you need them.

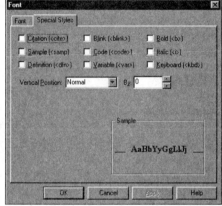

Figure 18-9:
The Special
Styles tab
of the Font
dialog box.

Aligning and indenting text

FrontPage Express lets you set the alignment and indentation for text by using the following buttons:

Align left	
Center	
Align right	
Increase indent	
Decrease indent	

Creating bulleted and numbered lists

By clicking one of the following buttons, you can create lists in which each paragraph in the list is marked by a bullet character or a number:

Bulleted list	
Numbered list	

However, for more precise control over the format of your list, use the Format➪Bullets and Numbering command. Choosing this command brings up the dialog box shown in Figure 18-10.

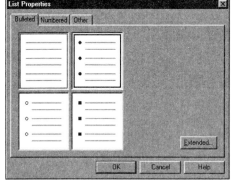

Figure 18-10:
The Bullets and Numbering dialog box.

The Bullets tab, which is pictured in Figure 18-10, enables you to choose from one of four different styles of bullet characters. To create a numbered list, click the Numbered tab to reveal the numbered list options, shown in Figure 18-11. Here, you have the option of using Arabic numbers, Roman numerals, or letters. And you can pick the starting number for the list by using the Start At control.

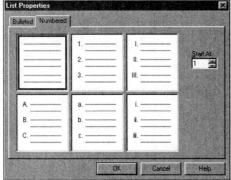

Figure 18-11:
The
Numbered
list options
in the
Bullets and
Numbering
dialog box.

Creating a Hyperlink

A *hyperlink* is a bit of text that, when clicked, links users with another page. The link can be to another location in the current Web page, another page at the same Web site, or a page at a different Web site somewhere else on the Internet.

To add a hyperlink to a FrontPage Express Web page, follow these steps:

1. Type some text that you would like to turn into a link.

For example, type **click here to go to my home page**.

If you prefer, you can insert a picture and turn it into a link. See the section "Inserting a picture" later in this chapter for more information.

2. Highlight the text you want to turn into a link.

3. Choose the Insert⇨Hyperlink command.

The Create Hyperlink dialog box appears, as shown in Figure 18-12.

4. Type the address of the Web page you want to link to in the URL field.

If the page is intended to reside at your own Web site, you don't have to type the complete URL. Instead, just type the filename for the HTML document you want to link to.

5. Click OK.

Your selected text is transformed into a link. To indicate that the text is a link, FrontPage Express displays it in blue underlined text. When Web users view your page on the Web, they can jump to the page referred to in the link by clicking the underlined text.

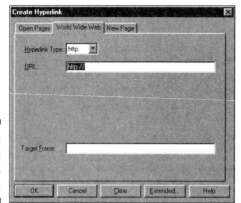

Figure 18-12:
The Create
Hyperlink
dialog box.

If an address change is in order for a linked page, you can update your hyperlink in FrontPage Express by selecting the link text and choosing the Edit➪Hyperlink command. Choosing this command brings up the Edit Hyperlink dialog box, which is identical to the Create Hyperlink dialog box. Change the address in the URL field, and then click OK to update the link.

Spicing Up Your Page with Graphics

FrontPage Express enables you to improve the appearance of your page by adding graphics, as described in the following sections.

Inserting a horizontal line

One of the commonly used formatting features in Web pages is the horizontal line, which is drawn across the page to visually separate groups of information. Figure 18-13 shows a Web page with two types of horizontal lines on it.

To insert a horizontal line, follow these steps:

1. **Position the insertion point where you want to insert the horizontal line.**

2. **Choose the Insert➪Horizontal Line command.**

   A plain, rather boring horizontal line is inserted into your document. For example, have a look at the first line shown back in Figure 18-13.

3. **Click the line to select it.**

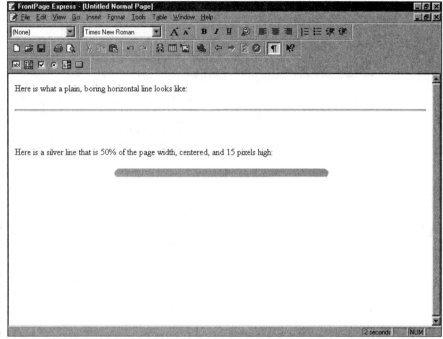

Figure 18-13:
A Web
page with
two types of
horizontal
lines.

4. Choose the Edit⇨Horizontal Line Properties command.

The dialog box shown in Figure 18-14 appears.

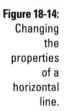 

Figure 18-14:
Changing
the
properties
of a
horizontal
line.

5. Set the line properties to something more interesting.

For example, to create the second line in Figure 18-13, I set the line width to 50 percent of the page, its height to 15 pixels, its alignment to Centered, and its color to Lime.

6. Click OK.

The line is formatted.

To remove a line later on, select it by clicking anywhere on the line and then press the Delete key.

Inserting a picture

Pictures attract attention, and nearly all Web pages are crafted with at least a few graphics. In some cases, the pictures are actual scanned photographs, but more often, the pictures are small graphic images created by a drawing program, such as Windows Paint (the free drawing program that comes with Windows 95).

Before you can insert a picture on your Web page, of course, you must first obtain the graphic file for the picture you want to add. Good news: You can find plenty of pictures you can use at Microsoft's online Web Gallery, located at www.microsoft.com/gallery. From this site, you can download all sorts of images suitable for use on your Web pages.

To insert a picture into a FrontPage Express Web page, follow these steps:

1. **Move the insertion point to the position where you want the picture inserted.**

2. **Summon the Insert⇨Image command.**

   Or, just click the Insert Image button in the Standard toolbar (shown in the margin). Either way, an Image dialog box like the one in Figure 18-15 appears.

3. **Click the Browse button.**

   Clicking this button summons the Image dialog box, shown in Figure 18-16.

Figure 18-15:
The Image
dialog box.

Figure 18-16:
Selecting
an image.

4. **Find and select the image you want to insert.**

You may have to navigate through the various folders on your hard disk to find the file.

5. **When you find the image you want, click Open.**

The image is inserted into your Web page.

Be careful about inserting large graphics in your Web pages. The larger your graphic, the more time it takes to download when a Web user views your page. If the page takes too long to download, expect the Web user to curse under his breath and vow to never visit your page again.

Inserting a marquee

A *marquee* is a bit of text that scrolls across the screen from one side to the other. To create a marquee in your Web page, choose the Insert➪Marquee command. Choosing this command brings up the dialog box shown in Figure 18-17. You can play with the various settings in this dialog box to set the text that you want to scroll, the direction and speed with which you want the text to scroll, the size of the area in which the text scrolls, and whether you want the text to scroll just once or to repeat in a loop.

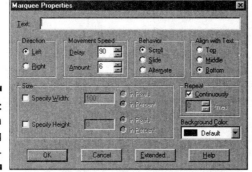

Figure 18-17:
Creating a
scrolling
marquee.

Adding a background image

Many Web pages use a background graphic that makes the page more attractive. You can add a background image to your Web page by following these steps:

1. **Choose the Format⇨Background command.**

   The Page Properties dialog box appears, as shown in Figure 18-18.

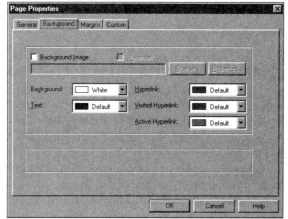

Figure 18-18: The Background dialog box.

2. **Select the Background Image option.**

3. **Click the Browse button.**

   A Select Background Image dialog box appears, as shown in Figure 18-19.

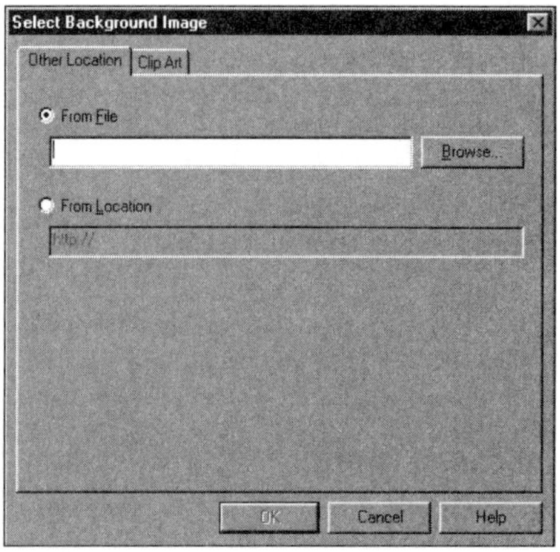

Figure 18-19: The Select Background Image dialog box.

4. Click Browse.

This summons another dialog box that allows you to search your files and folders for the image you want to use.

5. Locate the graphic file you want to use for your background image.

6. Click Open.

You return to the Page Properties dialog box.

7. Click OK.

The image you selected is used as the background image for your page.

Viewing HTML Source Code

Normally, FrontPage Express displays your Web pages pretty much as they appear when displayed by a Web browser such as Internet Explorer. However, there are occasions when you may want to view the actual HTML codes that comprise your Web page. To do so, just call up the View⇨HTML command. The HTML file for your Web page is displayed in a separate window, as shown in Figure 18-20.

Figure 18-20: Viewing the HTML for a Web page.

```
View or Edit HTML

<!DOCTYPE HTML PUBLIC "-//IETF//DTD HTML//EN">
<html>

<head>
<meta http-equiv="Content-Type"
content="text/html; charset=iso-8859-1">
<meta name="GENERATOR" content="Microsoft FrontPad 2.0">
<title>Home Page 5</title>
</head>

<body>

<h1>Home Page 5</h1>

<hr>

<h2><a name="top">Contents</a> </h2>

<ul>
    <li><a href="#jobinfo"><strong>Employee Information</strong></a>
    </li>
    <li><a href="#projects"><strong>Current Projects</strong></a>
    </li>
    <li><a href="#hotlist"><strong>Hot List</strong></a> </li>
    <li><a href="#contactinfo"><strong>Contact Information</strong></a>
    </li>
    <li><a href="#comments"><strong>Comments and Suggestions</strong></a>
    </li>
```

If you want to, you can actually edit the HTML in this window. Just click anywhere and start typing. Or, if you have better judgment, just look at the HTML for a moment, gasp in amazement that some people are actually interested in such arcane subjects, and click OK to close the HTML window.

Chapter 19

Publishing Your Web Pages

● ●

In This Chapter

▶ Using Microsoft's Web Publishing Wizard to transfer your HTML documents to your Web server

▶ Using the Personal Web Server to set up a Web server on your own computer

● ●

*A*fter you use FrontPage Express to create one or more Web pages, plunge right into copying those pages from your computer to the Web server, which actually hosts your Web site on the Internet. This chapter shows you how to accomplish that feat using the Microsoft Web Publishing Wizard, which works for most Web servers. The Web Publishing Wizard comes with Internet Explorer 4, so you probably already have it. If not, hop on over to the Internet Explorer 4 download site (`www.microsoft.com/ie/ie40/ download`) and grab it as soon as possible.

This chapter also shows you how to turn your own Windows 95 computer into a mini-Web server using a handy little program called Personal Web Server, which comes with Internet Explorer 4. Again, if you don't have Personal Web Server, you can get it from the Internet Explorer 4 download site (`www.microsoft.com/ie/ie40/download`).

Using the Web Publishing Wizard

The Web Publishing Wizard is designed to automate the task of copying HTML files from your computer to the Web server computer that hosts your Web site. Before you can use the Web Publishing Wizard, you need to know the following details:

✔ The Web address that is expected to access your Web page. For example, `www.myserver.com/me`.

✔ The name of the folder on your computer's hard drive where your Web pages are stored.

✔ The method your Internet service provider wants you to use to upload the files to its Web server. The choices are FTP, HTTP Post, or CRS. (You don't need to know what any of those acronyms stand for. Just which one your ISP uses.)

✔ The name of the folder on your Internet service provider's Web server where you're supposed to upload your files.

After you have this information, you can follow the procedure in the next section, "Using the Web Publishing Wizard the first time," to set up the Web Publishing Wizard for your Web server. After the Web Publishing Wizard has been set up, you can use the procedure under "Updating your Web files" to upload your HTML files to the Web server whenever necessary.

Using the Web Publishing Wizard the first time

The first time you use the Web Publishing Wizard, you have to supply the Wizard with the information it needs to configure itself for the Web server that hosts your Web page. To do so, follow these steps:

1. Click the Start button in the Windows 95 taskbar, and then choose the Programs⇨Internet Explorer⇨Web Publishing Wizard command.

The Web Publishing Wizard appears, as shown in Figure 19-1.

Figure 19-1:
The Web Publishing Wizard springs to life.

2. Click Next> to get started.

The Web Publishing Wizard displays the dialog box shown in Figure 19-2, asking you to provide the location of the HTML files you want to upload to the Web server.

Figure 19-2:
The Web
Publishing
Wizard
wants to
know what
files you
want to
upload to
the Web
server.

3. **Indicate the location of the file or files you want to upload to the Web server.**

   To upload a single HTML file, type the name of the file (along with the drive and folder that contains it) in the File or Folder Name field. Or, click the Browse Files button, select the file you want to upload in the dialog box that appears, and then click Open.

   To upload an entire folder of files, type the name of the folder in the File or Folder Name field or click the Browse Folders button, select the folder in the dialog box that appears, and click OK.

   In Figure 19-2, I indicate that I want to upload all the files in the folder C:\My Home Page.

   If you want to include files from any subfolders contained within the folder you specify, check the Include Subfolders check box.

4. **Click Next>.**

   The dialog box shown in Figure 19-3 appears, in which the Web Publishing Wizard asks you to provide a name for the Web server that you want the files uploaded to.

5. **Type a name for your Web server in the Descriptive Name field.**

   You can use any name you want. If you can't think of anything better, type **My Web Server**.

6. **Click the Advanced button.**

   You see the dialog box shown in Figure 19-4.

Figure 19-3:
The Web
Publishing
Wizard
needs a
name for
the Web
server.

Figure 19-4:
Now the
Wizard
wants you
to select
your
Internet
service
provider.

7. Choose the connection method your Internet service provider uses to upload files to the Web server from the drop-down list.

The choices are FrontPage Extended Web, FTP, HTTP Post, and Microsoft Content Replication System (also known as CRS). You have to ask your ISP which method it uses. Mine relies on FTP, so that's the method I illustrate for the remainder of this procedure. (The other methods are similar, but the Wizard asks for specific information based on the method you select.)

8. Click Next>.

The dialog box shown in Figure 19-5 is displayed.

Figure 19-5:
The Wizard
needs to
know the
URL for
your Web
page.

9. **Type the address for your Web page in the URL or Internet Address field.**

   For example, if the address for your home page is www.mycompany.com/me, that's what you type into the URL or Internet Address field.

10. **Click Next>.**

   The Web Publishing Wizard now asks for information that depends on the connection method you selected back in Step 7. For FTP, the dialog box resembles the one shown in Figure 19-6. The dialog box is be somewhat different if you choose FrontPage Extended Web, HTTP Post, or CRS.

Figure 19-6:
The Wizard
now needs
information
about
the FTP
connection.

11. Type the FTP Server name and the name of the subfolder on the FTP server that will contain your files.

You have to find out this information from your Internet service provider.

12. Click Nex**t>.**

The Wizard displays its final dialog box, as shown in Figure 19-7.

Figure 19-7: The Web Publishing Wizard is ready to upload your files to the Web server.

13. Click Finish.

The Enter Network Password dialog box appears, as shown in Figure 19-8.

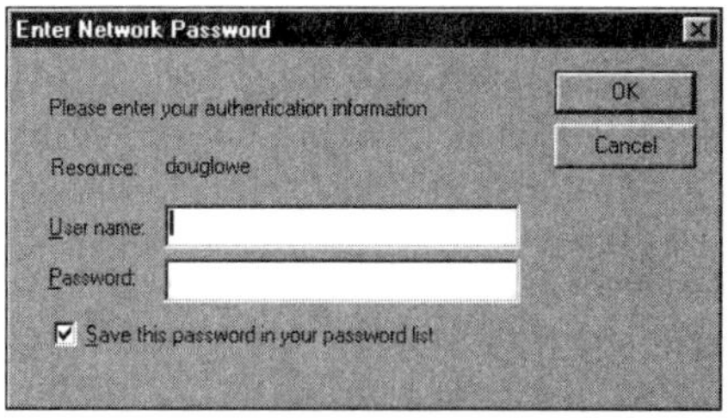

Figure 19-8: Enter your user name and password.

14. Type your user name and password, and then click OK.

The Web Publishing Wizard connects to your Web server, and then begins to copy the files from your computer to the server. A progress dialog box similar to the one shown in Figure 19-9 is displayed as the files are copied.

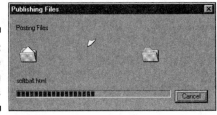

Figure 19-9:
Now we're
making
progress.

After the file copying business concludes, the dialog box shown in Figure 19-10 is displayed.

Figure 19-10:
Finished!

15. Click OK.

The Wizard vanishes. Your files are now successfully copied from your computer to the Web server.

Updating your Web files

The Web Publishing Wizard keeps track of almost everything it asks of you when you run it the first time. As a result, after you post your Web pages to your Web server once, you can upload updates quickly, without having to muddle through most of the Web Publishing Wizard screens.

The following procedure shows how easy it is to upload Web pages to your Web server after you've configured the Web Publishing Wizard:

1. Start the Web Publishing Wizard by choosing Start⇨Programs⇨ Internet Explorer⇨Web Publishing Wizard.

The Web Publishing Wizard appears. (The starting dialog box was shown back in Figure 19-1.)

2. Click Next>.

The Web Publishing Wizard asks which file or folder you want to upload. The Wizard defaults to the file or folder you uploaded the last time you ran the Wizard, so you don't have to do anything if you want to upload the same files again.

3. **Click Ne<u>x</u>t>.**

The Wizard asks which server to use. Again, the default is set for the same server you used the last time you ran the Wizard.

4. **Click Ne<u>x</u>t>.**

The Wizard displays its final screen (the one that was shown in Figure 19-7).

5. **Click Finish.**

The Wizard connects to the server, uploads the files, then displays a confirmation dialog box advising you that the files upload is a rousing success.

6. **Click OK.**

That's all there is to it!

Using the Personal Web Server

To publish a Web page on the Internet, you need a server computer that has a high-speed Internet connection and runs special Web server software. However, you don't have to go to such lengths if all you want to do is set up a set of Web pages that can run on your own computer or over a small network. Internet Explorer 4 comes with a program called Personal Web Server that's perfect for such tasks.

Starting Personal Web Server

To start Personal Web Server, follow these steps:

1. **Click the Start button in the Windows 95 taskbar, and then click <u>S</u>ettings⇨Control Panel.**

The Control Panel folder appears.

2. **Double-click the Personal Web Server icon in the Control Panel folder (or single-click if you are using the Active Desktop).**

This launches the Personal Web Server Properties dialog box, shown in Figure 19-11.

If you can't find the Personal Web Server icon in the Control Panel folder, you didn't install Personal Web Server when you installed Internet Explorer. Jump on the Internet and hop over to www.microsoft.com/ie/ie40/download to download and install Personal Web Server. With a 28.8 Kbps modem, this should take less than five minutes.

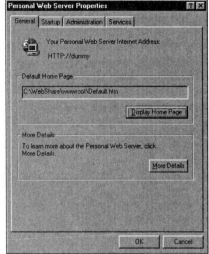

Figure 19-11:
The
Personal
Web Server
Properties
dialog box.

3. **Click the Startup tab at the top of the Personal Web Server Properties dialog box.**

   The Startup options appears, as shown in Figure 19-12.

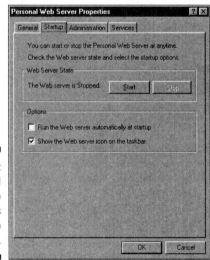

Figure 19-12:
Personal
Web
Server's
startup
options.

4. **Click the Start button.**

   The Personal Web Server responds.

If you want Personal Web Server to start automatically every time you start your computer, check the Run the Web Server Automatically at Startup option.

5. Click OK.

The Personal Web Server Properties dialog box is dismissed.

 After Personal Web Server starts, the icon shown in the margin appears in the Windows taskbar. You can double-click this icon at any time to summon the Personal Web Server Properties dialog box.

Personal Web Server comes with a set of Web pages that serve as Help files to give you an overview of how the Web Server works and how you can manage it. To access these help files, call up the Personal Web Server Properties dialog box and click the More Details button, which launches Internet Explorer for a view of the Help files.

Posting a Web page to Personal Web Server

Posting your HTML files to Personal Web Server so that you can view them using Internet Explorer from your computer or from another computer connected to your local area network is easy. Personal Web Server uses a folder named C:\WebShare\wwwroot as the root directory for your Web pages. To post an HTML file to Personal Web Server, all you have to do is save the file in the C:\WebShare\wwwroot folder.

To do that in FrontPage Express, just choose the File⇨Save As command. When the Save As dialog box appears, navigate your way to C:\WebShare\wwwroot, and then click Save to save the HTML file.

Accessing a Web page on Personal Web Server

To access a page stored in Personal Web Server, you need to know the Internet address for your Personal Web Server root directory. To find out, double-click the Personal Web Server icon in the Windows 95 taskbar or the Personal Web Server icon in Control Panel. The Personal Web Server Properties dialog box appears. Click the General tab (if it's not already selected). The Internet address of your Web server is shown.

To check out an example, look back at Figure 19-11. Here, the Internet Address for my Personal Web Server is HTTP://dummy.

The default Web page for Personal Web Server is default.html. Thus, if you have created a file named default.html in C:\WebShare\wwwroot, you can display that page simply by entering your Personal Web Server address in Internet Explorer's Address box. For example, if your Web Server address is dummy, just type **dummy** in the Address box to display your home page.

To display a different HTML file, type the filename after the Internet address, separated by a slash. For example, to display a page named softball.html, you type **dummy\softball.html**.

The Internet address used by Personal Web Server is based on your Windows 95 computer name, which you created when you first installed Windows 95 on your computer. If you want to change this name, open Control Panel and double-click the Network icon. This reveals the Network dialog box. Click the Identification tab, and then type a new computer name in the Computer Name field. When you click OK, your computer will restart, and then you can use the new name for your Personal Web Server Internet address.

Chapter 20

Making Your Pages Sing and Dance with Dynamic HTML

• •

• •

*I*n the battle for Web browser dominance, both Microsoft and Netscape continually introduce new HTML features for their browsers. What Microsoft and Netscape hope is that you and thousands of other Web-page developers can't resist a full-fledged commitment to using their unique HTML features.

This chapter shows you how to use Microsoft's latest entrant in the gee-whiz HTML battle: *Dynamic HTML*. As luck has it, the latest release of Netscape Navigator also sports a feature called Dynamic HTML. However, the Microsoft version of Dynamic HTML goes far beyond the Netscape version. As a result, when your Netscape-bigot friend says, "Big deal, we do Dynamic HTML too," don't take it to heart. Microsoft's Dynamic HTML is better than theirs.

This chapter assumes that you have a basic understanding of how Web pages are developed, including at least a rudimentary knowledge of *Hypertext Markup Language* (HTML), the programming language behind all Web pages. If you're new to Web page creation, or if you're just starting out with HTML, check out *HTML For Dummies,* 2nd Edition, by Ed Tittel and Steve James (published by IDG Books Worldwide, Inc.), for some really great tips on creating Web pages. And for detailed information about Dynamic HTML, you can get a copy of *Dynamic HTML For Dummies* by Michael Hyman (also published by IDG Books Worldwide, Inc.).

Also, be warned that the Dynamic HTML features described in this chapter will work only when your pages are viewed with Internet Explorer 4. If you use these features and someone views your pages using a different Web browser (including an earlier version of Internet Explorer), he or she won't be able to see the cool new features you worked so hard to put on your pages.

What Is Dynamic HTML?

Dynamic HTML is a collection of new HTML features that are designed to make Web pages more attractive, more interactive, and more efficient. Specifically, Dynamic HTML features the following:

- Additions to HTML that enable you to precisely control the placement of elements on the page.

- Additions to HTML that make it possible to handle events such as mouse movements for all of the elements on a page. You handle these events by creating a script using either the VBScript or JScript (Microsoft's implementation of JavaScript) scripting language.

- An *object model* that makes it possible to access every element on an HTML page from a script. You can use scripts to modify the content or style of any element on the page.

- A new feature called *data binding,* which lets you create HTML tables that are actually more like databases than tables. With data binding, you can specify a filter that determines which rows of a table are displayed and you can sort the table into any order you want.

- Special multimedia controls that enable you to create animation effects on a Web page.

A Little Review (Yuck!)

To get the full effect of Dynamic HTML's new features, you have to create scripts using the VBScript or JScript scripting language. Most of the new Dynamic HTML features also depend on styles, so you need to know how to use Cascading Style Sheets (also known as CSS). The following sections present a brief (and I mean brief!) review of both scripting and styles.

Scripts

A *script* is a program that can be embedded in an HTML document. Internet Explorer 4 enables you to choose one of two scripting languages to create scripts: VBScript, which is based on Microsoft's Visual Basic, and JScript, which is based on the Java programming language. In this chapter, I use VBScript.

A script can be inserted into an HTML document within a pair of `<script>` and `</script>` tags, as in this example:

```
<script language='VBScript'>
    Sub SayHello
        MsgBox "Hello World"
    End Sub
</script>
```

Procedures such as this are usually added to the `<head>` section of an HTML document. However, you can also associate a procedure with a form control such as a button. Then, the procedure is usually coded inline with the form control, like this:

```
<form name='myform'>
    <input name='button1' type='button' value='button1'>
    <script language='VBScript' for='button1'
    event='onclick'>
        MsgBox "Hello World!"
    </script>
</form>
```

In this case, the procedure is triggered when the user clicks the Button1 button.

As you see in the section "Style Sheets," Dynamic HTML includes a new method of introducing scripts into an HTML document to change the content or the style of any element on your Web page.

Style Sheets

HTML applies only rudimentary formats by using *paragraph tags* that associate a paragraph with a particular format. For example, headings are formatted using tags such as `<h1>`, `<h2>`, and `<h3>`; block quotations are formatted with `<blockquote>` tags; and normal paragraphs are formatted with `<p>` tags.

All Web browsers apply simple, basic formatting to your Web page text based on these HTML tags. For example, headings are always displayed with a larger type size than normal text. A *style sheet,* however, enables you to add additional formatting information to these standard HTML tags.

For example, with a style sheet, you can create a Web page in which all first level headings (using the `<h1>` and `</h1>` tags) are centered on the page and appear in 26-point Arial Bold font. Or you can create regular paragraphs (using the `<P>` and `</P>` tags) that are formatted as 9-point Century

Schoolbook font with a first line indent of $1/2$ inch. You can make your text different colors, italicize words you want to emphasize, or highlight sections of your Web page — you can really make your Web pages come alive using style sheets.

To give your Web pages life, color, and personality, Internet Explorer enables you to choose from more than a dozen formatting attributes that can be included in your HTML style sheets. For example, you can set the font using the `font-family` attribute, and you can set the point size using the `font-size` attribute. And the `color` and `background` attributes enables you to set the text color or the background color.

You can apply style sheets to your HTML documents in the following three ways. Each method is appropriate in different situations.

Embedded Style Sheets

The first type of style sheet is an *embedded style sheet,* which you include in the `<head>` section of your Web document. The embedded style sheet contains codes that specify the formats that should be applied to all text marked with a specific tag, which allows you to apply consistent text formatting throughout an entire HTML document. For example, if you specify in an embedded style sheet that headings (`<h1>` tags) should be formatted in 36-point Arial font, then *all* `<h1>` headings in a Web document are formatted with 36-point Arial font.

Here's an example of an embedded style sheet:

```
<style>
    H1 {font-family: Arial; font-size: 36pt}
    H2 {font-family: Times New Roman; font-size: 24pt;
    color: Red}
</style>
```

With this style sheet placed at the beginning of the document (in the `<head>` section), any `<h1>` heading appears in 36-point Arial, and any `<h2>` appears in 24-point red Times New Roman.

Linked Style Sheets

A linked style sheet contains a set of style definitions and exists as a separate file with a .css filename extension. You use a `<link>` tag in an HTML document's `<head>` section to link the Web document to the style sheet.

For example, suppose that you store your style sheet in a file named styles.css, located at `http://freedonia.gov/styles.css`. The style.css file looks like this:

```
H1 {font-family: Arial; font-size: 36pt}
H2 {font-family: Times New Roman; font-size: 24pt; color:
Red}
```

Notice that the `<style>` and `</style>` tags aren't required in the .css file.

To link an HTML document to the style.css style sheet, you include the following lines between the `<head>` tags of the HTML file:

```
<head>
<title>This document uses a linked style sheet</title>
<link rel=stylesheet
href="http://freedonia.gov/styles.css" type="text/css">
</head>
```

That's all there is to it. The REL attribute indicates that the LINK applies to a stylesheet, and the HREF attribute supplies the filename for the stylesheet to be used. As a result, this Web document is formatted using the style definitions found in the styles.css file.

Inline Styles

Occasionally, you may want to override one of the formatting options provided by the embedded style sheet or the linked style sheet. For example, suppose that your style sheet formats `<h1>` headings as 36-point text, but you have one heading that you want to emphasize by displaying it as 44-point text. You can override the style sheet settings by applying an *inline style.* You first apply an `<h1>` tag to the heading and then add an inline `style` attribute. This code overrides the `font-size` attribute of the `<h1>` tag (which is specified in the embedded style sheet, for example) and specifies the new, larger type size.

To override a formatting attribute for a tag, you add a `style` attribute to the tag, as in this example:

```
<h1 style="font-size: 44pt" >
```

Notice that the `style` attribute's value is a standard style definition enclosed in quotation marks. Thus, any of the formatting properties that can be used in a style sheet can also be used in a `style` attribute on *any* HTML tag.

The override formatting specified by an inline style attribute applies *only* to the tag in which the attribute appears. In the preceding example, for instance, all subsequent `<h1>` headings appear in the font size designated in the style sheet (that is, 36-point text).

To apply formatting to only a portion of a paragraph, you can use the `<span>` tag along with a `style` attribute. For example, suppose that you want to change the background color of a few words of text to yellow in order to give the text a highlighted appearance. You can format a portion of text using the `<span>` tag, as shown in the following code:

```
This is <span style="background: yellow">some text</span>
that has been highlighted.
```

In the preceding code, the `<span>` tag includes a `style` attribute that changes the background color to yellow for the words "some text."

The `style` attribute is also used in a `<div>` tag to apply style to a section of a document, or to the `<body>` tag to apply a style to the entire body of your Web page. In addition, you can use styles with many other types of tags, including `<img>` (used to insert an image), `<iframe>` (used to create a floating frame), and `<table>` (used to create a table).

Positioning Elements on a Page

At last, we're ready to learn some Dynamic HTML. The new positioning feature of Dynamic HTML enables you to precisely control the position of every element on a Web page. Before Dynamic HTML, you had only crude control over the position of page elements. With style sheets, you could set text alignment and margins, but for anything more than that, you had to fuss with tables or frames to control positioning.

With Dynamic HTML, you can specify the exact position of any element on the page using simple x and y coordinates. And you can layer objects on the page so that when objects overlap, you can control which one is visible — that is, which one appears to be on top.

Specifying an element's page position

To control an element's position on the page, you use three new style attributes:

✔ **position:** The `position` attribute tells Internet Explorer that you are going to set the position for the element. `position` can have one of two values: `absolute` or `relative`. I explain the difference between `absolute` and `relative` in the section "Using relative positioning." For now, just use `position=absolute`.

✔ **top:** Specifies the position of the top of the element.

✔ **left:** Specifies the position of the left edge of the element.

To see how these positioning attributes work, have a look at the following snippet of an HTML document:

```
<body style="font-family: Arial; font-weight: Bold; font-
size: 36">
Here is some text
<span style="position: absolute; top: 200; left: 300">
Here is some more text
</span>
</body>
```

In this example, the `<body>` tag uses a style attribute to set the default font for the document to 36-point Arial Bold. Then, "Here is some text" is displayed. Next, a `<span>` tag uses a style attribute to set the position of the text that follows to 200 pixels from the top of the page and 300 pixels from the left of the page. Figure 20-1 shows how this page appears when displayed in Internet Explorer 4.

Note that the top and left positions are given in pixels. (Pixels are the little dots that make up the image on your computer monitor.) If you prefer, you can use any of the measurements listed in Table 20-1 instead. Pixels, however, give you the most precise control over your layout.

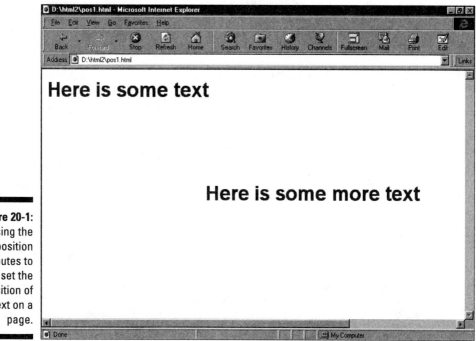

Figure 20-1:
Using the position attributes to set the position of text on a page.

Table 20-1	Measurement Units You Can Use
Measurement Unit	*Example*
pixel	top: 100 left: 200px
inches	top: 1in
millimeters	left: 10mm
centimeters	top: 2cm
points (1 point = 1/72 inch)	left: 72pt
picas (1 pica = 1/6 inch)	top: 12pc
em (height of the font)	top: 3em
ex (height of the font's letter *x*)	left: 22ex
percentage of page width or height:	left: 50%

Mixing positioned and unpositioned text

Be aware that positioning attributes apply only to the elements that are contained within the tags that specify the positioning. Once the tag is closed (for example, with a `</span>` tag), HTML reverts back to its normal mode of positioning elements on the page. This can sometimes lead to unexpected results.

For example, consider this bit of HTML:

```
<body style="font-family: Arial; font-weight: Bold; font-
size: 36">
Here is some text
<span style="position: absolute; top: 200; left: 300">
Here is some more text
</span>
Oh boy, here is even more text still!
</body>
```

This HTML is the same as the HTML that created the page shown back in Figure 20-1, except that I added another line of text following `</span>`. Figure 20-2 shows how this page appears in Internet Explorer 4. As you can see, the new text was placed immediately after the first line of text — on the very same line, in fact. That's because `</span>` canceled the effect of the style positioning, so HTML reverted to its normal positioning for the rest of the document.

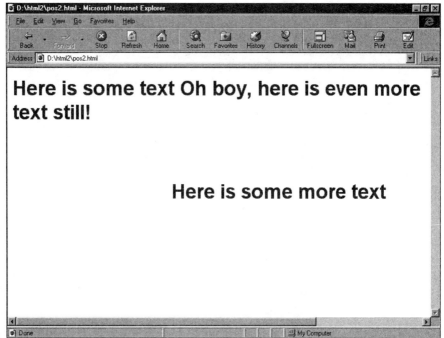

Figure 20-2:
Mixing
normal
positioning
and style
positioning.

Overlapping page elements

If you want, you can set up the positioning attributes of two or more page
elements to cause the elements to overlap. For example, you may want to
place a graphic background image on the page, and then place some text on
top of the image. Or, you may want to layer several images atop one another
to create an interesting graphic effect.

For example, consider this HTML code:

```
<body>
<img src="twoton.jpg" style="position: absolute; top: 100;
left: 100">
<span style="font-family: Arial;
font-weight: Bold;
     font-size: 36;
     position: absolute;
     top: 130;
     left: 200;
     ">
Here is some text
</span>
</body>
```

In this example, twoton.jpg is a clipart graphic file that I downloaded from Microsoft's Web Gallery (www.microsoft.com/gallery). The <img> tag inserts this graphic onto the page, positioning it 100 pixels from the top and 100 pixels from the left. Then, the <span> tag sets up the text so that it's positioned 130 pixels from the top of the page and 200 pixels from the left. As Figure 20-3 shows, this positioning centers the text over the graphic.

When two or more page elements overlap, Internet Explorer layers the elements one atop the other. Normally, elements are layered in the order in which they appear in the HTML file. Thus, the text in Figure 20-3 appears above the image because the text came after the <img> tag. Had I reversed the order of these elements, the text would not be visible because the image would be on top of it.

In other words, suppose the HTML for Figure 20-3 looks like this:

```
<body>
<span style="font-family: Arial;
font-weight: Bold;
     font-size: 36;
     position: absolute;
     top: 130;
     left: 200;
     ">
Here is some text
</span>
<img src="twoton.jpg" style="position: absolute; top: 100;
left: 100">
</body>
```

Because the <img> tag follows the text, it's placed on top of the text, rendering the text invisible.

However, you can control the layering order by using an additional positioning attribute: z-index. The z-index attribute determines the position of an element when elements are layered. Elements with greater z-index values overlap elements with lower z-index values.

Any element for which you do not specify a z-index value is given a z-index of zero. Thus, 0 is the default layer for text and other elements which form the bulk of your page. You only need to use the z-index attribute when you want to force an object to appear above or below this default layer. For example, to move a graphic image behind text, add z-index: -1 to the style for the graphic's <img> tag. Or, to place an element above the text layer, use z-index: 1.

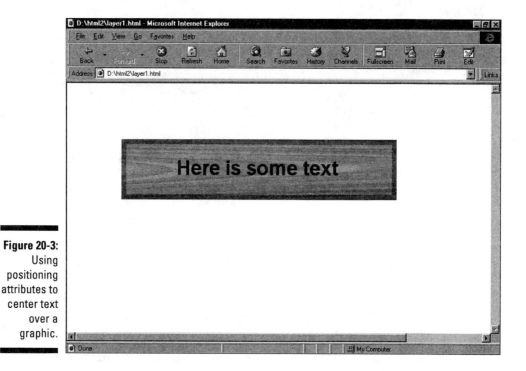

In our example, you would add z-index: -1 to the <img> tag for the twoton.jpg graphic file, like this:

```
<img src="twoton.jpg" style="position: absolute; top: 100;
left: 100; z-index: -1">
```

Then, the text properly overlays the twoton.jpg image, even though the <img> tag for the graphic file comes after the text in the HTML file.

Using relative positioning

So far, all the positioning examples I offer in this chapter have specified POSITION: ABSOLUTE. This tells Internet Explorer that the TOP and LEFT attributes give the element's position from the top left corner of the page. This *absolute positioning* enables you to disregard the position of other elements on the page when you are specifying an elements position.

The alternative to absolute positioning is *relative positioning*. To use relative positioning, include POSITION: RELATIVE in the style. Then, use the TOP and LEFT attributes to specify the element's position relative to the current position on the page rather than to the top left corner of the page. This allows you to control the position of elements yet preserve the element's flow within the Web page.

Here is an example that uses relative positioning to create a subscript:

```
<h1 style="font-face: Arial; font-size: 36; font-weight:
Bold">
H<span style="font-size: 24; position: relative; top:
+8pt">
2</span>0
</h1>
```

In this example, the `<h1>` tag includes a style that sets the font to 36-point Arial Bold. Then, the letter H is displayed. Next, a `<span>` tag changes the font size to 24 and uses relative positioning to move the top of the following text down 8 points. Then comes the numeral 2, followed by a `</span>` tag to end the spanned style and the letter O, which is displayed again as 36-point Arial Bold.

Figure 20-4 shows how this HTML appears when displayed in Internet Explorer. As you can see, the "2" is indeed shown as a subscript.

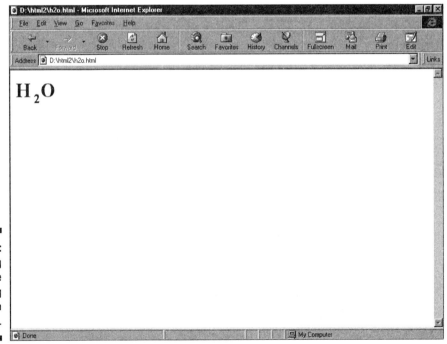

Figure 20-4:
Using
relative
positioning
to create a
subscript.

Handling Events with Scripts

An *event* is an action which triggers the execution of a VBScript or Jscript script. The most common type of events are mouse clicks. For example, you can set up a Web page so that a script is run whenever a user clicks a graphic image. The script can include whatever instructions you want carried out when the button is clicked.

Previous versions of HTML limited you to handling events such as mouse clicks only for form controls such as buttons and text fields. With Dynamic HTML, however, every single element on the page can have scripts associated with it to handle a wide variety of events. Thus, you can add scripts to control every aspect of your Web pages.

Intrinsic events

In Dynamic HTML, you don't need to use the `<script>` tag to insert a script into a document. Instead, you can use special attributes called *intrinsic events* to specify scripts that are invoked when various events occur. You can use these attributes in virtually any HTML tag. For example, you can use the `onclick` attribute in an `<h1>` to specify a script that is run whenever the heading is clicked. Or you can use an `onmouseover` attribute in a `<img>` tag to trigger a script whenever the mouse moves over an image.

Table 20-2 lists the most commonly used intrinsic events. There are others that are used less often; for a complete list, check out the Microsoft Site Builders Network at `www.microsoft.com/workshop/author/dynhtml`.

Table 20-2	Intrinsic Event Attributes
Event	*Explanation*
onclick	The user clicks the mouse over the element.
ondblclick	The user double-clicks the mouse over the element.
onmouseover	The user moves the mouse to the element.
onmouseout	The user moves the mouse away from the element.
onmousedown	The user presses down the mouse button over the element.
onmouseup	The user releases the mouse button while the mouse is over the element.
onmousemove	The user moves the mouse while the mouse is over the element.

(continued)

Table 20-2 *(continued)*

Event	Explanation
onfocus	The element receives input focus by pointing or by tabbing.
onblur	The element loses focus (see *onfocus*).
onkeypress	The user presses and releases a key while the element has input focus.
onkeydown	The user presses down a key while the element has input focus.
onkeyup	The user releases a key while the element has input focus.
onload	Internet Explorer finishes loading the page or frame (used only with <body> or <frameset>).
onunload	Internet Explorer unloads the page or frame (used only with <body> or <frameset>).

A simple script

Here's a simple example that demonstrates how to create a script (written in VBScript) that modifies the appearance of a text element when the user moves the mouse over the text:

```
<h1 onmouseover="this.style.color='red'">
Don't Make Me Angry!
</h1>
```

In this example, the script consists of a single line:

```
this.style.color='red'
```

In VBScript lingo, this line causes the style color attribute of the current object ("this") to be set to red. Because the script is contained in an onmouseover attribute, the script will be run whenever the user moves the mouse over the text. Thus, the text "Don't Make Me Angry!" turns red when the user points to it with the mouse.

Pay attention to the confusing syntax that's required when you embed a VBScript script within an HTML tag. The entire script must be contained within quotation marks. However, the script itself is bound to need quotation marks. To avoid confusion, I use apostrophes within the script. But be careful: It's easy to forget to add the closing quotation mark at the end of the script. When you do, your page won't work properly, but you probably won't see any error messages either. So always double-check the closing quotation marks.

How do you make the text turn back to black when the user moves the mouse away from the text? By adding a second script to the `<h1>` tag:

```
<h1 onmouseover="this.style.color='red'"
onmouseout="this.style.color='black'">
Don't Make Me Angry!
</h1>
```

Now, whenever the user moves the mouse out of the heading text, the `onmouseout` script is run and the color is set back to black.

Working with longer scripts

Most scripts require more than just one line of code to do anything interesting. To create longer scripts within an HTML tag, just separate the lines from one another with semicolons, as in this example:

```
<h1 onmouseover="this.style.color='red' ;
this.style.fontSize=48"
onmouseout="this.style.color='black' ;
this.style.fontSize=24">
Don't Make Me Angry!
</h1>
```

In this example, the text is changed to red and the font-size is increased to 48 points when the mouse moves over the heading. When the mouse leaves, the text is restored to 24-point and black.

However, coding longer scripts within quotation marks can get pretty cumbersome. For scripts longer than a few lines, you need to implement the script as a Sub procedure, which you can then call whenever you need it.

The only trick when creating Sub procedures for event handling is knowing how to refer to the HTML element that triggered the event. When you code the script directly in the HTML tag, you can use `this` to refer to the current element. When you create a Sub procedure, `this` won't work. Instead, you use the arcane but functional construct `window.event.srcElement`. Thus, to set the color of the element that triggered the procedure, you set `window.event.srcElement.style.color`.

I object to the object model!

The cornerstone of Dynamic HTML is the new HTML object model, which enables you to access each and every element of an HTML document from a script written in VBScript or Jscript.

Unfortunately, object models are troublesome to learn — especially if you're new to object programming. The good news is that the HTML object model is relatively straightforward. Most of the objects correspond directly to HTML elements you already know (well, assuming you already know some HTML). For example, you use the style object to access the style attributes of an element. Within the style object are additional objects which correspond to each style attribute. For example, style.color is used for an element's color.

Here are a few tricks you need to know:

✔ If an attribute name includes a hyphen, drop the hyphen, and capitalize the first letter that followed the hyphen. For example, font-face becomes fontFace and font-size becomes fontSize.

✔ To access a specific page element, use the id attribute in the element's HTML tag. Then, in the script, use the object document.all followed by the id you gave the element. For example, if you create a heading paragraph with the tag <H1 id=MyHeading>, you refer to it in your script as document.all.MyHeading.

✔ If the script is included directly in an HTML tag (for example, in an onmouseclick attribute), you can use this to refer to the element itself.

✔ If you use a Sub procedure, you can refer to the element that triggered the procedure by using the window.event.srcElement object.

Here's an example that changes the color and size of text when the mouse moves over the text, and then sets the color and size back when the mouse leaves the text using Sub procedures:

```
<head>
<script language='VBScript'>
Sub TurnItOn()
    window.event.srcElement.style.color="red"
    window.event.srcElement.style.fontSize="48"
End Sub
Sub TurnItOff()
    window.event.srcElement.style.color="black"
    window.event.srcElement.style.fontSize="24"
End Sub
</script>
</head>
```

```
<body>
<h1 onmouseover="TurnItOn()" onmouseout="TurnItOff()">
Don't Make Me Angry!
</h1>
</body>
```

Here, the `TurnItOn` Sub procedure sets the color to red and the font size to 48. Then, the `TurnItOff` Sub procedure restores the color to black and the font size to 24.

Notice in this example that both Sub procedures are listed in the `<head>` section of the document rather than the `<body>`. It's a good idea to place all your Sub procedures together in the `<head>` section of your document.

Referring to other objects

The `this` object is a handy way to refer to the element that triggered an event. But what if you want to change a different element? To do that, you first need to provide an identifying name for the element you want to change by using the `id` attribute. For example, here's a heading paragraph with an assigned `id`, "angry":

```
<h1 id=Angry>
You wouldn't like me when I'm angry!
</h1>
```

Now, you can refer to this element in a script command by using a special object called `document.all`. For example, to set the color of the Angry element to red, you use the following VBScript statement:

```
document.all.Angry.style.color = 'red'
```

You can put it together into a complete page, this time using the `visibility` style attribute rather than the color attribute. `Visibility` controls whether an element is visible or not; the possible values for visibility are `hidden` or `visible`. Here's the HTML:

```
<h1
onmouseover="document.all.Angry.style.visibility='visible'"
onmouseout="document.all.Angry.style.visibility='hidden'">
Don't Make Me Angry!
</h1>
<h1 id=Angry style="visibility: hidden; color: red">
You Wouldn't Like Me When I'm Angry!
</h1>
</body>
```

This example begins by displaying the ⟨h1⟩ paragraph "Don't Make Me Angry!" When the user moves the mouse over the text, an additional ⟨h1⟩ paragraph appears which says "You Wouldn't Like Me When I'm Angry!" The second heading disappears when the user moves the mouse away from the first heading.

How does it work? By setting the second heading's style visibility attribute to hidden, the heading is not displayed on the page. But when the user moves the mouse over the first heading, the onmouseover script changes the second heading's style visibility to visible. The onmouseout script changes the style visibility back to hidden to hide the second heading when the user moves the mouse away from the first heading.

Changing text on the page

Dynamic HTML also enables you to change the text of an element from within a script. The easiest way to do that is to use the innerText object property. InnerText enables you to replace the text of an element with new text. To see how it works, take a look at the following snippet of HTML:

```
<h1 onmouseover="this.innerText='You Wouldn\'t Like Me When
          I\'m Angry!'"
    onmouseout="this.innerText='Don\'t Make Me Angry!'">
Don't make me angry!
</h1>
```

This HTML starts by displaying the heading paragraph "Don't Make Me Angry!" When the user moves the mouse over the paragraph, the onmouseover script replaces this text with "You Wouldn't Like Me When I'm Angry!" Then, when the user moves the mouse away from the heading, the text changes back to "Don't Make Me Angry!"

There's a Lot More!

In this chapter, I only scratch the surface of what's possible with Dynamic HTML. For example, there are many more methods you can use to insert text or new elements into an HTML document from a script. There are also special positioning techniques you can use to create simple animations on a page. And I haven't even touched the new multimedia controls or data binding features. There's a lot to figure out. Sigh.

For more complete information about Dynamic HTML, check out Microsoft's Dynamic HTML Web site at www.microsoft.com/workshop/author/dhtml. There, you find technical articles about various aspects of using Dynamic HTML, a complete reference for Dynamic HTML, and plenty of examples.

Chapter 21

Creating Your Very Own Channel

● ●

In This Chapter

▶ Creating a channel

▶ Converting a Web site into a channel

▶ Creating a CDF file for your channel

▶ Using Liburnia, a free program that makes CDF files easier to create

▶ Allowing users to subscribe to your channel

● ●

*W*ouldn't it be fun to own your own channel? I'm not talking about a TV channel or the kind of channel that invites you to talk with dear, departed relatives, but rather the communications kind of channel available with Internet Explorer 4. If your channel is good enough, you may even put MSNBC or PointCast (two of the more popular Web channels) out of business!

This chapter shows you how to turn your existing Web site into a channel. After you turn your site into a channel, any Internet user can subscribe to your channel. After a user subscribes to your channel, he or she is automatically informed whenever you make changes to your channel.

For example, suppose you go to great lengths to create a Web site devoted to your daughter's high school marching band, the Rydell Marching Rangers (`www.rydell.edu/band.html`). You tell all your friends and relatives about the Rydell Band site, and they check it out once or twice. Some may even add your site to their Favorites. But even your closest friends and relatives probably lose interest after a few visits. So they likely miss out when the Rangers place 14th at the regional band festival and you update the Rydell Band site to gloat over this accomplishment. (Of course, you won't mention that only 15 bands entered in the festival, and one of the bands forgot to put their instruments on the bus.)

By converting the Rydell Band site into the Rydell Band Channel, however, your friends and relatives can subscribe to it. Then, whenever you update the Rydell Band Channel, your subscribers are notified that the channel's changed. Seeing that there is new information available, they call up Internet Explorer's Channel Viewer and tune in to the Rydell Band Channel to see what the big news is.

This chapter focuses on creating your own channel. For basic information about channels (such as what a channel is) and for the procedures you must follow to subscribe to a channel and view the channels you have subscribed to, see Chapter 6.

Turning a Web Site into a Channel

With Internet Explorer, you can easily turn any Web site you create into a channel. Creating a simple channel is not difficult. All you have to do is pull together the following elements:

- One or more HTML documents that provide the content of your channel. One of these documents is designated as the *main channel page,* while the others are known as *channel items.* The main channel page can be your existing Web site's home page, and any other pages in your Web site can become channel items. Note that you don't need to create separate HTML documents for your channel if you already created the HTML documents for an ordinary Web site. You can use the same HTML documents for both the channel and the Web site. (Of course, you can create a separate set of HTML documents for the channel if you want to.)

- Two graphic images that you must create using a graphics editing program. One of these images is a logo to display in the Internet Explorer Channels bar when a user subscribes to your channel. The other is an icon to appear when the user clicks Channels in the Favorites menu.

- A special file called a *CDF* file that spells out important details about your channel. (CDF stands for Channel Definition Format, but that won't be on the test.) Creating the CDF file isn't rocket science, but it is the most time-consuming part of turning a Web site into a channel. In fact, most of this chapter is devoted to showing you how to create a CDF file. After you create the CDF file, you place it on your Web server in the same folder that holds your channel's HTML documents.

- A way for users to subscribe to your channel. The easiest way to do this is to create a Web page that includes a link to the CDF file. When a user clicks on this link, Internet Explorer 4 automatically launches the Subscription Wizard to guide the user through the steps of subscribing to your channel.

The remaining sections in this chapter show you how to create each of these channel elements so that you can create your own channel.

A Sample Web Site

Throughout this chapter, I use a sample Web site for the Rydell High School Rangers Marching Band as I show you how to convert an ordinary Web site into a channel. For testing purposes, I placed this Web site on my own computer using the Personal Web Server using the Internet address `rydell`. When the site is actually placed on the Internet, it undoubtedly uses a more realistic Internet address, such as `www.rydell.edu`.

The sample Web site consists of a home page named `rangers.html`, which is illustrated in Figure 21-1. This home page includes a simple graphic and links to six other HTML documents:

- **Staff.html,** which gives biographical information about the band director and other members of the staff.

- **Band.html,** which provides interesting information about the band, such as how many members it has, who the drum majors are, what music the band plays, and so on.

- **Guard.html,** which lists information about the Rydell High Color Guard.

- **Sched.html,** which lists the competition schedule for the upcoming year.

- **Awards.html,** which provides information about how the band has done in each of its competitions so far this year. This is the page that's most likely to change as the marching band season progresses.

- **Fund.html,** which gives information about upcoming fund-raising events such as raffles, candy sales, and so on. This page is also one that changes frequently throughout the year.

To convert this Web site into a channel, all I have to do is create the two graphic files for the logo and icon and create a CDF file that lists the HTML files that comprise the channel. To keep things simple, I use the Web site's existing HTML files for the channel. The `rangers.html` home page becomes the main page for the channel, and each of the six pages that are linked to the home page becomes a channel item.

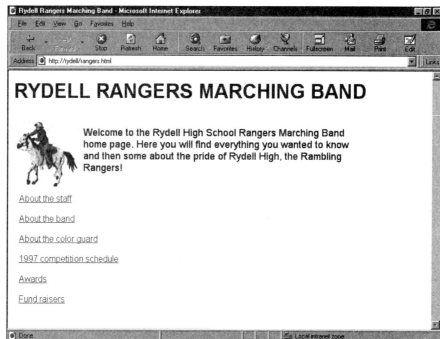

Figure 21-1:
The Rydell
High School
Rangers
Marching
Band home
page.

Creating the Logo and Icon Graphics

As mentioned before, you must create two graphic images for your channel: one to use as a logo that's displayed in the Channels bar, the other to use as an icon that's displayed in the Favorites menu. You can use any graphics drawing program to create these images.

The logo image should be 80 pixels wide and 32 pixels in height and should be stored in GIF format. The icon image should be 16 pixels by 16 pixels and can be stored in either GIF or ICO format. Both images should be posted to your Web server in the same folder as the other channel files.

Figure 21-2 shows the two graphic images I used for the Rydell High School Marching Band channel.

Figure 21-2:
The logo and icon graphics for the Rydell High School Marching Band channel.

Creating the CDF File

The heart of creating a channel is composing the CDF file that defines the HTML documents that make up the channel. A CDF file is a special type of text file containing CDF tags (which are similar to HTML tags) that detail all the information Internet Explorer 4 needs to know to access the channel.

CDF stands for *Channel Definition Format.* Although CDF is not officially a Web standard, Microsoft has submitted its specifications for CDF to the standards gurus at the World Wide Web Consortium, the same folks who oversee important Web standards such as HTML and HTTP. Whether or not the Consortium acts to make CDF a recognized standard, the mere fact that Microsoft created it and Internet Explorer 4 uses it makes CDF the "de-facto" standard for creating channels.

You can use any text editor, including NotePad (which comes free with Windows 95), to create a CDF file. The only trick is to be sure to assign a file name ending in .cdf when you save the file.

Internet Explorer 4 is very finicky about the syntax of CDF files. Unfortunately, Internet Explorer doesn't give you much help if you make a mistake in your CDF file. When you try to subscribe to a channel whose CDF file contains an error, Internet Explorer just sits there. No error message is displayed indicating that the CDF is in error. If something seems to be wrong with your channel, check — and double-check — your CDF to see if it contains errors such as missing quotation marks, < or > symbols, or slashes.

A sample CDF file

Listing 21-1 shows the complete CDF file for the Rydell Marching Band channel. As you can see, the CDF file loosely resembles an HTML document, with tags enclosed in < and > symbols. The following sections describe each of the tags in this CDF file.

Listing 21-1	The CDF File for the Rydell High Marching Band Channel

```xml
<?XML version="1.0"?>

<channel href="http://rydell/rangers.html" base="http://
rydell">
  <title>Rydell Rangers Marching Band</title>
  <abstract>Find the latest news and information
    about the Rydell High School Marching Rangers!
  </abstract>
  <logo href="logo.gif" style="image" />
  <logo href="icon.gif" style="icon" />
  <schedule>
    <intervaltime day="1" />
    <earliesttime hour="1" />
    <latesttime hour="5" />
  </schedule>

  <item href="staff.html" lastmod="1997-08-19">
    <title>Band staff</title>
    <abstract>Meet the band director, assistant director,
      color guard director, and other band
      staff.</abstract>
    <logo href="icon.gif" style="icon" />
  </item>

  <item href="band.html" lastmod="1997-08-19">
    <title>About the band</title>
    <abstract>Find out how the band has come together this
    year.</abstract>
    <logo href="icon.gif" style="icon" />
  </item>

  <item href="guard.html" lastmod="1997-08-19">
    <title>About the color guard</title>
    <abstract>Wondering what the color guard does all year?
    Here is where you will find the answers!</abstract>
    <logo href="icon.gif" style="icon" />
  </item>

  <item href="sched.html" lastmod="1997-08-19">
    <title>Schedule</title>
    <abstract>The complete band and color guard competition
    and performance schedule.</abstract>
    <logo href="icon.gif" style="icon" />
  </item>
```

```
<item href="awards.html" lastmod="1997-08-19">
  <title>Awards</title>
  <abstract>Find out how we've done.</abstract>
  <logo href="icon.gif" style="icon" />
</item>

<item href="fund.html" lastmod="1997-08-19">
  <title>Fund raisers</title>
  <abstract>None of this happens for free. Find out how
  you can help raise funds for the Marching Rangers.
  </abstract>
  <logo href="icon.gif" style="icon" />
</item>

</channel>
```

In the rest of this section, I explain each of the elements in this CDF file in detail.

The XML header

The first line in any CDF file is a line that indicates which version of XML is being used. XML, which stands for *eXtensible Markup Language*, is a set of rules that can be used for creating markup languages such as HTML or CDF. The XML line should appear exactly as follows:

```
<?XML version="1.0"?>
```

Because CDF is actually a type of XML file, all CDF files must begin with this XML header line.

The Channel element

The main section of a CDF file is the Channel element, which begins with the start tag `<channel>` and ends with the end tag `</channel>`. If you look back at Listing 21-1, you see that save for the XML header line, the entire CDF file is enclosed within the `<channel>` and `</channel>` tags.

Element is the technical term for a unit of text which, in most cases, is marked by a starting tag and an ending tag such as `<channel>` and `</channel>`. In this case, the Channel element consists of the `<channel>` and `</channel>` tags, plus everything that appears between them. Some elements, such as the Logo elements, which I explain in the section "The Logo element," are self-contained within a single tag. In that case, there is no end tag and the element consists solely of the tag itself.

The `<channel>` tag for the rangers.cdf file looks like this:

```
<channel href="http://rydell/rangers.html" base="http://
rydell">
```

A `<channel>` tag should always include an `href` attribute, which names the HTML document that's used as the main page for the channel. In this example, the main page is a document named rangers.html on a Web server named rydell. Note that this `href` attribute is identical to the HREF attribute you would use in a `<a>` tag in an HTML document.

Following the `href` attribute is a `base` attribute. The `base` attribute provides the base address for other `href` tags that appear in the CDF file so that you don't have to keep repeating this portion of the address. For example, skip down a line in Listing 21-1 to the first `<logo>` tag. Here, you can see the `href` attribute `href="logo.gif"`. Because of the `base` attribute in the `<channel>` tag, this `href` attribute is treated as if I typed the full address, `href="http://rydell/logo.gif"`.

A number of other tags that appear between the `<channel>` and `</channel>` tags are described in the following sections.

The Title and Abstract elements

The Title element in a CDF file provides a name for the channel, just as the Title element in an HTML document provides the title for a Web page. The title itself should be sandwiched between a pair of `<title>` and `</title>` tags. The Title element in Listing 21-1 is

```
<title>Rydell Rangers Marching Band</title>
```

The title is displayed along with the channel's logo or icon when you view channels from the Channels bar or the Favorites menu.

You can provide more information about your channel by including an Abstract element. Here is the Abstract element from Listing 21-1:

```
<abstract>Find the latest news and information
  about the Rydell High School Marching Rangers!
</abstract>
```

Internet Explorer displays the Abstract text when the user points the mouse cursor at the channel's logo in the Channels bar.

The Logo element

Every channel should have two Logo elements to indicate the graphics files that are used for the channel's logo and icon. The two Logo elements in Listing 21-1 are

```
<logo href="logo.gif" style="image" />
<logo href="icon.gif" style="icon" />
```

To indicate the graphic file used for your channel's logo, list the name of the logo file in the HREF attribute and specify image for the style attribute. For the icon, list the name of the icon file in the href attribute and specify icon in the style attribute.

The Logo element is peculiar in that it doesn't have an end tag. Instead, you type a slash immediately before the closing > symbol. If you forget this slash, your CDF won't work.

The Schedule element

The Schedule element is used to tell Internet Explorer how often the Web site is usually updated. Like the Title and Logo elements, the Schedule element should fall within the Channel element. The Schedule element begins with a <schedule> start tag and ends with a </schedule> end tag. Between the <schedule> and </schedule> tags, you should include the following three additional tags:

- <intervaltime>: Indicates how often the schedule repeats itself.
- <earliesttime>: Indicates the start of the update period.
- <latesttime>: Indicates the end of the update period.

All three of these tags can include three attributes: day, hour, and min (which stands for Minutes).

The <interval>, <earliesttime>, and <latesttime> tags do not have corresponding end tags. Instead, you must include a slash character immediately before the final > symbol. For example, to indicate that the schedule should repeat itself every day, you would use the following tag:

```
<intervaltime day="1"/>
```

Although you can use these attributes to create just about any imaginable type of schedule, most CDF files include a Schedule element that allows for daily updates in the wee hours of the morning. For example, consider the Schedule element from Listing 21-1:

```
<schedule>
  <intervaltime day="1" />
  <earliesttime hour="1" />
  <latesttime hour="5" />
</schedule>
```

In this example, scheduled updates occur every day between the hours of 1 a.m. and 5 a.m.

Suppose you want to allow updates between midnight and noon once a week. In that case, you write the Schedule element tags like this:

```
<schedule>
  <intervaltime day="7" />
  <earliesttime hour="0" />
  <latesttime hour="12" />
</schedule>
```

The Item element

For each channel item you want your channel to have, you must create an Item element in the CDF. The Item element begins with an `<item>` start tag and ends with an `</item>` end tag. Between these tags, you can include a `<title>` tag to give the channel item a title, an `<abstract>` to provide a description of the channel item, and a `<logo>` tag to endow the item with its own icon.

The `<item>` tag itself includes several attributes, the most important of which is `href`. The `href` attribute is used to supply the address of the Web page that is displayed when the user views the channel item.

Another important `<item>` tag attribute is `lastmod`, which gives the date on which the channel item was most recently changed. Internet Explorer 4 uses the `lastmod` date to determine if the channel item has changed since the user last looked at your site. As a result, you should be sure to update the `lastmod` values in your channel's CDF whenever you make a change to any of the channel's pages.

Here's a look at the first Item element in Listing 21-1:

```
<item href="staff.html" lastmod="1997-08-19">
  <title>Band staff</title>
  <abstract>Meet the band director, assistant director,
    color guard director, and other band
```

```
      staff.</abstract>
   <logo href="icon.gif" style="icon" />
</item>
```

In this example, the channel item named "Band staff" displays the staff.html Web page when the user views the channel. The Web page was last modified August 19, 1997. The abstract spells out the contents of the channel item, and the `<logo>` tag gives the item its own icon.

The rest of the CDF file in Listing 21-1 consists of nothing more than five additional Item elements, one for each of the remaining five items in the channel. Each of these Item elements is similar to the first, the only differences being the name of the item's HTML document, the title, and the abstract.

Liburnia to the Rescue

Microsoft offers a free program called *Liburnia* that can help you create CDF files. Liburnia uses a series of Wizards to fill in the details required by each CDF tag. With Liburnia, you must still learn all the details of CDF tags. But Liburnia helps ensure that you don't accidentally omit required elements from your CDF tags or make syntax errors.

You can get Liburnia free from Microsoft by downloading Microsoft's Internet Software Development Kit (also known as the InetSDK) from the following address:

```
www.microsoft.com/msdn/sdk/inetsdk
```

The download takes about 20 minutes to download with a 28,800 bps modem.

To use Liburnia to create a CDF file, first download and install the Liburnia program from Microsoft's Web site. Then, follow these steps:

1. **Start the Liburnia program.**

   Unfortunately, the InetSDK Setup program doesn't add a Start menu item for Liburnia. So to start Liburnia, you have to open a My Computer window and then navigate to the C:\InetSDK\Bin folder and double-click the Liburnia.exe icon. When Liburnia comes to life, it displays the screen shown in Figure 21-3.

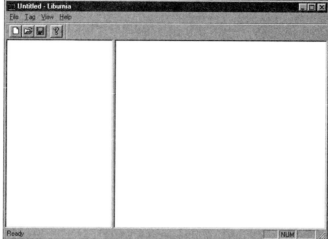

Figure 21-3:
Liburnia
comes to
life.

2. Choose the File⇨New command.

The Channel dialog box shown in Figure 21-4 appears.

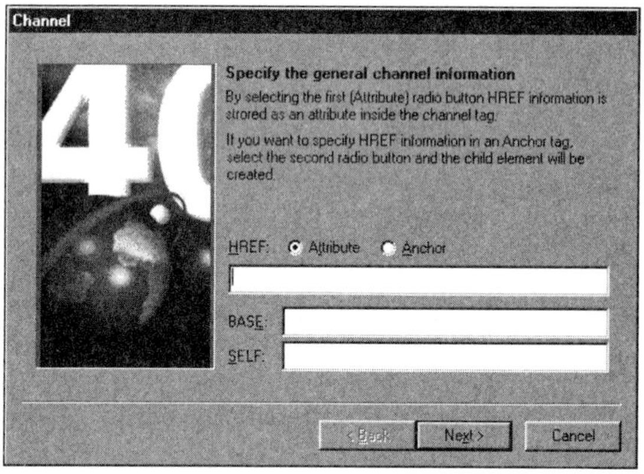

Figure 21-4:
Liburnia
asks for
information
about your
channel.

3. Supply all the information Liburnia requests for your channel. Click Next> to move from screen to screen.

Liburnia asks for the Internet address of the channel's main page, the channel's title and abstract, the update schedule, and the Internet address for the channel's icon and logo files. Liburnia also asks for two additional decisions about personal preferences: whether to keep a log or to require users to log in. You can safely disable both logging and the login requirements.

4. When you reach the last screen, click the Finish button to create the CDF tags needed to set up your channel.

The Channel dialog box disappears, and you return to the Liburnia main window. As Figure 21-5 shows, Liburnia creates several tags for your CDF file.

Figure 21-5:
CDF tags
created by
Liburnia
when you
create a
new
channel.

5. To add an item to your channel, choose the Tag➪New➪Item command.

The Item dialog box appears, as shown in Figure 21-6.

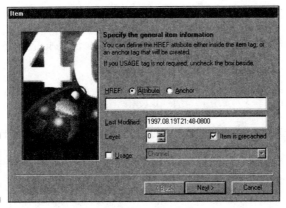

Figure 21-6:
The Item
dialog box.

6. **Supply all the information Liburnia requests for the channel item. Click Next to move from screen to screen.**

   Liburnia asks for the Internet address of the item's Web page, the item title and abstract, and the address of the item's icon file.

7. **When you reach the last screen, click the Finish button to create the CDF tags for the item.**

   The Item dialog box vanishes, and the tags for the item you just created are inserted into the CDF file, as shown in Figure 21-7.

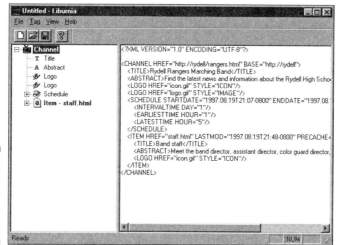

Figure 21-7:
Liburnia
creates the
CDF tags for
an item.

8. **Repeat Steps 5 through 7 for each additional item you want to add to your channel.**

9. **To save the CDF file, choose the File⇨Save command. When the Save As dialog box appears, type a file name, select the folder in which you want the CDF file saved, and click Save.**

That's all there is to it. After you finish, exit the program by choosing the File⇨Exit command (save your work, of course).

Here are a few additional thoughts to consider when you work with Liburnia:

✔ Liburnia gives you a handy tree view of your CDF file in the left side of its main window. This tree view gives you an overall picture of the structure of your channel.

✔ You can use Liburnia to edit an existing CDF file. Just choose the File⇨Open command to open the CDF file, make any changes you want to make, and then use the File⇨Save command to save the changes.

✔ If you try to open a CDF file that contains an error, Liburnia displays an error message indicating what the error is and which line contains the error. Even if you don't want to use Liburnia to create your CDF files, Liburnia is still a handy tool for checking the validity of your CDF files. If you can open a CDF file in Liburnia, you can be certain that the file does not contain any syntax errors.

Allowing Users to Subscribe to Your Channel

After you create a CDF for your channel and place it on a Web server along with the logo and icon image files and the actual Web pages that make up your channel, only one step remains to make your channel usable: You must provide some method for Internet users to subscribe to your channel. The easiest way to do that is to create a link to the channel's CDF file. When the user clicks on this link, Internet Explorer launches its Subscription Wizard so that the user can subscribe to the channel.

If you want, you can create a separate Web page that contains the subscription link. This Web page might describe the features of your channel, such as what type of information it includes and how often you update it. Then, if the user is so inclined, he or she can click the subscription link to subscribe.

To create a simple text link to a CDF file, use an Anchor element such as the following:

```
<a href="http://rydell/rangers.cdf">Click here to subscribe
    to the Rydell Rangers Marching Band Channel!</a>
```

In this example, the user subscribes to the channel by clicking the "Click here to subscribe to the Rydell Rangers Marching Band Channel!" text link.

Microsoft recommends that you employ a graphic link, rather than a simple text link, using the special button shown in Figure 21-8. You can download this button from Microsoft's Web site at the following address:

```
www.microsoft.com/workshop/prog/ie4/channels/button.gif
```

Point Internet Explorer to this address, and then right-click the button that appears and choose the Save Picture As command to save the button on your own computer. Then, you can post the button.gif file along with your other HTML and graphic files on your Web server.

Figure 21-8:
Microsoft's
standard
channel
subscription
button.

To create a button link to subscribe to your channel, use an `<IMG>` tag within an Anchor element, such as this:

```
<a href="http://rydell/rangers.cdf">
<img src="button.gif" width="110" height="24" border="0"
    alt="Subscribe to channel">
</a>
```

Simple as that. When the user clicks on the button, the Subscription Wizard launches so the user can subscribe to your site.

Part VII
The Part of Tens

The 5th Wave   By Rich Tennant

JEEZ—YOU'D THINK THESE PEOPLE NEVER SAW A LAPTOP BEFORE!

GATE 9   ATE 8

In this part . . .

If you keep this book in the bathroom (where it rightfully belongs), the chapters in this part are the ones destined to gain the most readership. Each of these chapters offers up ten (more or less) things that are worth knowing about various aspects of using Internet Explorer.

Without further ado, here they are, direct from the home office in Fresno, California. . . .

Chapter 22

Ten Hot Internet Explorer 4.0 Features

*O*nce again, Microsoft has outdone itself — as it proves with release of the fourth-generation browser, Internet Explorer. Internet Explorer 4 boasts many new features that make it a major improvement over Internet Explorer 3. This chapter describes ten of those important developments. The folks at the Microsoft ad agency stay up late at night trying to come up with catchy slogans for these features, so look out. You can only imagine what wild Explorer-ations await!

The Internet Connection Wizard

Internet Explorer 4 comes with a handy program called the Internet Connection Wizard that can automatically (well, *almost* automatically) take care of signing you up for an Internet connection. The Connection Wizard even finds an Internet service provider for you in your area. When you choose the provider, the Connection Wizard handles the sign-up and configures Internet Explorer to work with the provider you prefer. Taking the first step toward the Internet has never been easier.

The New Explorer Bar

I love the new Explorer bar. It's a type of toolbar that occupies about one-fourth of the left side of the Internet Explorer window. There are four variations of the Explorer bar:

- ✔ **Search bar:** The Search bar provides a quick means of searching the Internet for a specific topic.

- ✔ **Favorites bar:** The Favorites bar enables you to access your favorite Internet locations without having to wade through the Favorites menu.

- ✔ **History bar:** The History bar displays a list of Web sites you recently visited.

- ✔ **Channels bar:** The Channels bar displays a list of channels you subscribe to.

What makes the Explorer bar so cool is that it remains on the screen while you're viewing your Web pages. For example, you can search for Web pages about armpits, and then browse the pages that come up while keeping the search results visible in the Explorer bar. Figure 22-1 shows the Explorer bar in action. (It's true: Endoscopic Transthoracic Sympathectomy is a surgery that's performed through the armpit.)

You find plenty of information about the various uses of the Explorer bar in Chapters 3, 4, 5, and even 6.

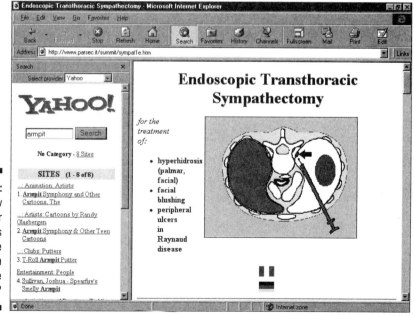

Figure 22-1:
See how Search bar remains visible while you explore the Web?

Dynamic HTML

No, this is not HTML that explodes if you drop it. *Dynamic HTML* refers to the latest and greatest version of the HTML language that Web authors use to create the fabulous pages you see when you browse the Web. Dynamic HTML enables Web authors to create pages that look and act like full-featured Windows programs. A favorite trick of Dynamic HTML is to create objects that respond in some way when you pass the mouse over them. For example, a button might change color or text might increase in size. Oooh! Ahhh!

I'd show you a picture of a Dynamic HTML page, but that would miss the point. You can't capture *movement* in a picture, and the whole idea of Dynamic HTML is to make pages that move and groove. You have to experience it to appreciate it. If you're a Web author who wants to learn how to create your own Dynamic HTML pages, turn to Chapter 20 to find out how.

The Active Desktop

The Active Desktop, known as the Windows Desktop Update, is a major new feature of Internet Explorer 4 — one that transforms your Windows 95 desktop into something that looks like the Web. The idea behind the Active Desktop is that it makes sense to use the same interface to browse both the Internet and your computer's own hard drive.

The Active Desktop enables you to place active components directly on the desktop. Internet Explorer comes with one such component, called the Channels bar, which lets you quickly access the channels you subscribe to. You can download others, such as a stock ticker, a weather map, or an up-to-date news page, from Microsoft's Web site.

The Active Desktop also enables you to customize your folders by assigning a different background image for each folder. Or, if you have the time and inclination, you can create an HTML Web page for your folders.

Active Desktop also includes several minor but useful improvements to the way Windows 95 works. For example, you can now create your own toolbars to place on the desktop, in addition to the standard Windows 95 taskbar. And the taskbar has new buttons that enable you to instantly launch Internet Explorer, Outlook Express, view your channels, or minimize all the windows that are cluttering up your desktop.

Figure 22-2 shows what the Active Desktop looks like. For complete information about the Active Desktop, turn to Chapters 16 and 17.

Figure 22-2:
The Active
Desktop
changes
the way
Windows 95
looks and
feels.

Channels

A *channel* is a special new type of Web site that's designed to enable your computer to automatically download updates on a regular basis and alert you when new content is available. To receive these regular updates, you must first subscribe to the channel. Microsoft managed to talk a few hundred content providers into creating channels on the Internet for you to subscribe to.

You find more information about channels in Chapter 6.

FrontPage Express

FrontPage Express is a scaled-back version of Microsoft's popular FrontPage program for creating and editing Web pages. FrontPage Express enables you to create sophisticated Web pages without worrying about all the details of HTML coding. FrontPage Express even includes several wizards that automatically generate HTML documents for you.

Figure 22-3 shows FrontPage Express in action.

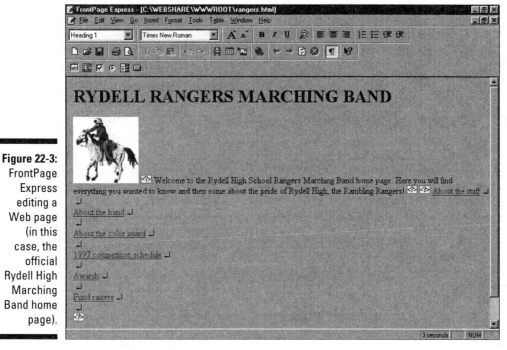

Figure 22-3:
FrontPage
Express
editing a
Web page
(in this
case, the
official
Rydell High
Marching
Band home
page).

Outlook Express

It seems as if Microsoft can't make up its mind which e-mail program it wants us to use. When Windows 95 came out, Microsoft introduced the ultimate e-mail program, Microsoft Exchange. Exchange was great, but it was painfully slow. Then, when Microsoft Office 97 arrived on the scene, we got another ultimate e-mail program: Microsoft Outlook. It was even better and slower than Exchange.

When Internet Explorer 3 came out, we were blessed with a slim and trim e-mail program called Microsoft Internet Mail, which I loved because it was about ten times as fast as Exchange or Outlook.

Now, with Internet Explorer 4, Microsoft seems to have realized that speed matters in an e-mail program. So Internet Explorer includes a tight version of Outlook called Outlook Express. Actually, Outlook Express is a beefed-up version of Internet Mail, combined with Internet Mail's sister program, Internet News. Outlook Express can handle both your e-mail and Internet newsgroups, so you don't need to use separate programs to read your e-mail and your newsgroups.

Figure 22-4 shows Outlook Express. For complete information about Outlook Express, turn to Chapters 8 and 9.

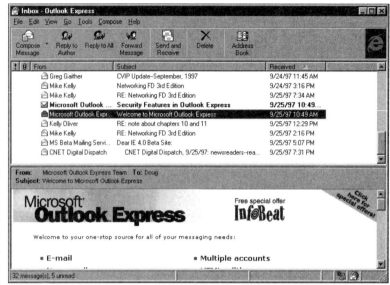

Figure 22-4:
Outlook
Express, the
lean, mean
e-mail
machine.

Microsoft Chat

With Internet Explorer 3, Microsoft introduced a new program that enabled you to participate in online Internet chats. For better or worse, someone at Microsoft thought it was cute to show the chats in the form of an ongoing cartoon strip rather than just a bunch of plain text. The result is novel, interesting, and sometimes downright silly.

Unfortunately, the first version of what was then called Microsoft Comic Chat was just too limited to be useful as a serious chatting program. But for Internet Explorer 4, Microsoft has beefed up its chat program — and removed *Comic* from the program's name to emphasize that Microsoft Chat is now a contender. Microsoft Chat still presents that silly comic-strip mode, as Figure 22-5 shows. However, it also packs the powerful features that make online chat-junkies drool. For more information about Microsoft Chat, see Chapter 10.

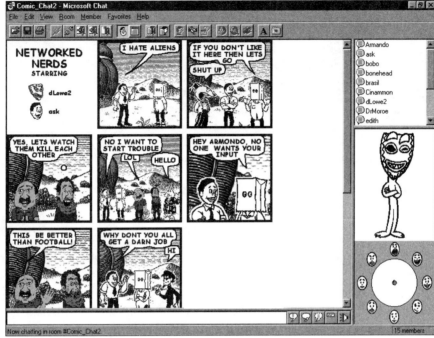

The Easter Egg

Artists sign their paintings. Authors get to put their names on the covers of their books. Journalists have their bylines. What about lowly programmers?

They're sneaky. Many of today's programs have the names of the developers buried deep inside the program. You have to know the secret combination of unlikely commands to unlock these hidden treasures. These signatures are called *Easter eggs*.

The programmers who wrote Internet Explorer 4 left a nifty Easter egg which lists just about everyone who was involved with the project, plus a few interesting and humorous tidbits. Here's how to conjure up this Easter egg:

1. **Start Internet Explorer 4.**

2. **Choose the Help⇨About Internet Explorer command.**

   The About Internet Explorer dialog box appears, as shown in Figure 22-6.

Figure 22-6:
The About
Internet
Explorer
dialog box.

3. **Press and hold down the Ctrl key. Then point the mouse at the "e" in the upper-right corner of the About Internet Explorer dialog box and, pressing down the left mouse button, drag the "e" to the left, over the globe. Then move the "e" straight to the right towards the word "Internet."**

   If you do it right, the words *Microsoft Internet Explorer 4.0* slide off the screen, revealing a button labeled Unlock.

   If the button isn't revealed, don't panic. Just click OK to dismiss the About Internet Explorer dialog box and start over. Eventually, you'll get it to work.

4. **Release the mouse button and let go of the Ctrl key, and then click the Unlock button.**

   The globe starts to pulsate.

5. **Hold down the Ctrl key again, and then use the left mouse button to drag the "e" back over the pulsating globe. Release the "e" over the globe.**

   The globe explodes. Then, a list of the names of everyone who worked on Internet Explorer 4 is displayed.

The list is very long. But let it run all the way through. There are a few humorous interludes along the way that are worth watching.

It's Still Free

Remarkably, Internet Explorer is still free. You can download Internet Explorer 4 from the Microsoft Web site (`www.microsoft.com/ie/ie40/download`) and use it with no fee of any kind. Microsoft does ask you to register Internet Explorer after you download it, but you don't have to pay a fee for registering or using the software.

Chapter 23
My Top Ten Web Site Picks

. . . .

In This Chapter
▶ The Library of Congress
▶ Microsoft
▶ The House of Representatives
▶ The Smithsonian Institution
▶ The National Park Service
▶ NASA
▶ Late night television
▶ Free stuff from the Microsoft Network
▶ Games Domain
▶ MSNBC

. . . .

*I*t's a sign of the times: In addition to their favorite TV shows, movies, and rock stars, people now have preferred Web sites. This chapter presents ten of mine. All ten of these Web sites are in my Favorites folder, and I visit them frequently. Some of these Web sites contain genuinely useful information, and others lean toward more frivolous pursuits.

The Library of Congress

```
www.loc.gov
```

The Library of Congress home page, shown in Figure 23-1, is one of the better pages anywhere on the Web. Apparently, I'm not alone in my pick of a favorite: About 45,000 pages are retrieved from this site *every day.*

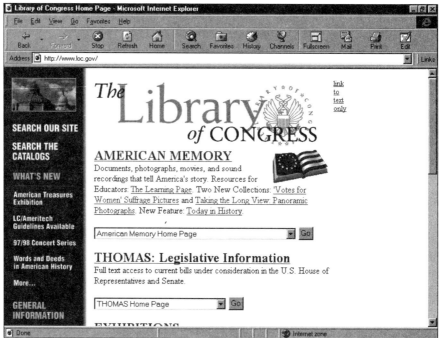

Figure 23-1:
The Library
of Congress
Web page.

In addition to allowing you to search through its vast catalogs of books, this home page provides special exhibits of the library's fascinating collections. For example, the following special exhibits were available in August 1997:

- ✔ American Treasures of the Library of Congress

- ✔ For European Recovery: The Fiftieth Anniversary of the Marshall Plan

- ✔ Dresden: Treasures from the Saxon State Library

- ✔ Creating French Culture: Treasures from Bibliothéque Nationale de France

- ✔ The Russian Church and Native Alaskan Cultures

- ✔ Rome Reborn: The Vatican Library and Renaissance Culture

- ✔ Revelations from the Russian Archives

- ✔ Frank Lloyd Wright: Designs for an American Landscape, 1922–1932

- ✔ African-American Culture and History

- ✔ Declaring Independence: Drafting the Documents

- ✔ Temple of Liberty: Building the Capitol for a New Nation

- ✔ The Gettysburg Address
- ✔ Women Come to the Front: Journalists, Photographers, and Broadcasters During WWII
- ✔ 1492: An Ongoing Voyage
- ✔ Scrolls from the Dead Sea

Plus, the Library of Congress offers an online library called *American Memory* that includes documents from the Continental Congress and Constitutional Convention, digitized images of Walt Whitman's notebooks, thousands of photographs from the Civil War, early motion pictures that you can download and play on your computer, and much more. The American Memory collection is an ongoing project, so new features are periodically added.

Microsoft

www.microsoft.com

Microsoft has one of the more active pages on the World Wide Web. The page serves as a portal to all kinds of information and support provided free by Microsoft. The opening page for the Microsoft Web site is shown in Figure 23-2.

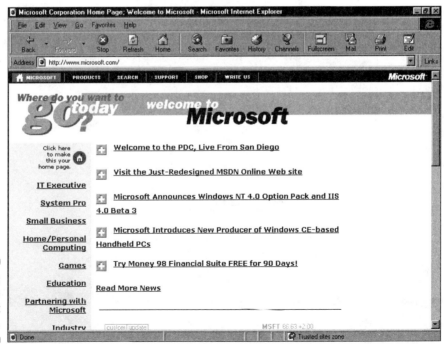

Figure 23-2: The Microsoft Web page.

Microsoft is confident that you want to visit its Web site frequently, so the company built a link to the Microsoft home page right into Internet Explorer. All you have to do is open the Links toolbar by double-clicking on the word Links, and then click the Microsoft icon.

The Microsoft Web site offers many different features, including product information, schedules of upcoming events, and press releases. When you have a problem, you can find the most useful information in the support section, shown in Figure 23-3. (To access the Support Online page, click the Support icon on the Microsoft home page.)

Several support services are available from this Web page:

✔ For information about a specific product, select the product you're interested in from the drop-down list at the top of the page and then click Go! Product-specific Web pages are available for most Microsoft products.

✔ The Knowledge Base is a searchable database of answers to thousands of technical questions about Microsoft software. The Knowledge Base is usually the best place to begin your quest for help because someone has probably already solved whatever problem you're experiencing.

Figure 23-3:
The
Microsoft
Support
Online
page.

✔ The download area contains updated program files and drivers. If you purchase a new printer but can't find a driver for it, check here.

✔ Microsoft maintains its own news server with newsgroups for each of its products. To access these newsgroups, click the Visit Our Newsgroups tab. In the newsgroups, you can post a specific question and then check back the following day to review the responses.

Of course, Microsoft also maintains a Web site devoted entirely to Internet Explorer 4 (see Figure 23-4), which you can find at the following address:

```
www.microsoft.com/ie/ie40
```

From the Internet Explorer home page, you can download the latest version of Internet Explorer and its add-on components, view a showcase of sample pages that demonstrate the coolest new features of Internet Explorer 4.0, and find out about the latest Internet Explorer features.

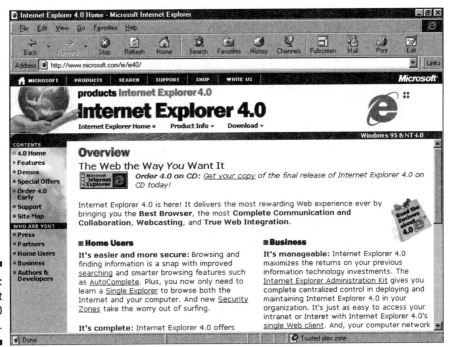

Figure 23-4:
The Internet Explorer 4.0 page.

If you are a Web developer or HTML author, you should also check out the following two addresses within the vast Microsoft Web site:

- ✔ `www.microsoft.com/workshop/author/default.asp`, which takes you to the Microsoft Site Builder Network where you will find detailed information about Internet Explorer 4's new features such as Dynamic HTML and Channel Definition Format (CDF) files.
- ✔ `www.microsoft.com/msdn/sdk/inetsdk`, where you can download the Internet Software Development Kit, which provides useful tools and documentation for Web developers.

The U.S. House of Representatives

`www.house.gov`

All the major branches of government have Web pages, but my favorite is the Web page for the House of Representatives, shown in Figure 23-5.

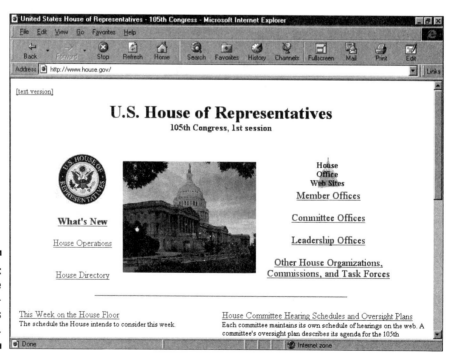

Figure 23-5:
The House of Repre-sentatives Web page.

Here are some of the services that are available from the House of Representatives Web page:

- ✔ The complete text of all bills introduced during the current Congress. (If you read this stuff, consider yourself a step ahead of the representatives who actually vote on it!)
- ✔ Information about the status of current bills, amendments, voting records, committees, and so on
- ✔ The names, addresses, and phone numbers of all legislators
- ✔ Information about visiting Capitol Hill
- ✔ A schedule of legislative activity

The Smithsonian Institution

`www.si.edu`

Take a tour of the nation's premier museum by checking out the Smithsonian Institution's Web site. From the home page, you can visit any of the Smithsonian's 18 museums, including the National Air and Space Museum, the National Museum of American History, the National Museum of American Art, and the National Zoo. You can also visit Smithsonian research institutions, and you can make use of a travel planner that helps you plan a trip to the nation's capital. The opening page of the Smithsonian Web site is shown in Figure 23-6.

A visit to any of the museums leads you to digitized images of the museum's most priceless treasures. For example, you find images of the Apollo 11 command module, which is displayed in the entrance gallery of the National Air and Space Museum along with other milestone aircraft, including the Wright Brothers' original flyer and The Spirit of St. Louis.

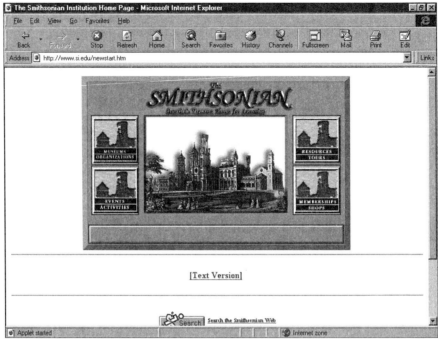

Figure 23-6:
The
Smithsonian
Web site.

The National Park Service

www.nps.gov

The National Park Service maintains an excellent Web site, called ParkNet, which offers information about hundreds of national parks, monuments, and historical sites. Figure 23-7 shows the NPS home page.

You can find the following information at the National Park Service Web site:

- ✔ Information about national parks and monuments, indexed by park name or searchable via regional map
- ✔ Camping and park reservation information
- ✔ Suggestions for visiting the national parks
- ✔ Historical information about the national parks
- ✔ Educational resources

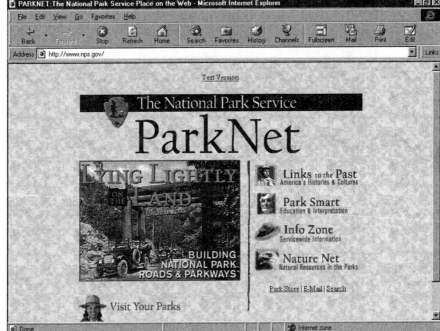

Figure 23-7:
The
National
Park
Service on
the Web.

NASA

www.nasa.gov

I'm a space nut, so the NASA site is one of my favorite places to visit on the Internet. The images from the Pathfinder rover that NASA posted on its Web site were spectacular. Figure 23-8 shows the NASA home page.

The NASA Web site includes the following interesting features:

- A gallery of pictures, sounds, and videos from NASA
- Detailed flight information for all the NASA manned flights, dating back to the Mercury program
- Information about the Space Station project
- Links to other NASA centers, such as Jet Propulsion Laboratory in Pasadena, California; Dryden Flight Research Facility at Edwards Air Force Base, California; and the Johnson Space Center in Houston, Texas

Figure 23-8:
The NASA
Web page.

Late Show Web Pages

    www.cbs.com/lateshow

    www.nbctonightshow.com

Couldn't stay up late enough last night to watch the *Late Show with David Letterman?* Check out the Late Show with David Letterman Web page for the current Top 10 list or to access an archive of past Top 10 lists. You can also find information about guests and news about the show and read David's best jokes from recent shows.

Not to be outdone, Jay Leno also has a Web site for *The Tonight Show.* In addition to guest lineups, *The Tonight Show* page includes quips from Jay's recent monologues, plus excerpts from his regular Monday night Headlines feature.

The Microsoft Network

www.msn.com

Microsoft's online service, The Microsoft Network (also known as MSN), is a subscription service which you must pay a monthly fee to access. However, as an enticement to get you to join, Microsoft makes portions of MSN available free for the asking. All you have to do is check out www.msn.com, pictured in Figure 23-9.

The MSN free Web site gives you access to several useful services. Here are my favorites:

- ✔ **Encarta Concise Encyclopedia** is a scaled-back version of Microsoft's popular Encarta encyclopedia. The Concise version, which you can access freely from www.msn.com, includes 16,000 of the full Encarta's 31,000 articles. To get to this site directly, go to encarta.msn.com.

- ✔ **Cinemania** offers reviews of the major movies currently playing in theaters, a collection of reviews for the more popular rental videos, and film industry news. The Web address for the MSN Cinemania service is cinemania.msn.com.

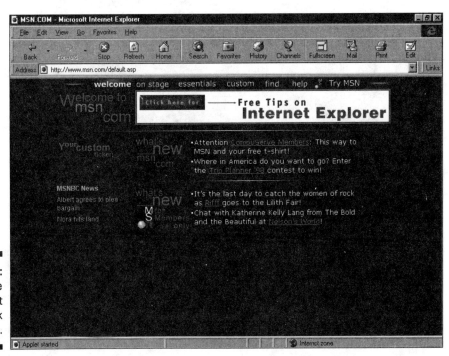

Figure 23-9:
The Microsoft Network home page.

✔ **Carpoint** is a great way to research a new or used car purchase. It gives you detailed descriptions and dealer price lists for most makes of cars, vans, and trucks. To go directly to Carpoint, use the address `carpoint.msn.com`.

✔ **Expedia** is an online travel service which lets you research and actually purchase airplane tickets, hotel reservations, and car rentals. You can reach Expedia directly at `expedia.msn.com`.

Games Domain

`www.gamesdomain.com`

All work and no play makes for boring Internet exploring. Fortunately, the World Wide Web is full of fun, frivolous, and sometimes freaky places to visit. Games Domain, shown in Figure 23-10, is one of the more complete gaming Web sites you can find. Domain maintains a library of more than 5,000 games you can download for free and play on your computer. This should be enough to keep you playing for a while!

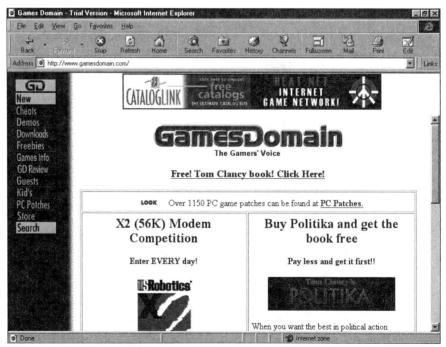

Figure 23-10: Games Domain.

In addition to games, Games Domain also includes FAQ (Frequently Asked Questions) files for hundreds of games, plus links to hundreds of other game-related Web sites.

If you find yourself stuck in a game, you can also check out one of the *walkthroughs,* which provide complete solutions for more than 400 computer games. Of course, reading one of these walkthroughs spoils the game for you, so read them only if you are *really* stuck.

MSNBC

www.msnbc.com

MSNBC is a partnership of Microsoft and broadcasting giant NBC to create a news site that complements NBC's broadcast news. There are many other sources of news on the Internet, but MSNBC is my personal favorite. Figure 23-11 shows a recent MSNBC page.

MSNBC is also available as a channel, which means you can arrange to have MSNBC delivered to your computer each day at a predetermined time (for example, 2:00 a.m.). Then, you can read MSNBC offline whenever you want, without having to wait for each picture and each story to download. For more information about channels, refer to Chapter 6.

Figure 23-11:
MSNBC is
an excellent
source for
news.

Chapter 24

Ten Things That Sometimes Go Wrong

● ●

In This Chapter

▶ Finding you don't have Internet Explorer

▶ Missing out on a modem connection

▶ Forgetting your password

▶ Getting strange messages about unexpected errors

▶ Being unable to find Internet Explorer

▶ Losing a file you know you downloaded

▶ Getting cut off from the Internet in the middle of a big download

▶ Forgetting where to find your favorite Web page

● ●

*A*ctually, it's probably accurate to say that more like 10,000 things *can* go wrong, but this chapter describes some (okay, so I list nine, not ten — but who's counting) of the things that often get out of kilter.

I Don't Have Internet Explorer!

No problem. Internet Explorer is available from many sources, and it's free. If you have any type of access to the Internet, you can find Internet Explorer at the Microsoft Web site, located at the following URL:

```
www.microsoft.com/ie/ie40/download
```

If you don't have access to the Internet, you can purchase Internet Explorer 4 at your local computer store for a modest charge or order it directly from Microsoft for $5.00 to cover shipping and handling. Microsoft's phone number is 1-800-426-9400.

I Can't Connect to the Internet!

You double-click the Internet Explorer icon, the Connection Manager dialog box appears, and you type in your name and password, but you can't get any further. For some reason, you are unable to connect to the Internet. Arghhhhh!

Many, *many* things could be wrong. Here are a few general troubleshooting procedures that can help you solve the problem, or at least narrow down the possibilities:

✔ Make sure that the modem is securely connected to the telephone wall jack and to the correct jack on the back of the modem. Phone cables sometimes jar loose. They go bad sometimes, too, so replacing the cable may solve the problem. If you're not sure which jack is the correct one, consult the manual that came with the modem.

✔ Make sure that the modem is not in use by another program, such as a fax program or the Windows 95 Hyperterminal program.

✔ Make sure that your teenager isn't talking on a phone that shares the same phone line as the modem. (This very thing happened to me several times.)

✔ Try calling your Internet access number on a regular phone to see if it answers. If you get a busy signal or if it just rings on and on and on, something may be wrong with the local access number. Try again later, and call your Internet service provider's customer service if the problem persists.

✔ Double-check the phone number in the Connection Manager dialog box. If your Internet service provider supplies an alternate phone number, try that one instead.

If you just installed the modem or if the modem never has worked right, you should make sure that the modem is configured to use the proper Communications Port within your computer. To change the port setting, follow these steps:

1. **Click the Start button on the taskbar and choose Settings⇨Control Panel.**

2. **Double-click the Modems icon.**

3. **Click the Properties button.**

4. **Change the Port setting for the modem.**

5. **Click OK twice.**

6. **Try dialing in again.**

Sometimes, removing and reinstalling the modem within Windows 95 solves the problem. If all else fails, try this:

1. **Click the Start button on the taskbar and choose Settings⇨Control Panel.**

2. **Double-click the Modems icon.**

3. **Click the modem to select it and then click the Remove button.**

4. **Click Add.**

5. **Follow the Install a New Modem wizard to reinstall the modem.**

I Forgot My Password!

Didn't I tell you to write it down and keep it in a safe place? Sigh. If you really did forget your password, and you didn't write it down anywhere, you have to call your Internet service provider for assistance. If you can convince the person on the other end of the line that you really are who you say you are, he or she can reset your password for you.

Now, to avoid this kind of time-consuming mess, write down your password and store it in a secure location. Here's a list of several not-so-secure places to hide your password:

- In a desk drawer, in a file folder labeled *Not My Internet Password*
- On a magnet stuck to the refrigerator (No one, including you, will ever be able to pick it out from all the other junk stuck up there.)
- On the inside cover of this book, in Pig Latin so that no one can understand it
- Carved on the back of a park bench
- On the wall in a public restroom
- Tattooed on your left buttock, backward so that you can read it in a mirror

I Got an Unexpected Error Message!

Sometimes, when you try to follow a link to a cool Web page, or you type a URL yourself and press Enter, instead of getting the page you expected, you face a dialog box with a message that looks something like this:

```
Internet Explorer cannot open the Internet site http://
            www.whatever.com
A connection with the server could not be established.
```

Sometimes no dialog box appears, but instead of the page you're looking for, you just get a page with some bland text that says something like:

```
HTTP/1.0 404 Object Not Found
```

These error messages and others like them mean that your Internet Explorer couldn't find the page you tried to access. Several possible explanations may account for this error:

- ✔ You typed the URL incorrectly. Maybe it should have been `www.whoever.com` instead of `www.whatever.com`.

- ✔ The page you're trying to display may no longer exist. The person who created the page may have removed it.

- ✔ The page may have been moved to a new address. Sometimes you get a message telling you about the new address, sometimes not.

- ✔ The Web site that hosts the page may be having technical trouble. Try again later.

- ✔ The page may be just too darn popular, causing the server to be busy. Try again later.

The Internet Explorer Window Disappeared!

You know that you are signed in to the Internet, but you can't seem to find Internet Explorer anywhere. The window has mysteriously vanished!

Here are a few things to check before giving up in despair:

- ✔ Find the taskbar, that Windows 95 thingy that usually lurks down at the bottom of your screen. The taskbar has a button for every window that's open. If you find the Internet Explorer button in the taskbar, clicking it should bring the window to the front. (You may have to move your mouse all the way to the bottom edge of the screen to make the taskbar appear. Also, if you moved your taskbar, it may be on the top, left, or right edge of the screen rather than at the bottom.)

- ✔ If no Internet Explorer window appears in the taskbar, you may have closed Internet Explorer but remained connected to the Internet. To make Internet Explorer come alive again, just double-click on the desktop Internet Explorer icon or click Start and choose Internet Explorer from the Programs menu. Because you're already connected to the Internet, you don't have to reconnect.

✔ You may have been disconnected from the Internet for one reason or another. Normally when that happens, a dialog box appears, informing you that you have been disconnected and offering to reconnect. If no dialog box appears, you can reconnect by clicking Start and choosing Programs⇨Accessories⇨Dial-Up Networking, and then double-clicking the icon for your Internet connection.

You can tell whether you're connected to the Internet by looking for the little connection icon in the corner of the taskbar, next to the clock; it looks like two little computers strung together with kite string. If the icon is present, you're connected. If the icon is missing, you're not.

I Can't Find a File I Downloaded!

Don't worry. The file is probably around; you're just not looking in the right place. Internet Explorer offers a Save As dialog box that you must complete before downloading a file, so presumably you know where the file has been saved. However, you can all-too-easily click OK without really looking at this dialog box when it appears.

Fortunately, all you have to do is choose File⇨Save As to recall the Save As dialog box, which by default opens the same folder the dialog box was opened to last. Just check the Save In field at the top of the dialog box to find out the folder where you saved your file.

If you can't remember the name of the file you downloaded, here's a trick that may help you find it:

1. **Open a My Computer window for the folder in which you saved the file.**

   Click My Computer and then navigate your way through your drives and folders until you come to the one where you saved the file.

2. **Choose View⇨Details and make sure that your toolbar is visible.**

3. **Choose View⇨Arrange Icons⇨By Date.**

   The list of files is sorted into date sequence, with the newest files appearing at the top of the list.

4. **Look at the files at the top of the list.**

   With luck, one of these files rings a bell.

I Was Disconnected in the Middle of a Two-Hour Download!

Wow. Tough break. Unfortunately, the Internet doesn't have any way to restart a big download, picking up where you left off. The only solution is to download the entire file again.

Don't blame me; I'm just the messenger.

I Can't Find That Cool Web Page I Saw Yesterday!

I've faced this problem myself. The Web is such a large place that you can easily stumble into a page you really like and then not be able to find it again later.

If you can't seem to retrace your steps, you may still have a record of where you were. Click the History button to display links to all the pages you recently visited. With some luck, you can find the page in the history folder. If you do, double-click it, and you're on your way.

To avoid the frustration of misplacing the Web sites you love, use the Favorites⇨Add to Favorites command any time you come across a Web page you think you may want to visit again. That way, you can always find the page again by choosing it from the Favorites menu. If you later decide that the page isn't so great after all, you can always delete it from Favorites.

I've Started a Nuclear War!

If you're minding your own business, enjoying a nice game of Global Thermonuclear War at www.wargames.com, and you suddenly hear air-raid sirens and see mushroom clouds on the horizon, don't panic. See if you can interest the computer in a nice game of chess instead.

Just kidding. Nothing you do can start a nuclear war from the Internet. Experienced computer hackers have been trying to start nuclear wars on the Internet for years, and no one has succeeded, at least not yet.

Chapter 25

Ten Safety Tips for Kids on the Net

● ●

In This Chapter

▶ Safety tips for kids and their parents

▶ Ways to help keep the Internet a safe place for everyone

● ●

*T*he Internet is an inherently risky place for kids (and adults, too). Along with pictures of Neil Armstrong on the moon, your kids can just as easily find images you probably don't want them to see. And although chatting online can be fun and enlightening, it can also be unhealthy and possibly even dangerous.

This chapter lists ten important safety tips that parents should drill into their kids' heads before they allow them to go online.

I really don't want to be an alarmist here. Overall, the Internet is a pretty wholesome place. Don't be afraid to let your kids venture out online, but don't let them go it alone, either. Make sure that they understand the ground rules.

Don't Believe That People Really Are Who They Say They Are

When you sign up with an Internet service provider, you can type anything you want for your user ID. And no one makes you tell the truth in e-mail, newsgroups, or chats. Just because someone claims to be a 16-year-old female is not reason enough to believe it. That person can be a 12-year-old boy, a 19-year-old girl, or a 35-year-old pervert.

Never Give Out Your Address, Phone Number, Real Last Name, or Credit Card Number

If you're not sure why Rule No. 2 exists, see Rule No. 1.

Never Pretend to Be Someone You're Not

The flip side of not believing who someone says he or she is, is that other people may believe that you are who you say you are. If you are 13 years old and claim to be 17, you're inviting trouble.

We all like to gloss over our weaknesses. When I'm online, I don't generally draw attention to the fact that a substantial portion of my hair is gone, and I'm a bit pudgy around the waistline (well, okay, I'm a *lot* pudgy around the waistline). But I don't represent myself as a super athlete or a rock star, either. Just be yourself.

Save Inappropriate Postings to a File So That You Can Show Them to an Adult

If someone sends you inappropriate e-mail, not just something that makes you feel angry or upset, but something that seems downright inappropriate, choose File➪Save As to save the message as a file. Then show it to an adult.

If Someone Says Something Inappropriate to You in a Chat, Save the Chat Log

If someone is vulgar or offensive in an online chat, save the chat log to a file. Then show it to an adult.

Watch Your Language

The Internet isn't censored. In fact, it can be a pretty rough place. Crude language abounds, especially on Usenet. But that doesn't mean you have to contribute to the endless flow of colorful metaphors. Watch your language while chatting online or posting messages.

Don't Obsess

The Internet can be fun, but there's more to life than going online. The best friendships are the ones in which you actually spend time in the presence of other people. If you find yourself spending hour upon hour online, maybe you should cut back a bit.

Report Inappropriate Behavior to an Adult

If something seems really amiss in your Internet experience — for example, if you think someone is harassing you beyond what should be normal, or if someone asks you questions that make you uncomfortable — tell an adult.

You can also complain by sending e-mail to the administrator of the perpetrator's Internet service provider. If the perp is clever, you may not be able to figure out his or her true e-mail address. But you often can. If you receive harassing mail from `idiot@jerk.com`, try sending a complaint to `postmaster@jerk.com`.

If You Feel Uncomfortable, Leave

Don't stick around in a chat session if you feel uncomfortable. Just leave.

Similarly, don't bother to reply to inappropriate e-mail messages or newsgroup articles.

Parents: Be Involved with Your Kids' Online Activities

Don't let your kids run loose on the Internet! Get involved with what they are doing. You don't have to monitor them every moment they are online. Just be interested in what they're doing, what friends they have made over the network, what they like, and what they don't like. Ask them to show you around their favorite Internet pages.

Glossary

Active Desktop

An optional feature of Internet Explorer 4 that allows Internet Explorer to take over your Windows 95 desktop. When you turn on the Active Desktop, you browse both the Internet and the files and folders on your local computer using Internet Explorer. Active Desktop also enables you to customize your desktop and individual file folders with HTML documents.

Active Desktop control

An object that you can place directly on your desktop when you have installed the Active Desktop feature of Internet Explorer 4. Active Desktop controls can be connected to the Internet so that your desktop constantly displays up-to-the-minute information such as stock reports and weather maps.

ActiveX

The Microsoft Web-based object technology that enables intelligent objects to be embedded in Web documents to create interactive pages. See *object linking and embedding*.

ActiveX control

An ActiveX object that can be embedded in a Web page. Most ActiveX controls are user-interface gadgets, such as list boxes and command buttons, but some provide behind-the-scenes functions, such as timers.

Address Book

A file that stores the Internet e-mail addresses of the people with whom you correspond regularly. Outlook Express maintains an Address Book for your e-mail.

AFK

Away from keyboard, an abbreviation commonly used when chatting. See *IRC*.

America Online

A popular online information service that also provides Internet access. America Online is often referred to as *AOL*. To send e-mail to an AOL user, address the message to the user's America Online name followed by the domain name (@aol.com). For example, if the user's AOL name is Barney, send an e-mail message to Barney@aol.com.

anonymous FTP

An FTP site that allows access to anyone, without requiring an account.

AOL

See *America Online*.

applet

A program written in the Java language and embedded in an HTML document. An applet runs automatically whenever someone views the Web page that contains the applet.

ARPANET

The very first incarnation of the Internet, built by the Department of Defense in Summer of Love.

article

A message posted to a Usenet newsgroup.

ASCII

The standard character set for most computers. Internet newsgroups are *ASCII-only,* meaning that they can support only text-based messages.

attach

Sending a file along with an e-mail message or newsgroup article. Internet Explorer automatically encodes and decodes attachments.

attachment

A file attached to an e-mail message or a newsgroup article.

AutoComplete

A mostly useful but sometimes annoying feature of Internet Explorer that anticipates what you are trying to type and tries to complete your Web address for you before you finish typing it.

AVI

The Microsoft standard for video files that can be viewed in Windows. AVI is one of the more popular video formats on the Web, but other formats such as QuickTime and MPEG are also widely used.

bandwidth

The amount of information that can flow through a network connection. Bandwidth

is to computer networks what pipe diameter is to plumbing: The bigger the pipe, the more water allowed through.

baud

See *bits per second.* (Actually, a technical difference does exist between *baud* and *bits per second,* but only people with pocket protectors and taped glasses care.)

binary file

A non-ASCII file, such as a computer program, a picture, a sound, or a video.

BITNET

A large network connecting colleges and universities in North America and Europe through the Internet. BITNET mailing lists are presented as Usenet newsgroups under the bit hierarchy.

bits per second (bps)

A measure of how fast your modem can transmit or receive information between your computer and a remote computer, such as your Internet service provider. You won't be happy browsing the Internet using anything less than a 28,800 bps modem (commonly referred to as a *28.8 modem*). Note that the term *Kbps* is often used to designate thousands of bits per second. Thus, 28,800 bps and 28.8 Kbps are equivalent.

BRB

Be right back, an abbreviation commonly used when chatting. See *IRC.*

browser

A program, such as Internet Explorer, that you can use to access and view the World Wide Web. Internet Explorer is, at its core, a browser.

cache

An area of your computer's hard disk used to store data recently downloaded from the network so the data can be redisplayed quickly.

cappuccino

An Italian coffee drink that blends espresso, steamed milk, foam, and (if you're lucky) a dash of cinnamon. Not to be confused with *Java*.

CDF

See *Channel Definition Format*.

Certificates

An online form of identification that gives one computer assurance that the other computer is who it claims to be. Certificates are a common form of security on the Internet.

channel

A special type of Web site that can deliver information to you automatically (typically in the wee hours of the morning) so you can later view the information without having to wait while each page downloads. A channel informs you whenever new information is available. See *subscription*.

Channel Definition Format

A special file format that you must use to create a CDF file, which is used to set up your own channel.

Channel Guide

A special channel sponsored by Microsoft that lists noteworthy channels you can subscribe to.

CGI

Common Gateway Interface. A method of programming Web sites, mostly used to handle online forms. CGI utilizes script programs that run on the server computer, as opposed to Java or VBScript programs, which run on client computers. Because client-side programming is more efficient, CGI is losing popularity.

chat

See *IRC*.

chat room

A place where two or more Internet users gather online to hold a conversation. See *IRC*.

chat server

An Internet server that hosts a chat.

Chaucer

A dead English dude who didn't spell very well.

compressed file

A file that's been processed by a special *compression program* that reduces the amount of disk space required to store the file. If you download the file to your computer, you must decompress the file before you can use it using a program such as WinZip or PKUNZIP.

CompuServe

A popular online service that also provides Internet access. To send Internet mail to a CompuServe member, address the mail to the user's CompuServe user ID (two groups of numbers separated by a comma), followed by `@compuserve.com`. However, use a period instead of a comma in the user ID. For example, if the user's ID is 55555,1234, send e-mail to 55555.1234@compuserve.com. You have to use the period because Internet e-mail standards don't allow for commas in e-mail addresses.

connect time

The amount of time you're connected to the Internet or your online service. Some Internet service providers limit your monthly connect time or charge you by the hour.

Connection Manager

A new gizmo that comes with Internet Explorer 4 to take care of dialing in to your Internet service provider and logging you on to the Internet.

Content Advisor

An Internet Explorer 4 feature that lets you block Web sites based on their ratings. See *ratings*.

cookie

A file that a Web server stores on your computer. The most common use for cookies is to customize the way a Web page appears when you view it. For example, customizable Web pages such as www.msn.com use cookies to store your viewing preferences so that the next time you visit that Web page, only the elements that you request are displayed.

cyberspace

An avant-garde term used to refer to the Internet.

decode

The process of reconstructing a binary file that was encoded using the uuencode scheme, used in e-mail and newsgroups. Outlook Express automatically decodes encoded files.

decompression

The process of restoring compressed files to their original states. Decompression is usually accomplished with a program such as WinZip and PKUNZIP. (You can download the shareware version of PKUNZIP at www.pkware.com.)

decryption

See *Tales from Decrypt*. Just kidding. Decryption is the process of unscrambling a message that has been encrypted (scrambled so that only the intended recipient can read it). See *encryption*.

dial-up script

A special file that contains the instructions used to log you in to your ISP so you can connect to the Internet.

"Dixie"

A happy little tune that you can whistle while you are waiting for a Web page to finish downloading.

DNS

Domain Name Server. The system that allows us to use almost intelligible names, such as www.microsoft.com, rather than completely incomprehensible addresses, such as 283.939.12.74.

domain

The last portion of an Internet address (also known as the *top-level domain*), which indicates whether the address belongs to a company (com), an educational institution (edu), a government agency (gov), a military organization (mil), or another organization (org).

domain name

The address of an Internet site, which generally includes the organization domain name followed by the top-level domain, as in www.idgbooks.com.

download

Copying a file from another computer to your computer via a modem.

Dynamic HTML

A new flavor of HTML that is supported by Internet Explorer and that allows you to create Web pages in which every element on the page (text and graphics alike) can by dynamically changed as the user interacts with the page.

e-mail

Electronic mail, an Internet service that enables you to send and receive messages to and from other Internet users.

emoticon

Another word for a *smiley* — an expressive face you can create with nothing more than a few keystrokes and some imagination :-)

encode

A method of converting a *binary file* to ASCII text, which can be sent by Internet e-mail or posted to an Internet newsgroup. When displayed, encoded information looks like a stream of random characters. But when you run the encoded message through a decoder program, the original binary file is reconstructed. Outlook Express automatically encodes and decodes messages, so you don't have to worry about using a separate program for this purpose.

encryption

Scrambling a message so that no one can read it, except, of course, the intended recipient, who must *decrypt* the message before reading it.

ETLA

Extended three-letter acronym. A four-letter acronym.

event

In Dynamic HTML, a user action (such as moving the mouse) that can be handled by a VBScript or JScript program. See *Dynamic HTML.*

Explorer

A Windows 95 program that enables you to view the contents of folders alongside a hierarchical representation of the computer's folders. Essentially, Explorer is the Windows 95 version of the old Program Manager and File Manager programs found in Windows 3.1. With the Internet Explorer 4 Active Desktop feature, Internet Explorer itself replaces that old Windows 95 Explorer so you can browse your folders in the same way you browse the Internet.

Explorer bar

The left one-third or so of the Internet Explorer main window, which Internet Explorer periodically uses to display a special toolbar when you click the Search, History, Favorites, or Channels buttons.

FAQ

A *frequently asked questions* file. Contains answers to the most commonly asked questions. Always check to see if a FAQ file exists for a forum or Usenet newsgroup before asking basic questions. (If you post a question on an Internet newsgroup and the answer is in the FAQ, expect to be flamed for sure.)

Favorites

A collection of Web page addresses that you visit frequently. Internet Explorer enables you to store your favorite Web addresses in a special folder so that you can recall them quickly.

File Transfer Protocol (FTP)

A system that allows the transfer of program and data files over the Internet.

finger

An Internet program that enables you to obtain information about another Internet user.

flame

A painfully brutal response to a dumb posting on a Bulletin Board System (BBS) or Internet newsgroup. (On some newsgroups, just having `aol.com` in your Internet address is enough to get flamed.)

freeware

Software that you can download and use without paying a fee.

FrontPage Express

A WYSVRWYG (what-you-see-vaguely-resembles-what-you-get) HTML editor that comes with Internet Explorer 4. FrontPage Express is actually a scaled-back version of Microsoft's powerful HTML editor, FrontPage.

FTP

See *File Transfer Protocol.*

FTP site

An Internet server that has a library of files available for downloading with FTP.

gateway

A computer that enables other computers on a local area network (LAN) to access the Internet.

GIF

Graphic Interchange Format. A popular format for picture files. The GIF format uses an efficient compression technique that results in less data loss and higher quality graphics than other formats, such as PCX.

home page

(1) The introductory page at a Web site; sometimes refers to the entire Web site. (2) The first page displayed by Internet Explorer when you start it. By default, the home page is set to `home.microsoft.com`, but you can change the home page to any Web page you want.

host computer

A computer to which you can connect via the Internet.

HTML

Hypertext Markup Language. A system of special tags used to create pages for the World Wide Web.

HTTP

Hypertext Transfer Protocol. The protocol used to transmit HTML documents over the Internet.

hyperlink

A bit of text or a graphic in a Web page that you can click to retrieve another Web page. The new Web page may be on the same Web server as the original page, or it may be on an entirely different Web server halfway around the globe.

hypermedia

A variation of hypertext in which hyperlinks can be graphics, sounds, or videos, as well as text. The World Wide Web is based on hypermedia, but the term *hypertext* is often loosely used instead.

hypertext

A system in which documents are linked to one another by text links. When the user clicks on a text link, the document referred to by the link is displayed. See *hypermedia.*

IBM

A big computer company.

Information Superhighway

Al Gore's pet name for the Internet.

Internet

A vast worldwide collection of networked computers, the largest computer network in the world.

Internet address

A complete address used to send e-mail to someone over the Internet. Your Internet address consists of a user ID plus the host name of your Internet service provider. For example, if your user ID is `JClampet` and your service provider's host name is `beverly.hills.com`, your Internet address is `JClampet@beverly.hills.com`.

Internet Connection Wizard

A program that comes with Internet Explorer 4 to help you get connected to the Internet.

Internet Explorer

The Microsoft program for browsing the Internet.

Internet Relay Chat

See *IRC.*

Internet service provider

Also known as *ISP.* A company that provides access to the Internet.

IP

Internet Protocol. The data transmission protocol that enables networks to exchange messages; serves as the foundation for communications over the Internet.

IRC

Internet Relay Chat. A system that enables you to carry on live conversations (known as *chats*) with other Internet users.

ISDN

A digital telephone line that can transmit data at 128 Kbps. ISDNs still cost a bit too much for the average home user. Watch, though; the price will come down.

ISP

See *Internet service provider.*

Java

An object-oriented programming language designed to be used on the World Wide Web, created by Sun Microsystems. Java is one way to add sound, animation, and interactivity to Web pages. Although Internet Explorer supports Java, Microsoft prefers that you use VBScript instead.

JavaScript

A version of Java used with Netscape Navigator that enables Web-page authors to embed Java programs in HTML documents. *JScript* is the Internet Explorer version of JavaScript.

JPEG

Joint Photographic Experts Group. A popular format for picture files. JPEG uses a compression technique that greatly reduces a graphic's file size, but results in some loss of resolution. For photographic images, this loss is usually not noticeable. Because of its small file sizes, JPEG is a popular graphics format for the Internet.

JScript

The Microsoft implementation of JavaScript for use with Internet Explorer.

KB

An abbreviation for *kilobyte* (roughly 1,024 bytes).

Kbps

A measure of a modem's speed in thousands of bits per second. Two common modem speeds are 14.4 Kbps and 28.8 Kbps.

LAN

See *local area network.*

Liburnia

A program that is available from Microsoft for editing CDF files. See *Channel Definition Format.*

link

See *hyperlink.*

Links toolbar

A special Internet Explorer toolbar that lets you quickly access a handful of the sites you visit most frequently.

LISTSERV

A server program used for mailing lists, which are basically e-mail versions of newsgroups. See *mailing list.*

local area network

Also referred to as a *LAN.* Two or more computers that are connected to one another to form a network. A LAN enables the computers to share resources, such as disk drives and printers. A LAN is usually located within a relatively small area, such as a building or on a campus.

LOL

Laughing out loud. A common abbreviation used to express mirth or joy when chatting on IRC, in e-mail messages, or in newsgroup articles.

lurk

To read articles in a newsgroup without contributing your own postings. Lurking is one of the few approved forms of eavesdropping. Lurking for a while in a newsgroup before posting your own articles is the polite thing to do.

macro

In Microsoft Chat, a feature that enables you to store an entire response or message and recall it with a simple keyboard shortcut.

mailing list

An e-mail version of a newsgroup. Any messages sent to the mailing list server are automatically sent to each person who has subscribed to the list.

MB

Megabyte. Roughly a million bytes.

Microsoft

The largest software company in the world. Among other things, Microsoft is the maker of MS-DOS, Windows 95, and the Microsoft Office suite, which includes Word, Excel, PowerPoint, and Access. Oh, and I almost forgot — Internet Explorer, too.

Microsoft Chat

The Internet chatting program that comes with Internet Explorer 4. Microsoft Chat has the unique ability to display chats in the form of a comic strip.

Microsoft Exchange

A Windows 95 program that handles e-mail and fax communications. Outlook Express is easier to use than Exchange, and it's a lot faster.

MIME

Multipurpose Internet mail extensions. One of the standard methods for attaching binary files to e-mail messages and newsgroup articles. See *uuencode.*

modem

A device that enables your computer to connect with other computers over a phone line. Most modems are *internal* — they're housed within the computer's cabinet. *External* modems are contained in their own boxes and must be connected to the back of the computer via a serial cable.

moderated newsgroup

A newsgroup whose postings are controlled by a moderator, which helps to ensure that articles in the newsgroup follow the guidelines established by the moderator.

Mosaic

The original Web browser, available free of charge. Internet Explorer, which is also available free of charge, is much better. So why bother with Mosaic?

MPEG

Motion Picture Experts Group. A standard for compressing video images based on the popular JPEG standard used for still images. Internet Explorer includes built-in support for MPEG videos.

MSN

The Microsoft Network, a commercial online service. Although you have to pay to access all the MSN services, some of the most useful features of MSN such as Encarta, Cinemania, and Expedita are available to all Web users free of charge.

NetMeeting

A program that comes with Internet Explorer 4 and enables you to have online meetings with other Internet users.

Netscape

The company that makes the popular *Netscape Navigator* browser software for the Internet. Internet Explorer and Navigator are currently duking it out for the title of "Best Web Browser."

Network Wizards

An organization that monitors the growth of the Internet. Check out their Web page at www.nw.com to find out how big the Internet really is.

newsgroup

An Internet bulletin board area where you can post messages, called *articles,* about a particular topic and read articles posted by other Internet users. Thousands of different newsgroups are out there, covering just about every conceivable subject. You can access newsgroups with Outlook Express.

news server

A host computer that stores newsgroup articles. You must connect to a news server to access newsgroups; your Internet service provider probably has its own news server to which you can connect. Microsoft uses its own news servers for its product support newsgroups.

object linking and embedding

Commonly known as *OLE*. A funky feature of Windows that enables you to embed documents (or portions of documents) from other programs into a document. For example, you can embed an Excel spreadsheet in a Word document. When you double-click the spreadsheet object, Excel takes over to enable you to edit the spreadsheet. It turns out that Microsoft's new ActiveX technology is just another reincarnation of OLE.

object model

An important aspect of Dynamic HTML that enables scripts written in VBScript or JScript to access any element of an HTML page. See *Dynamic HTML*.

OIC

Oh, I see. A commonly used abbreviation in chats or e-mail messages.

OLE

See *object linking and embedding*.

online

Connecting your computer to a network, to an online service provider, or to the Internet.

Outlook Express

A scaled-back version of the Microsoft Outlook program that comes with Internet Explorer 4. (You can get the full Outlook program with Microsoft Office 97.)

Personal Web Server

A program that comes with Internet Explorer 4 and lets you turn your computer into a Web server.

PKZIP

A popular shareware program used to compress files or to expand compressed files. You can get your copy at www.pkware.com.

PMJI

Pardon me for jumping in. A commonly used abbreviation in newsgroup articles.

posting

Adding an article to a newsgroup.

PPP

Point to Point Protocol. The protocol that enables you to access Internet services with Internet Explorer.

protocol

A set of conventions that govern communications between computers in a network.

public domain

Computer software or other information that is available free of charge. See *shareware*.

push technology

A buzzword that refers to a new type of Internet technology in which Web servers send information to users without the users first having to request the information. *Channels* are a form of push technology.

QuickTime

A video format popularized by Apple for its Macintosh computers. Internet Explorer provides built-in support for QuickTime movies, so you don't need separate software to view QuickTime files.

rating

A voluntary system of rating the contents of Internet sites, similar to the ratings used for movies and television. Internet Explorer lets you block Web sites based on their ratings.

RSAC

Recreational Software Advisory Council, the organization that developed and oversees the use of Internet ratings.

ROFL

Rolling on the floor laughing. A common abbreviation used in chats, newsgroup articles, and e-mail messages. You may see variations such as ROFLPP and ROFLMAO. Figure those out yourself — this is a family book.

script

A type of program that you can embed in an HTML document. Internet Explorer allows scripts that are written in one of two languages: VBScript or JScript.

Search bar

A special toolbar that appears in the left one-third or so of the Internet Explorer main window when you click the Search button. See *Explorer bar.*

server

A computer that provides services to other computers on the Internet or on a local area network. Specific types of Internet servers include news servers, mail servers, FTP servers, and Web servers.

service provider

See *Internet service provider.*

shareware

A software program that you can download and try — free of charge. The program is not free, however. If you like the program and continue to use it, you are obligated to send in a modest registration fee. See *public domain.*

shortcut

An icon that can represent a link to a location on the Internet. You can place shortcuts just about anywhere, including on your desktop, in a Windows 95 folder, or even in a document.

signature

A fancy block of text that some users routinely place at the end of their e-mail messages and newsgroup articles. Outlook Express lets you use signatures. Also see *stationery.*

SLIP

Serial Line Internet Protocol. A method for accessing the Web, now largely replaced by PPP connections.

smiley

A smiley face or other *emoticon* created from keyboard characters and used to convey emotions in otherwise emotionless e-mail messages or newsgroup postings. Some examples include:

: -)	Feelin' happy
: - D	Super-duper happy
8 ^)	Smiling Orphan Annie (Leapin' lizards!)
; -)	Conspiratorial wink
: - o	You surprise me
: - (	So sad
: - |	Apathetic

spam

Unsolicited e-mail or newsgroup postings that do not relate to the topic of the newsgroup. Spam is the electronic equivalent of junk mail.

stationery

An Outlook Express feature that lets you add a background graphic, a signature, and a font style to your e-mail messages and newsgroup postings.

style

In HTML, a style is a special type of element that provides formatting information for other HTML elements.

subscription

An Internet Explorer 4 feature that enables you to check a Web site or channel for changes automatically and download Web pages at a scheduled time, such as in the middle of the night while you are fast asleep. You can then view the Web site or channel without having to connect to the Internet and wait for each page to download.

taskbar

A Windows 95 feature that displays icons for all open windows, a clock, and the Start button, which you use to run programs. Normally, the taskbar appears at the bottom of the screen, but it can be repositioned at any edge of the screen you prefer. If the taskbar is not visible, try moving the mouse to the very bottom of the screen, or to the left, right, or top edge of the screen. The Active Desktop feature of Internet Explorer 4 adds some extra goodies to the taskbar.

TCP/IP

Transmission Control Protocol/Internet Protocol. The basic set of conventions that the Internet uses to enable different types of computers to communicate with one another.

Telnet

A protocol that enables you to log in to a remote computer as if you were actually a terminal attached to that remote computer.

TIFF

Tagged Image File Format. A format for picture files. TIFF files are large compared with other formats such as JPEG and GIF, but they preserve all of the original image's quality. Because of their large size, TIFF files aren't all that popular on the Internet.

thread

An exchange of articles in a newsgroup. Specifically, an original article, all of its replies, all the replies to replies, and so on.

TLA

Three-letter acronym. Ever notice how just about all computer terms can be reduced to a three-letter acronym? It all started with IBM. Now, there's URL, AOL, CGI, and who knows what else. I guess I shouldn't complain; this book is being published by IDG.

Uniform Resource Locator

Also knows as a *URL.* A method of specifying the address of any resource available on the Internet, used when browsing the Internet. For example, the URL of IDG Books Worldwide, Inc., is `www.idgbooks.com`.

UNIX

A computer operating system that is popular among Internet users. The Internet was developed by UNIX users, which is why much of the Internet has a UNIX look and feel — especially when you leave the World Wide Web and venture into older parts of the Internet, such as FTP sites.

upload

Copying a file from your computer to the Internet.

URL

See *Uniform Resource Locator.*

Usenet

A network of Internet newsgroups that contains many of the more popular newsgroups. You can access Usenet from Outlook Express, which comes free with Internet Explorer 4.0.

uuencode

A method of attaching binary files, such as programs or documents, to e-mail messages and newsgroup articles. The other method is called MIME.

VBScript

A version of Visual Basic that enables you to create programs that can be embedded in HTML documents.

virus

An evil computer program that slips into your computer undetected, tries to spread itself to other computers, and may eventually do something bad like trash your hard disk. Because Internet Explorer doesn't include built-in virus detection, I suggest that you consider using one of the many virus-protection programs available if you're worried about catching an electronic virus.

Visual J++

The Microsoft Java compiler, which programmers can use to create ActiveX controls in their Web pages. Visual J++ provides a sophisticated visual development environment that's similar to the popular Visual C++ environment.

Web

See *World Wide Web.*

Web browser

A program that can find pages on the World Wide Web and display them on your home computer. Internet Explorer is an example of a Web browser.

Windows Desktop Update

Another name for the Internet Explorer 4 new Active Desktop feature. See *Active Desktop.*

Web page

An HTML document available for display on the Word Wide Web. The document may contain links to other documents located on the same server or on other Web servers.

Web Publishing Wizard

A program that comes with Internet Explorer 4 that makes it easy to post to a Web server HTML documents that you have created.

Web server

A server computer that stores HTML documents so that they can be accessed on the World Wide Web.

wide area network

Commonly called *WAN.* A computer network that spans a large area, such as an entire campus, or perhaps a network that links branches of a company in several cities.

WinSock

Short for *Windows Sock*ets. The standard by which Windows programs are able to communicate with TCP/IP and the Internet. Fortunately, you don't have to know anything about WinSock to use it. In fact, you don't even have to know you're using it at all.

Windows 95

The newest version of the Microsoft Windows operating system. Windows 95 is the main operating system for Internet Explorer 4, although versions of Internet Explorer exist for Windows NT, Windows 3.1, and Macintosh computers.

WinZip

A Windows version of the popular PKZIP compression program.

World Wide Web

Abbreviated *WWW* and referred to simply as *the Web.* This relatively new part of the Internet displays information using fancy graphics. The Web is based on *links,* which enable Web surfers to travel quickly from one Web server to another.

XML

eXtensible Markup Language. A definition of the rules used to create markup language such as HTML and CDF.

zipped file

A file that has been compressed using the PKZIP or WinZip program.

Index

• •

(continued)

(continued)

• K •

(continued)

(continued)

IDG BOOKS WORLDWIDE
BOOK REGISTRATION

Register This Book and Win!

We want to hear from you!

Visit **http://my2cents.dummies.com** to register this book and tell us how you liked it!

- ✔ Get entered in our monthly prize giveaway.

- ✔ Give us feedback about this book — tell us what you like best, what you like least, or maybe what you'd like to ask the author and us to change!

- ✔ Let us know any other *...For Dummies* topics that interest you.

Your feedback helps us determine what books to publish, tells us what coverage to add as we revise our books, and lets us know whether we're meeting your needs as a *...For Dummies* reader. You're our most valuable resource, and what you have to say is important to us!

Not on the Web yet? It's easy to get started with *Dummies 101*®: *The Internet For Windows*® *95* or *The Internet For Dummies*®, 4th Edition, at local retailers everywhere.

Or let us know what you think by sending us a letter at the following address:

...For Dummies Book Registration
Dummies Press
7260 Shadeland Station, Suite 100
Indianapolis, IN 46256
Fax 317-596-5498

BUSINESS AND GENERAL REFERENCE BOOK SERIES FROM IDG

COMPUTER BOOK SERIES FROM IDG